Children's
mathematics 4–15

Children's mathematics 4–15

Learning from errors and misconceptions

Julie Ryan and Julian Williams

Open University Press

Open University Press
McGraw-Hill Education
McGraw-Hill House
Shoppenhangers Road
Maidenhead
Berkshire
England
SL6 2QL

email: enquiries@openup.co.uk
world wide web: www.openup.co.uk

and Two Penn Plaza, New York, NY 10121-2289, USA

First published 2007

A catalogue record of this book is available from the British Library

ISBN-13: 978 0 335 22042 7 (pb) 978 0 335 22043 4 (hb)
ISBN-10: 0 335 22042 8 (pb) 0 335 22043 6 (hb)

Library of Congress Cataloging-in-Publication Data
CIP data applied for

Typeset by RefineCatch Limited, Bungay, Suffolk
Printed in Poland by OZ Graf. S.A.
www.polskabook.pl

The McGraw·Hill Companies

To Leonore, John, Jean and Reg

Contents

Acknowledgements

We thank all those who helped with this manuscript by reading and commenting: Thekla Afantiti-Lamprianou, Laura Black, Pauline Davis, Constantia Hadjidemetriou, Yvette Solomon, Ian Sugarman, Howard Tanner; and Diane Brooks for artwork on the discussion prompt sheets (Appendix 2).

More broadly, we would like to thank all the colleagues and students who, through joint work, which is cited in references, and many conversations, which are not, have helped us to formulate our ideas, especially those colleagues and post-docs involved in previous research projects on Argumentation, Situated Intuition, Maths@work, and various assessments, particularly Mathematics Assessment for Learning and Teaching: Brian Doig, Susie Groves, Constantia Hadjidemetriou, Andreas Koukkoufis, Jason Lamprianou, Thekla Afantiti-Lamprianou, Liora Linchevski, Barry McCrae, Maria Pampaka, Lawrence Splitter, Geoff Wake, Lawrence Wo, and too many others to list.

We recognize the essential contribution of the many children, students and teachers who have participated in related research projects over the last decade, mostly in England and Australia, but also in Israel. The validity of the text depends on the authenticity with which we have re-presented their voices.

Julie Ryan and Julian Williams

1 Introduction

What is the problem with mathematics education?

Learners, teachers, parents, academics, business leaders, politicians all say there is a serious problem with mathematics education, so it must be true. It is repeatedly asserted by government inquiries and reports in the UK (the most recent is the Smith Inquiry following the Roberts Review).[1] Furthermore this has become a worldwide phenomenon, courtesy of international assessments such as PISA (the Organisation for Economic Co-operation and Development's Programme for International Student Assessment) and TIMSS (the International Association for the Evaluation of Educational Achievement's Trends in International Mathematics and Science Study); even in Japan there is a now a crisis over standards of mathematics.[2]

In addition, there is growing evidence that state-mandated projects that claim significant improvements in standards are politically motivated and unsupported by rigorous research evidence. These projects typically tie accountability to performativity: performance on 'high stakes' state-wide tests, comparative pupil/school or teacher league tables, leading to the practice of 'teaching to the test'. The 'Texas miracle' and similar projects throughout the western world show that, typically, such efforts lead to short-term, superficial and in many cases illusory improvements in test scores without genuine, substantial gains in children's understanding.[3]

Here are some data from our own analyses of a large, cross-sectional survey of some 15,000 children aged 4 to 15 years taken in the year 2005 in the UK (see Figure 1.1).[4] Note the plateau in performance between ages 11 to 14 years, the very focus of government initiatives recently in this country. The slope of children's progress looks so slow that it appears to cease altogether for some years.

A little explanation about this data set is in order as we will be drawing on it periodically throughout the book (for more, see Appendix 1). The large representative sample of 15,000 children was drawn nationally for the purposes

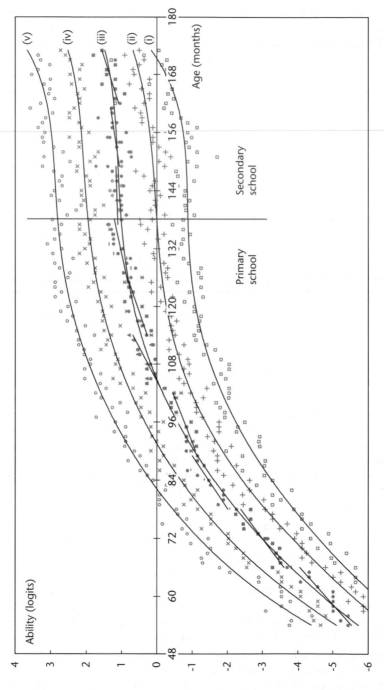

Figure 1.1 Mathematical ability against age for 5- to 14-year-old children.

Note: the five graphs show the (i) 10th percentile, (ii) lower quartile, (iii) median, (iv) upper quartile and (v) 90th percentile of all children's ability (logits) for ages 54 (4½ years) to 173 months (14½ years).[5]

of age standardization, and the middle graph shows the series of age-standardization lines drawn for the median pupils for each test from 'age 5' to 'age 14' (that is, Reception to Year 9 in the UK, thus when we refer to '5-year-olds' we actually mean mainly 54- to 66-month-old children). Each dot on the graph is the median score of the children with the given age in months (that is, the median of the hundred or so children with that particular birth month). Each median line is the best fit for those months that relate to that year's test, and was used to age-standardize the median score. Scores on each test year were vertically equated to a common scale, expressed in Figure 1.1 in 'logits'.

The curve fitted to this series of data points and lines therefore shows the expected performance of 5-year-old to 14-year-old children as a compromise between maturation within the year group and progress across the years. Similar curves were fitted for the 10th, 25th, 75th and 90th percentile at each age, and the difference between these curves is approximately the same (about 1 logit, which is recorded as 5 'scale score' points in Appendix 1) across most of the age range.[6] Scores on the different tests were 'vertically' equated using common tests (across persons) and common persons (across tests); this means that the common scale on the 'y-axis' can legitimately be used to compare scores on tests with at least that of the year above and the year below. As well as the scores of persons, the items of all the tests are put on the same scale too, and this again means that comparisons across at least three age groups can be drawn (see Appendix 1).[7]

The data confirm what previous research has often suggested: children currently learn and improve in mathematics only very slowly, almost plateauing after the age of 11 years for several years, with large disparities between the top 10 per cent and the median average, and again between the median average and the bottom 10 per cent. These differences (of 2 logits or 10 scale score points) represent the same change as might be expected of the average child between the ages of 90 and 130 months – that is, over three years of development. Put another way, the difference between what the top 10 per cent and the bottom 10 per cent can do is approximately (4 logits) the same as the difference between the average at 70 months and 130 months, or five years of relatively rapid development. By choosing different points on the graph it is easy to replicate the '7-year gap' between children on many core number topics reported in the 1980s.

Interpreting this graph as a measure of mathematical competence as measured by national assessment-type tests, it appears that the average child makes practically no progress between the ages of about 11 and 14 years. Increases of about 1 scale score mark (for example, 1 out of 45) per year are observed at most. This is about one-fifth of the difference between the average and the 75th percentile, likely to be judged the 'abler' performer.

The pattern described for the average child between 11 and 14 years is not significantly different for the 'abler' or the 'less able' child, as interpreted by the 75th or 25th percentile, nor even for the 'gifted' 90th percentile or 'at risk' 10th percentile. For all these children the interpretation of the plateauing is the same: it signifies very slow progress, especially when compared to the variation in performance within the year group; that is, the growth of 1 scale score point per year represents about one-tenth of the interquartile range (one-tenth of the difference between the 'abler' 75th percentile and the 'less able' 25th percentile). At this rate of progress it would take ten years of extra teaching for a 'less able' to catch up with an 'able' classmate, and five years for the 'less able' to achieve as well as the average.

To put this another way: the annual rate of progress between ages 11 and 14 years is about the same as one-twentieth of the difference between the ablest 10 per cent likely to be labelled 'gifted' and the least able 10 per cent, likely to be labelled as 'having a special educational need'. It would suggest at this rate that the equivalent of ten years of extra teaching would be required to advance the performance of the very least able to the average.

Another interesting feature of the graph is the discontinuities between the lines of best fit year on year. It seems that there is a jump of about 0.4 logits between the score of the 66-month-olds in Year 1 and Year 2 of schooling. A natural interpretation here is that the Year 2 children have had up to a year longer in school, and this extra teaching and curriculum exposure is reflected in enhanced performance. What then do we make of the reverse discontinuity between the lines later on? It might seem that the youngest in the class in the secondary school is expected to do worse than the oldest in the previous year, despite (or because of) the extra year's exposure to schooling. Of course, interpretations have to be made with caution: there is, for instance, a measurable effect in this data set at Year 2 (7-year-olds), Year 6 (11-year-olds) and perhaps Year 9 (14-year-olds), which might reflect the fact that children are being prepared for tests in those years. It is probable that the curve represents a better model of mathematical development than each line of best fit. Nevertheless this effect does add to the concern about what schooling is doing for children's learning of mathematics.

If extra exposure to the curriculum, assessment and teaching, especially in secondary school, has such a small effect, then one must question what is happening. One interpretation might be to look to the relative success of learning in the primary school years. Yet it is clear that the rate of progress in the graph is on the decline throughout the primary years. Perhaps not all ills should be laid at the door of teaching, schools and classrooms: learners' needs change as they develop and teaching must be adjusted accordingly.

What is the solution?

The point of view we adopt is that the problem lies with the *lack of an adequate pedagogy* in our education system, and especially in pedagogy that is unresponsive to learners and their needs. By this we do not mean to 'blame the teachers', but rather to point to the inadequacies of the whole system that leads to inadequate classroom practices. By 'pedagogy' we refer to the 'theory and practice of teaching'; our contention is that the problem is one of 'theory and practice', or praxis. In addition, we believe that recent/contemporary attempts to change practice have mostly been superficial and as such have become part of the problem and not the solution.

While it is widely acknowledged that there is a problem, the nature of the problem and its solution are contested. There is still resistance to the contention that league table performance linked to national or state-wide testing is a failed policy. However, the tendency in the political system to implement changes in such a way is probably with us for good, and we have to find ways to work with it. To put this another way, there are objective reasons why the nature of the problem and its solution will remain contested. On the one hand there is the need for practical and political action; for politicians this works to a four- or five-year timetable. Indeed it is not unreasonable for children and parents to want to see improvements in their educational 'lifetime'. On the other hand there is the need to develop the education system and teaching profession on a rigorous foundation of *research and inquiry*: we view this as a long-term task requiring long-term commitment from practitioners and researchers, teachers and academics.

At this point in time we are fortunate in the UK to have a policy that includes an emphasis on 'learning from errors and misconceptions' as part of an 'assessment for learning' strategy.[8] This interest is mirrored in the USA, Australia and other countries. It provided us with the starting point for this book: you will find in Appendix 1 a set of common errors that are expected to arise in each year, and the frequency with which these occurred in a national sample of children, with our interpretation based on the research literature. In this way we hope to provide every teacher with a resource that connects research with their daily teaching in a practical way.[9]

We have chosen this approach because we believe that the answer to the mathematics problem lies in the long term, in the slow process of improving mathematics pedagogy; that is, in developing *the theory and practice of teaching*. We believe the place to start is in understandings of mathematics learning in the teaching context. A caveat: we do not believe the 'miracle' will arise from improvements in pedagogy 'in general', or only in general, but rather from mathematics pedagogy in particular. While our entry to the book is therefore through research into children's learning, especially the overt manifestations of current interest to teachers (that is, errors and misconceptions), the book deliberately progresses gently to research in pedagogy and mathematics pedagogy for itself.

Outline of the book: from categories of errors and misconceptions to a theory of pedagogy

Appendix 1 provides the most recent data we have from the MaLT national survey of performance, errors and misconceptions. In general these results are consistent with the previous studies of the 1970s, and the actual tests are widely available now in print and electronic format.[10]

The book itself, however, starts in Chapter 2, 'Learning from errors and misconceptions', by organizing these errors into categories that can help teachers make sense of all these data, and so provide means to interpret and understand learners' behaviours in mathematics. We focus in particular on diagnoses of conceptual problems related to: 'modelling', 'prototyping', 'overgeneralizing' and 'process–object' linking. These concepts are grounded in recent large-scale data and draw on examples from across the age range 4 to 15. In each case we show that these errors involve learners' intelligent, constructive activity that is important to conceptual development; they often indicate important learning opportunities. Such diagnoses of errors are therefore to be celebrated.

In Chapter 3, 'Children's mathematical discussions', we describe a generic 'dialogical' pedagogy of argumentation and discussion designed to support effective conceptual learning. This is the first step towards a classroom practice that recognizes the nature of students' learning as both learner-driven and socioculturally mediated. The general nature of the pedagogy is, however, qualified: in regard to learning particular concepts, quite specific pedagogical strategies are needed. We believe this point emerges from the examples there that we have drawn from our own small-group and whole-classroom research.

Chapters 4 and 6 focus on some knotty problems in 'Developing number' (specifically counting, multi-digit subtraction and multiplication) and conceptual development 'From number to algebra'. The evidence of research is that a learner's progress in specific conceptual domains is often very slow, and conceptual obstacles can be very persistent. In this context, we discuss the effect of scaffolding on performance and suggest a simple scaffolding pedagogy. In dealing with specific well-known persistent obstacles, we argue that effective pedagogy should use models and modelling to help children and students formulate mathematics in *intuitive* ways. This modelling, we argue, is best applied to 'situated intuitions' that students bring from outside mathematics or from more familiar, elementary mathematics to the case in point. Examples given include the structure of egg boxes, the practice of buying and selling, the intuitive sense of fairness in games, and so on. Additionally, however, we discuss the need for new mathematical signs to be introduced – a delicate moment when teachers use their status as the 'expert mathematician' in the schooling context to introduce new mathematics.

Chapter 5 focuses on these ideas in the context of 'Shape, space and measurement' topics. This is also an excuse to celebrate the significance of visuospatial contexts for a pedagogy of mathematics, and hence the notion of embodiment, gesture, talk (especially metaphor) and internalization in a Vygotskian theory of learning and pedagogy. This is worked out in the context of van Hiele's model of development of shape and space, and in measurement. We argue for a pedagogy that connects number, measurement, and shape-and-spatial aspects of mathematics; again the essential concept is modelling.

Chapter 7 addresses the topics of 'Data handling, graphicacy, probability and', very briefly, some 'statistics'. The significance of context and situation is again elicited, and we argue for experimentation based in social and historical analyses of mathematical concepts. In each case we introduce the reader to recent research in mathematics education that may be followed up in classrooms, and point to the need for more research.

Chapter 8, 'Pre-service teachers' mathematics subject matter knowledge', is concerned with recent research into teacher trainees and teachers' errors and misconceptions, and how teacher educators and their trainees might make use of this work – for example, through personalized diagnostic assessment tools. We introduce some new approaches to such research and to methods that may be of interest to teacher educators and teacher education researchers.

Finally, Chapter 9, 'Learning and teaching mathematics: towards a theory of pedagogy', attempts to make a case for a sociocultural, cultural-historical activity theory approach to pedagogy that integrates the 'reinvention' pedagogy of Freudenthal. Picking up many of the strands of concepts developed in previous chapters, we argue not just for the importance and significance of a theory of pedagogy but for a theory of *mathematics* pedagogy, informed by understandings of the particular cultural and historical significance of mathematics.

How might the book be 'used' or 'read' by different audiences?

The book addresses as its audience all those with an interest in mathematics education. We report our own recent empirical and theoretical research (and that of many colleagues, students and others) for our research community, but we have simultaneously tried to address teachers and teacher educators, especially those new to research but looking for practical ideas and implications. We introduce theory gently in relation to understanding empirical results, on the grounds that 'there is nothing so practical as a good theory'. Finally, by implication, we aspire to inform policy, the general public, and parents and students with a general interest in mathematics education.

. . . by a teacher, looking for ideas for classroom practice

A teacher preparing to teach a topic might have very practical questions in mind: for example, 'What does research say about the errors and misconceptions related to the topic I am about to teach?' We have provided in Appendix 1 a fully indexed set of errors arising from a major survey; finding a particular topic and error there, a teacher might go to the indexed parts of the book where there is related discussion about such errors and how they might be understood or managed. Perhaps, by dipping in and out, we hope that interested teachers may decide to find the time to study the book more thoroughly.

A teacher with sufficient interest will then find in Chapters 2 and 3 a wide-ranging set of common diagnostic errors organized according to a typology, together with a pedagogical approach to handling these in the classroom. This approach provides a strategy for eliciting and handling errors in a relatively productive way, and offers a contrast to the typical approaches we have often seen in classrooms (and indeed in 'exemplary practice' videos) where errors are simply and unproductively corrected. Some 'Discussion prompt sheets' are provided in Appendix 2 for teachers experimenting with classroom 'dialogue', which have children's ideas organized around a 'problematic' that a class might be provoked to discuss.

These two chapters, together with Appendix 1, aim to provide a basic conceptual toolkit for a 'diagnostic' teaching approach, or pedagogy, which takes seriously the learner's current state of knowledge. Some might say it provides the basis for a mathematical 'assessment for learning' pedagogy.

Chapters 4–8 are more specialized investigations for teachers, teacher trainers and researchers who want to understand in greater depth aspects of learning trajectories in various key topics, and their implications for teaching. We have used recent research and theory to tell these stories in as simple terms as we can, but much of the necessary research is not complete and the craft implications still require more working out. Part of the conclusion of these chapters is the need for new language and theory, as well as new empirical research: the everyday discourse of the typical staffroom seems inadequate to discuss the pedagogical issues raised, and we look to the research community and its discourses for this missing language.

In Chapter 9 we confront the need for a theory of pedagogy directly; there is an introduction to theoretical frameworks that inevitably involve some new terminologies. Introductions to important and recent literature on theory and mathematics education are to be found in notes throughout the book. If these are biased towards our own work then we do not apologize; it is after all the work we understand best.

. . . by a researcher, looking for recent, relevant research into errors and misconceptions, mathematics education and pedagogy

An experienced researcher may wish to consume the book in one go: there are extensive citations where research literature underpinning the work is described and referenced. We hope you will find our typology in Chapter 2 and our approach to argumentation in Chapter 3 helpful and original, while heavily indebted to and grounded in the literature in mathematics education and in classroom discourse inter alia. There is substantial new 'topic-related' research underpinning Chapters 4–8 too, as is evidenced in the citations: some of this is learner-focused and some arises from studies of pedagogy. The argument in Chapter 9 (and implicitly developed in many of the early chapters) attempts to situate Freudenthal's Realistic Mathematics Education perspective within work in situated cognition and Cultural Historical Activity Theory (CHAT); as such it seeks fresh insights into a theory of mathematics pedagogy. We imagine some researchers and theorists will be surprised that we are content to use the terminology of 'errors' and 'misconceptions' within a CHAT or social practice perspective; this is worked out in Chapters 2, 4–7 and 9.[11]

. . . by the practitioner-researcher or research student, looking for ideas, concepts and research problems

The new researcher or research student looking for ideas will find here simple introductions to research that adopts many different methods, and many unanswered questions that might be developed into research projects. Suggestions for these are made explicit from time to time and in the notes referred to throughout the chapters.

In particular we hope that you will explore the findings of the MaLT project laid out in Appendix 1; here errors are to be found whose interpretations might be investigated in classrooms or through group interviews with children in the manner of our research cited in several chapters. In addition, a student with an interest in a particular topic might collect a set of tasks together in a hierarchy (as explained in Chapter 4) and interpret it as a possible developmental scale. Furthermore, we suggest (in Chapter 8) how those interested might use tasks (with interesting errors) to investigate and develop teachers' pedagogical content knowledge.

We hope also that the way we have organized the book, becoming progressively more formal and theoretical as the sections advance, will help the new researcher to become gradually acclimatized (let us not yet say 'enculturated') to research perspectives. It will soon become obvious that we have no truck with the quantitative–qualitative dichotomization of methods; perhaps an attraction of this book might be that research is drawn on as and when the narrative requires it, independently of the type of research method/ methodology employed. If we have oversimplified the literature here and there, our impression from experience of masters and beginning doctoral students leads us to believe this will be welcomed.

. . . by policy makers, researchers and consumers

The thrust of the book's argument intends to persuade the reader of a mathematics-specific approach to pedagogy. While we certainly allow for, and require, a dialogical pedagogy that can be argued to be of general validity in teaching, we nevertheless argue that there are significant limitations to generalization of or from mathematics education. The very specific mathematical details we offer are essential for preparing teachers to teach; but in fact the details we offer here are only illustrative and but a small part of the toolkit that teaching requires in practice.

Likewise, while we allow that the sociocultural approach to pedagogy we argue for can be developed as the core of theory of any 'science' education in general, this very theory essentially contextualizes mathematics education in the sociocultural reality of mathematics. Some approaches to pedagogy – and 'assessment for learning' may be one of them – are in danger of losing sight of the specific subject matter-relatedness of pedagogy. For instance, it is evident that the 'meanings' of errors in teaching middle-school technology or science are quite different from those of mathematics. But we now have policy makers formulating identical phrases for 'dealing with errors and misconceptions' in these different subjects.

So, we argue that while there are important general features of good discussion (listening, responding, reflecting, and so on) the essence of good argumentation is in fact predicated on 'good mathematics'. A good discussion will not necessarily evoke good mathematics. There are distinctly 'socio-mathematical' norms of good discussion as well as good 'social' norms. So, we make a contribution to the subject-specific aspects of pedagogy, and relate specifically to teachers' pedagogical content knowledge throughout this book. For instance, we cite a Year 1 teacher who taught her children that an 'odd' number arises from things being organized in pairs (socks) but then 'losing one' in the washing. Such a teacher understands not only the context of her children's lives (essential pedagogical knowledge) but also the algebraic structure of arithmetic (even $= 2n$; odd $= 2n - 1$) underpinning the concept of 'odd and even' in mathematics.

Additionally, we argue that at the core of a sociocultural theory of pedagogy is an appreciation of mathematics as a social and cultural activity – that is, as Freudenthal said, an essentially human, contextualized and culturally historically situated activity. In this view mathematics starts in every person's social world (and mathematics is truly for all), but it is the job of schooling to make the mathematical-scientific view of this everyday human activity visible. To paraphrase this formulation in terms of 'talk': schooling allows the learner to talk *mathematically* about the everyday phenomena in which mathematics is 'embedded'. Thus the joke:

> An astrophysicist, a physicist and a mathematician are out walking together in the Scottish Highlands. Suddenly, out of the mist in front of them appears a black sheep. 'That proves it!' says the astrophysicist, 'All sheep in Scotland are black!' 'No, that's too sweeping a generalization,' says the physicist, 'All we can say is that, in Scotland, some of the sheep are black.' 'No, no,' objects the mathematician, 'All we can say is that, in Scotland, there exists at least one sheep, at least one side of which is black.'[12]

While similar theoretical formulations might be made of the teaching of mathematics as of 'science' or any other discipline, this implies that there is an essential uniqueness in the context of the discipline, namely the particular social, historical, cultural and political context of the domain of mathematics. We hope a flavour of this is captured in the book as a whole.

Notes

1 Smith (2004) is the UK report to government on the mathematics crisis, following the Roberts Review (2002) on the UK science base.
2 PISA (2003, 2004, 2005); Jones *et al.* (2005) PME Research Forum.
3 See Tymms (2004) on the 'Texas miracle', an apparently remarkable set of data showing improved standards, which was later shown to be largely illusory.
4 From the MaLT project; see Williams *et al.* (2005).
5 Williams *et al.* (2005).
6 This is to be expected of a normal distribution: a logit represents approximately the difference between 70 per cent and 50 per cent of the population.
7 This means care must be taken when comparing performance between 'distant years' such as between Year 2 and Year 9, for instance, because the curriculum differences between these years make 'vertical equation' invalid.
8 Black *et al.* (2003, 2004).
9 Hence the book seeks to bridge the gap between research and practice – that is, between research in the psychology of learning mathematics and mathematics teaching practice (see Williams and Ryan, 2000).
10 MaLT (2005).

11 On account of the Smith, DiSessa and Roschelle (1993–94) argument based on 'a constructivist theory of learning that interprets students' prior conceptions as resources for cognitive growth within a complex systems view of knowledge'. Their theoretical perspective aimed 'to characterize the interrelationships among diverse knowledge elements rather than identify particular flawed conceptions; it emphasizes knowledge refinement and reorganization, rather than replacement, as primary metaphors for learning; and it provides a framework for understanding misconceptions as both flawed and productive' (p. 115).

12 Along the same lines of difference but this one does not involve mathematicians: A physicist, a chemist and a computer scientist are driving along in a car when it breaks down. 'Try the spark plugs,' suggests the physicist, 'perhaps the gap is too wide.' 'Try the choke,' suggests the chemist, 'The fuel–air mix is wrong.' Then the computer scientist says, 'Why don't we all get out of the car, and then get back in again and see if it'll start?'

2 Learning from errors and misconceptions

We think therefore we err[1]

Introduction

In classifying the errors children make on standardized assessments and national tests[2] we found, in addition to 'slips' and errors of 'uncertain diagnosis', several categories of significant, developmental errors that we explained as due to: 'modelling'; 'prototyping'; 'overgeneralizing'; and 'process–object' linking. In this chapter we describe each of these, give examples from across the curriculum, and conclude that the latter four types of errors are the result of intelligent constructions that should be valued by learners and teachers alike. Later in the book (Chapters 3–8) we provide more detailed discussions of some of these errors and misconceptions, and their implications for teaching.

However, we should first consider errors with no obvious developmental, conceptual explanation. Children, like adults, do make slips when they misread, misremember facts, suffer from 'cognitive overload' or 'jump to conclusions'.[3] We have often found, for instance, that when presented with a problem requiring two steps or a solution meeting two conditions, children often respond by performing just the one step, or provide a solution appropriate to just one of the two conditions required. (There are many examples of these in Appendix 1). When asked to select an odd factor of 28, for instance, some will identify an odd number but not a factor, and some will identify an even factor, suggesting lack of concentration, cognitive overload or reading difficulties. Such errors are also very common when reading tables of information – as those of us who have waited in vain for the non-existent 10:26 train on a Sunday may recall!

In cases such as that shown in Figure 2.1 it may be difficult if not impossible to say that the child who responds with 4½ or 5 has a concept or

In a competition children get points for how quickly they can type 10 words. Ben took 50 seconds. How many points did he get?	Time in seconds	Points
	Under 20	6
	Under 40	5
	Under 60	4
	Under 80	3
	Under 100	2
Common errors: 4½ and 5	Under 120	1

Figure 2.1   Reading and interpreting a table of information.

conceptual structure that needs replacing, developing or otherwise fixing. It is even possible that the superficial level of the thinking involved in a child's erratic response is symptomatic of the mode of assessment: one wonders if the child would be so careless if the task was a 'real life' one in which the correct answer 'really mattered' to them, such as in a 'real' competition.

Some researchers have found that even professional scientists make the mistakes that research claims to be typical of young learners – when interpreting graphs of an academic nature, for instance.[4] These failures are in contrast to their actual working practices, where they make few if any mistakes. In some previous research we found that a lack of motivation (coupled with low levels of anxiety) may affect children's test performance adversely, perhaps because of the many slips they make when poorly motivated.[5] On the other hand, we are also aware that high levels of anxiety can lead to blind panic and rushing, which can also cause errors. Errors due to the assessment conditions such as these are not informative for learning and have no developmental interest – that is, they may be important to improving test scores but are of little interest to learning and teaching proper.

In some cases an error in a 'two part' problem may also relate to a significant misconception. For instance, when asked to find the median of a set of numbers, children will commonly choose the middle number while forgetting to first put the set of numbers in order. It might be the case that this follows from a faulty conception of 'median': perhaps the child really believes that the median is 'the middle' of the set of numbers without regard to order. On the other hand, it is just as likely that the response was an incomplete performance, with the requirement that the set be ordered merely forgotten in the moment.

In response to such errors one can emphasize problem-solving strategies: (i) to read and think about the task carefully before beginning; (ii) to consider alternatives before leaping to conclusions; (iii) to make notes of relevant information and write down working out and partial answers to reduce cognitive load; and (iv) to always check answers and look back to the context for sense (to identify errors that might be correctable).[6] We are aware that such problem-solving strategies and heuristics could fill a book in itself, but we have little to say about these important strategies for improving performance and problem solving here.

Uncertain and problematic diagnoses of errors as indicators of development

In addition, we have to accept a degree of uncertainty in 'diagnosing' an error as indicative of a conceptual problem in any test-like assessment; a surer way to develop a diagnosis is to engage the children in discussion of their *reasoning* in relation to a diagnostic task. Many researchers have interviewed children about interesting categories of response to written assessments in order to access the reasons underpinning errors and other responses.[7] At this deeper level we can analyse and interpret the conceptual knowledge basis that diagnoses their developmental needs and thus help inform teaching that can support children in correcting these conceptual faults.

Table 2.1 summarizes this. The first level suggests relatively accessible and observable, 'surface' behaviour, usually involving procedures, responses to tasks, and so on.[8] The second, 'deep', level indicates the conceptual underpinning or mode of reasoning, its diagnosis and interpretation. We choose the terms 'surface' and 'deep' in deference to Skemp, who also articulated this kind of difference in mathematics in several books and papers in the 1960s and 1970s.[9] The connections between surface and deep structures will concern us throughout this book.

The surface level is relatively accessible to experienced teachers, who can recognize or even predict many of the errors that their children make in assessment tasks. Even though they may have no explanatory theory they can recognize, and even perhaps anticipate, some of these errors.[10] This level of assessment typically leads teachers to identify the error and provide a correct alternative, perhaps with a reason. The deeper level is more problematic, however, even for experienced teachers, and demands some theoretical

Table 2.1 Surface and deeper levels of knowledge, assessment and pedagogy

	Pupil knowledge	Assessment	Pedagogy
Surface: task response	Procedure/error	Record/observe/ categorize	Correct the error
Deeper: explanation/ reasoning/justification	Mis/conception Backing/ justification	Diagnose/explain Interpret/theorize	Dialogue with misconception/ reasoning/conflict

conceptions to organize a diagnosis and a related teaching design or strategy that engages or conflicts with the underlying mis/conceptions and reasoning directly. Notice that the surface level is principally behavioural, while the deeper level is more richly explanatory and discursive.

While some errors we have found are not obviously related to identifiable misconceptions or conceptual limitations, some clearly *are*. For example, for many children a diamond (a square orientated so that it 'sits on a corner') is not identifiable as a type of square; later on, again, for many children, a rectangle is not recognized as a type of parallelogram. These errors relate to limitations in their mathematical concepts and are quite typical of children's knowledge at a certain stage in their conceptual development. We believe that diagnosis involves understanding the stage of the learner's development and is critical to effective, conceptual teaching; the consequence of *not* understanding may be repeated re-presentation of a failing curriculum.

Understanding such errors can make all the difference to pedagogy and should be prized accordingly. These are the errors that will chiefly interest us in this book. They offer a window onto the conceptual structures that children are building and hence can be suggestive of appropriate intervention – for example, through the design of productive tasks, argumentation and cognitive conflict in discussion (see especially Chapter 3).

Modelling

We sometimes find that a problem or task context is understood or represented by a child 'inappropriately' – that is to say, in a way other than was intended, other than in the 'mathematical way' the teacher or assessor had in mind. When we refer to 'modelling' we refer to the way mathematics is connected with a 'real' everyday world – the everyday world being then represented by the mathematics. One can say perhaps when a child has a 'modelling error' that the child has their own 'model' of the situation, in conflict with the 'mathematical model' expected in the academic context of school. A well-known story tells of a nursery teacher who asks a new pupil to 'wait there for the present' – the poor child is dreadfully disappointed after waiting for an age not to duly receive her present. Then again, later on, she is asked in a test to tick the 'right' angle in a set of angles, and asks 'When it says "right" angel, does that mean the wings should be the right way up?'

These stories tell of children wrong-footed by the particular meanings attached to 'schooling' and 'doing school mathematics' in particular: what we refer to as the 'mathematical voice'.[11] It is easy enough to be fooled by being asked to 'divide 6 by a half' in an everyday context: even many graduates in teacher training often respond automatically with '3'. We put this down to the naturally intuitive everyday interpretation of 'divide by a half' as 'divide in half' or 'divide into halves', instructions one expects to find in daily tasks. Only in school do you ask for a number to be divided *by* a half!

Hughes' work with nursery children revealed a particularly important mathematical barrier.[12] Typically the pre-schooler can answer problems such as 'I have one brick, then I get two more bricks, how many bricks do I have now?' when bricks are handled in the task, even if some of the time they are not visible. But when asked 'What is one add two?' the same children can be struck dumb. It is as if they want to say 'One? One what?' This problem can be thought of as a matter of learning the rules of the new game of school mathematics. We refer to it as a modelling problem because it also involves connecting the mathematics of everyday life with this new game. The game in school involves doing sums like '1 add 2', but it can be mastered only by connecting it with the world of everyday mathematics, where one brick and another two bricks makes three bricks.

In an interview about the probability of spinning one particular number with a triangular spinner, an 11-year-old girl told us that she did not like to answer 'one-third'. She said, 'Well I usually go for "one-in-three" because usually when I think of fractions I think of splitting things up instead of probability and stuff.' We think this suggests a lack of ease with the mathematical voice and a preference for the everyday form of language of odds and chance. Of course her preferred answer here is not actually 'incorrect', but it is not helpful later to think of probability in this way when probabilities become subject to calculation: imagine for instance trying to multiply one-in-three by one-in-five less than three-in-four! In addition, the game of school mathematics demands that probability is tackled with fractions and decimals: this girl is beginning to be aware that her 'preference' is good for everyday life but not for the school game.

Sociologists of education have explained the differential performance of different social classes in education by the different demands that 'learning the game of school' makes of people from different class backgrounds. Bernstein in particular explains the relative ease that children from middle-class backgrounds have in accessing the rules of discourse that school demands. Since the middle classes mostly spend their lives in discourses that are largely mediated by textual symbol systems of one kind and another, the discourses of schooling are less strange to their children. Hasan's work with pre-schoolers has shown how these differences manifest themselves in mother–child talk.[13] In fact children from the lower social classes are acculturated to discourses that are relatively direct and contextualized, rarely indirectly mediated by 'distancing' language genres. Children who find the rules of the game a mystery are thereby likely to be regarded as just 'dumb' or, worse, culturally deprived.

The transition from informal-and-contextual to formal mathematical language is a delicate and important one. It is a matter of pedagogical judgement to decide when to accept the informal and when to introduce formal mathematical language. For instance, it is common in everyday life to hear sports commentators speak of 'point thirty-two' of a second when announcing decimal finishing times in sporting events. This informal use of language might provide a pedagogically helpful resource in translating '0.32' as 'thirty-two hundredths'. But it can be dangerous when dealing with decimals of different length, such as '0.5' and '0.32', since it is suggestive of the common misconception that 'point five should be less than point thirty-two'.

In general, everyday contexts provide an essential resource for building mathematics. In the case of fractions, we use the model of dividing a cake into equal shares because we know that the child brings knowledge of cake-sharing into the classroom and that we can make use of this. The child already knows how a cake should be cut to share it between two, four or more persons. Later, when the child suggests that one of the pictures in Figure 2.2 shows a shading of ¼, we can appeal back to the cake-sharing context and ask if they would believe this ¼ was a *fair* share of the cake.[14]

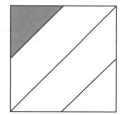 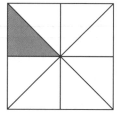

Figure 2.2   Unfair 'quarters' of a cake.

But while one can ask how many half-cakes make 6 whole cakes and how one could share 6 cakes between 12 people, one cannot concretely 'divide' 6 whole cakes 'by a half' to get 12. The sharing of cakes proves a helpful entry point but an incomplete context for fractions in this respect.[15] Rarely is any one model, context or representation in itself completely satisfying or even adequate for developing a branch of mathematics: usually at least several contexts, models and representations are needed, and one needs to switch and connect flexibly between them.

Consider the context of money for decimals; this is apparently good when all figures under consideration are to two decimal places. But metric lengths, despite being less familiar, provide a better context in allowing flexibility of decimal places and unit. What about visuo-spatial models? Shading areas on a hundred square is helpful for representing the relative sizes of the different places of the decimal, but the number line is better for emphasizing the order of decimals.

Many investigators have researched children's use of models to help build up their mathematics, and researchers have demonstrated their central role in learning. The number line has been particularly widely studied, and its importance demonstrated empirically and theoretically.[16] Lakoff and Nunez, and others, have analysed it from a metaphorical and 'embodied cognition' point of view, and suggest that it allows the learner to situate themselves bodily and spatially in the mathematics in a powerful way.[17] In general such models encourage the learner to communicate and articulate using actions and gestures as well as words.

The use of such representations (we include metaphors, contexts and models in this) brings 'meaning' to mathematics by providing connections between mathematics and what is already intuitively known.[18] Without the hundred square, the function machine, the number line, fractions of pies, money/length contexts for decimals, and the Cartesian grid, mathematics would be purely formal and very difficult for humans to learn or to use. But these concretizations of mathematics always bring with them *limitations*; if the context or the model were an exact, 'error-free' match with the mathematics, then they would almost *be* the mathematics. Thus errors and misconceptions often reveal a gap between the child's use of the model, context or metaphor and the targeted mathematics. They thereby reveal a 'learning zone' that pedagogy should address.[19]

In addition, however, to return to the question of the socialization of learners into the games of mathematics, research by Cooper and Dunne, and others in the Bernstein tradition, has shown that some children have particular difficulty in playing the game of 'contextualized mathematics'.[20] When presented with tasks in which mathematics is supposed to be used in a supposedly 'practical' way, many children can be fooled into interpreting the task too practically, bringing to bear all kinds of practical knowledge not given in the task and not expected by the teacher. For instance, in one much referenced test question, a lift is supposed to carry up to 14 people, and 269 people have to go up in the lift. The question is 'How many times must the lift go to transport them all?' Any practical response would, of course, have to deal with considerations like people getting fed up with waiting and taking the stairs; but a pupil with a 'feel for the game' of school maths knows that there is a mathematical structure, just the one answer, and that in tests all the information necessary is there in the question. It seems, however, that many children are not disposed by birth, upbringing, and so on, to decode this 'feel' for such games.[21] Most teachers take this feel for the game for granted; consequently these rules remain 'invisible'.[22] Perhaps this accounts for the failure rates of many working-class children, and suggests that pedagogy needs to make the rules of the game explicit. Indeed a mathematically literate pedagogy should perhaps make clear that mathematics is a particular game with its own rules, language, conventions, and so on.

Prototypes versus mathematical concepts

When we learn concepts we tend not to learn them 'mathematically' – that is, in the way they are defined mathematically. It seems humans evolved a way of developing concepts that is more 'prototypical'.[23] By a *prototype* for a concept we mean a culturally 'typical example' of the concept. Lakoff has drawn attention to the prototypical 'bachelor' by asking the question 'Is the Pope a bachelor?'[24] In some formal definitions of the concept of bachelor, the answer might be yes. But the Pope is not a *prototypical* bachelor: the prototype arises in our culture as part of a normative narrative. Thus, a boy matures into a young man, and a young man becomes a bachelor when he starts to be marriageable. Later still, he is married, and may become widowed, separated or divorced, but he may never be quite the same prototypical bachelor again.

An experiment we have found useful with teachers and students is as follows. Imagine in your mind's eye a rectangle. What does it look like? Does it 'lie flat' with its longest side horizontal? Is its height about half to a third of its length?[25] In a class of adults, in our experience, one typically finds that all but one or two draw a prototypical rectangle like the rectangle marked with a tick in Figure 2.3; it would be most unusual – and unnatural – to draw a square. Thinking prototypically, then, one would not include a square as an example of a rectangle; such an error is therefore diagnostic of prototypical thinking.

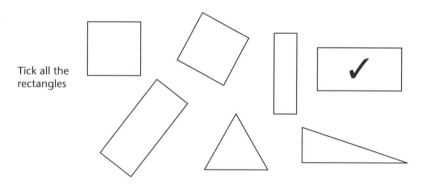

Tick all the rectangles

Figure 2.3 Rectangles and squares: the prototypical rectangle is ticked.

Thus children often recognize a square or a rectangle *only* if it is lying 'flat' with its base horizontal, and at a higher level they may refuse to recognize that a square is a rectangle, or that any rectangle is also a parallelogram. Thus we find errors arising within mathematics because humans naturally develop concepts informally and intuitively in 'non-mathematical', prototypical ways. The mathematical definition of a concept generally follows from a series of examples and defining relationships: not a prototypical way of thinking at all.[26] Once one recognizes that prototypical thinking is natural and intuitive, many other errors can be seen as prototypical in character: typically children will count up in steps of 1, or perhaps 10, or 100 when reading a scale, leading to common errors in reading graphs and handling data.

The common error of reading the scales (see Figure 2.4) as 2.2 instead of 2.4 can also be understood as prototypical: commonly children will have met scales that increase by 1, and increments of 2 or 4 are rarer. They are therefore predisposed to this prototype. Does this mean that such children are not 'able' to read scales that increment by 2s or 4s? This is less certain; if in such cases the child counts up through the scale to the next marker, they usually will see their error and re-compute, often on a trial-and-improve basis. Reflection on this conflict can suggest the need to develop new procedures for such tasks; this is suggestive of the general method of 'cognitive conflict' proposed by neo-Piagetians.[27] (For more on this see Chapters 3 and 9.)

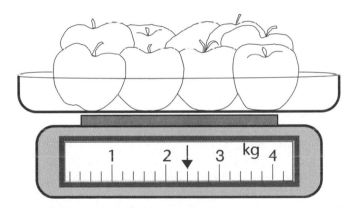

Figure 2.4 Reading scales: commonly misread as 2.2 kg (for example, by 35 per cent of 10-year-olds; see Appendix 1, M10.18).

We also label as 'prototypical' those errors in shape and space involving reflecting, or otherwise transforming shapes, that occur when children incorrectly adopt a prototypical mirror line (or centre of rotation). The prototype is usually a vertical or horizontal line, one that passes along an edge of the shape to be transformed, or at least that is conveniently parallel to the lines in the shape (see Figure 2.5).[28]

In a deep psychological sense, *the* prototypical mirror line is vertical because this is the symmetry of a human face, the first identifiable figure a baby recognizes and objectifies. Psychologists have even established that more symmetrical faces are rated as more 'beautiful or attractive' by adults under test conditions. Such considerations may suggest that children should at some point turn the object (or paper) of their reflection so that its mirror line *is*

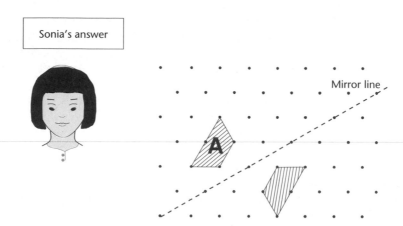

Figure 2.5 Reflection line is often taken 'conveniently', using a prototypical mirror line.

vertical – asymmetries tend then to become immediately and intuitively obvious.

Similarly, our embodied experience of rotation is that of one's hand on the end of one's arm rotating about the shoulder (and so on), or of a hand on a clock rotating about the centre of the clock (as clocks *used* to!). The fact that the centre of rotation is at the end of the arm or clock hand is important here: rotation of a shape about a point *not* on the object is known to be much, much harder to manage. Again, teaching that is sensitive to the prototypical rotation will make use of this: children can be invited to reach out a hand from the centre of rotation (the shoulder) to get hold of the shape with their 'hand' and rotate the arm. Thus pedagogy can recognize the prototypicality of an intuitive conception and make use of it.

Later prototypes look increasingly like taught overgeneralizations. Consider for instance the linear prototype in graphicacy common in the performance of 11- to 18-year-olds – that is, the tendency to draw straight-line graphs in all cases.[29] Might this not be a result of the habit of providing data that are almost always linear for graphing, especially in science curriculum contexts?

Faced with this prototypical view of concept formation, psychologists have advocated the need to work with a 'rational' set of examples – that is, a set of examples and counterexamples that can be used to illustrate the rational formation of the properties of a concept. Thus, one seeks a set of examples that includes all the most important irrelevant properties, and a set of counterexamples that illustrate all the relevant missing properties of the concept. For example, consider the concept of triangle, defined as a three-sided, three-angled polygon. Irrelevant properties include orientation, size of angles, lengths of sides, and so on. Relevant missing properties for counterexamples would be the number of sides, but might also include the straightness of the sides. One might further want to consider the triangular face of a three-dimensional object, or the 'triangle' formed by the three lines of longitude on a sphere. (See Chapter 5 for more on this.)

If prototypes are the result of 'typicality' in experiences then the limitations of prototypical thinking can presumably be 'fixed' only by providing for experience with a rationally diverse set of tasks or experiences – that is, for 'definition' moves with a set of rational examples. It will be vital, then, for examples of triangles to include a rational set of non-prototypical 'unusual' cases – cases that are 'only just' triangles, and cases that are 'only just not'. This might lead to all sorts of creative, anti-prototypical 'monsters': is the figure ABC, where A, B and C lie on a straight line, a 'triangle'? A mathematician might approve, since it seems to have 'the usual' properties (for example, its 'internal' angles sum to 180 degrees, its circumcentre lies at the point at infinity where its perpendicular bisectors meet, and so on). If so, then what about the 'triangle' ABB?[30]

Intelligent overgeneralization

Closely allied to errors due to prototypes are overgeneralizations. One early overgeneralization occurs when children subtract two-digit numbers by 'taking the smaller digit from the larger' (so that $32 - 17 = 25$). Perhaps because the children were taught to perform a two-digit subtraction algorithm 'without carrying' or decomposing first, they develop methods that work for these cases but that then do not generalize to all cases of two-digit subtraction. If the children did meet two-digit subtraction (without carrying) first as an algorithm, then this could be put down to a thoughtless curriculum, but we believe that this is rare nowadays.[31] It is still the case that the 'smaller from larger' error is likely to be developed by some children taught to solve such tasks using a vertical algorithm; this may be because the first experience of subtraction tasks has been to take the smaller from the larger (they may even have been taught this explicitly as in, 'You can't take seven from four, so . . .').

An important example of an overgeneralization later on is the belief that 'multiplication makes bigger' (or division makes smaller); this generalization is true enough when applied to (most) whole, natural numbers. Furthermore, in the models of multiplication used, such as 'times', set combinations, and so on, it is intuitively obvious.[32] This generalization can lend support to errors such as agreeing that $0.3 \times 0.2 = 0.6$, $120 \times 0.1 > 120$, that 0.5^2 must be bigger than 0.5, and so on. The most common errors (for ages 8 to 16 years) we attributed to overgeneralization (see Chapter 4) involved variations on this theme; that is, they almost all involved working with rules that had been established for the whole numbers into domains like fractions, decimals and negative numbers.[33]

At the simplest level, it is quite common for children to ignore the sign that indicates they should be dealing with a decimal, fraction, percentage or negative number. Thus 30% is treated as 30, the integer −5 is just read as 5, or the decimal point is 'ignored' as in $1.2 + 3 = 1.5$. This is usually indicative of a simple rejection of all but the whole numbers: at least it indicates a strong preference or comfort zone in whole numbers and their arithmetic. It may be that intuition, visualization and confidence are restricted to this zone in such cases. Similarly we categorize the computations $5 − 9 = 4$ and $1 ÷ 7 = 7$ as typical errors due to a restriction of perspective to the whole numbers: 'God made the natural numbers; all else is the work of man' (attributed to Kronecker).

However, more sophisticated overgeneralizations include the reading of decimals as a pair of whole numbers separated by a point; while all is then well with $1.3 + 3.5 = 4.8$, or even $1.5 + 3 = 4.5$, we find that '2 point 5' is smaller than '2 point thirty-two' because, ignoring the whole number parts, the 5 is smaller than 32. Furthermore, this leads to calculations with decimals such as: $2.3 + 1.47 = 3.50$, $2.5 × 2.5 = 4.25$, and hybrids like $4.7 × 100 = 4.700$.

Very commonly, one also sees the same thinking with the negative integers: the integer is conceived of as a 'combination of the sign and the number'. The minus is understood to mean smaller numbers than the plus, so −1, −2 and −3 come before +1, +2, +3, possibly in that order, giving . . . 0, −1, −2, −3, +1, +2, +3, . . . or maybe −1, −2, −3, 0, +1, +2, +3. . . . Then computations children make with these integers typically involve first combining the 'numbers' and, second, manipulating the signs: thus $−2 + 8 = −10$, and $+3 − −8 = +$ or −5.[34] These procedures are typically articulated as in 'I added the 2 and the 8 to get 10, then the signs are minus and plus, so it's minus . . . −10.' There may be very little by way of justification for these procedures, it is 'just so'. (This is discussed further in Chapter 6.)

Another important overgeneralization involves the overuse of the 'additive' strategy when a multiplicative strategy is required. This leads to cancelling down fractions by subtracting the same number from the top and bottom: $^7/_{18} = ^5/_{16}$ or $⅚ = ¾$. In ratio tasks this error is very frequent, so 4:10 is the same as 6:x yields $x = 12$. This proves extraordinarily resistant to change, enduring across contexts and right through from primary to secondary school, at least to the age of 16 for many children.[35] (This is discussed in detail in Chapter 4.)

Perhaps the most important conclusion here is the paradox that 'all generalizations are, or perhaps become, overgeneralizations' when the set of cases to which they are applied becomes inappropriately extended (or perhaps restricted). Thus errors due to overgeneralization are endemic in mathematics, which is largely about generalizing. Pedagogy could usefully develop an awareness of this metacognition in mathematics learning: perhaps pedagogy might usefully pose the question 'When does this (generalization) *not* apply?'

Process, object and structural conceptions

One of the earliest problems children have with number is recognizing that, when answering 'How many buttons?', the answer is the last numeral they use to count the set. When asked 'How many buttons?' a second time, the child may begin to *count* the set for the second time. Thus, 'How many . . .?' signals the *process* to count, and the sequence of numerals is read out 1, 2, 3, 4, . . ., 8. But this counting process is not yet realized as being about the formation of the object '8' – that is, both the result of the counting process and at the same time the numerosity (actually the cardinality) of this set of buttons.[36]

Learning mathematics involves many such process–object relations, and errors do often diagnose the child's lack of completion of the process–object 'reification' (Gray and Tall call this duality a 'procept').[37] Consider the child who answers 548 to the missing addend sum: ? − 1452 = 2000. This suggests an attempt to understand the task with an inadequate, 'process' conception of the equals sign.[38] The child's first understanding of the sign is often in the context of an instruction to carry out an arithmetical process, such as $3 + 5 = ?$ This 'process' view of the sign is often indicated by a reading of it as 'makes' as in '3 add 5 makes 8'. And yet, when this process is later understood as a number sentence, the equals sign acquires an additional meaning as 'is' or 'is the same as' or even 'is equal to'. The sum $3 + 5 = 8$ then becomes a number sentence that can equally be read as '3 and 5 is 8' or '8 is the same as 3 and 5'. This is an important conceptual change.

Full mastery of a process–object conception involves such a flexible switching and connection of the two perspectives: it is both true that the process 3 add 5 makes, or is, 8 *and* that 8 is the resulting object of adding 3 and 5. It is sometimes convenient to focus on the process, and other times helpful to focus on the object. The understanding of the process–object nature of '−5' implicates both (i) the process of subtracting 5, and (ii) a single object, the number 'minus 5', the result of subtracting 5 from zero (among many other things). These seem to be different conceptions, and can lead to inappropriate attempts to combine the two, as in interpreting − (−5) as 'take away . . . subtract 5'. In such difficulties, children may retreat into formal manipulations using rules without reasons; such children will treat the integer −5 as a combination of two signs to be considered and manipulated separately somehow (see the discussion above about overgeneralization). But for some, perhaps for many, grasping the 'object' conception needed to handle integer arithmetic may never happen. So, 'minus times minus is plus, the reasons why we must not discuss'. And, for many, the beginning of the withdrawal of their intelligence from mathematics begins. (This topic is discussed in more detail in Chapter 6.)

In the context of a measurement such as length, children may have difficulty identifying the relation between the numeral that labels the measure and the process of measuring that gives rise to it. Thus the label 5 on the ruler indicates that there are 5 units (for example, centimetres) of length that can be counted 'up to that point' from an origin on the ruler (labelled zero). Note that these 5 units are intervals between numerals, and that there are actually 6 numerals involved in the process of measuring a length of 5 units, namely: 0, 1, 2, 3, 4, 5. Lack of awareness or understanding of this relation may explain many errors with numerals and scales when measuring or even when counting on a number line. Thus, a child may say $18 - 4 = 15$, by counting down the four numerals 18, 17, 16, 15, or counting the ticks on a ruler or number line instead of the intervals between them. (See Chapter 5 for further discussion on this.) One can similarly reflect that a child who does not realize that 2 divided by 3 is 'obviously' simply ⅔, or who has no intuitive belief in the cancellation of fractions such as $^{10}/_5 = 2$, has not achieved a process–object conception of fractions as the object of the process of division (yet).

A particularly interesting problem that some older students have with interpreting graphs involves the reading of a graph as a picture. When asked to interpret the travel graph in Figure 2.6, a child may say that the person represented walks up a hill, then along for a while, then down again. In this case the process of graphing has been quite removed from its resulting pictorial graphical object: the graph has become a black box, its inner workings/processes are hidden from view.[39]

The diagnosis of a conception limited to a process perspective suggests the need for 'reification' (object-formation) to take place. This generally involves the use of appropriate contexts and models that represent the result of the process as an object and the naming of the object, sometimes merely

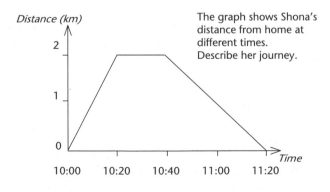

'Shona walks up a hill, along for a while, and then down again.'

Figure 2.6 Graph-as-picture misconception.

Figure 2.7   Equivalence of length of (2 + 3) and 5 with rods.

a grammatical shift from a verb to its noun (hence adding and 'addition', dividing and 'division', and so on).

To take the simple case of '2 add 3 makes 5', the use of beads or rods that represent this process as an equivalence is demonstrated before one's eyes (see Figure 2.7).[40] The naming of the equivalence as '2 and 3 is the same (length/ size/amount) as 5' begins to establish the number sentence and the concept of equivalence inherent in the equals sign. In practice the elision of the bracketed units, such as length, is only gradually achieved, and the re-introduction or reconnection of the model to the number sentence may be needed to help build the chain of meaning over quite an extended period of development.

A similar visual demonstration of the relation $(n + 1)^2 = n^2 + 2n + 1$ can help to provide a structural conception of the relation previously understood as a process of multiplying out of brackets (see Chapter 6). When the equals sign here is understood as signifying an *identity*, then it is both a statement about multiplying out brackets and equally a statement of factorization. It is an equation with an infinity of solutions *and* an algebraic identity.

Conclusions

We have examined four developmental categories of errors that seem to explain most of the errors of interest that we have found as due to: modelling, prototyping, overgeneralizing and process–object linking. All have some features in common: first, these errors diagnose (somewhat uncertainly) the child's state of knowledge; second, they are a natural outcome of intelligent mathematical development, involving connections, generalizations and concept formation; third, they signal a learning opportunity or zone, and so potential for development – for example, through targeted teaching.

In general, we see the learner's underpinning knowledge (for example, the conceptions or misconceptions) as the object that teaching must expose and engage with; the error itself is merely the superficial, visible behavioural response to a task. The obvious implication is that simply correcting the error is, for the child, unlikely to be an adequate teaching response; unless it engages with reason this correction may possibly do more harm than good, teaching the child to regard mathematics as a meaningless, arcane activity. What, then, should be the teacher's response to errors? We have suggested several specific, category-related strategies in this chapter. In the next chapter we describe an approach that makes use of specific local content knowledge but that has a general, dialogical framework that can be used in most such contexts. In subsequent chapters we return to some of the suggestions introduced in this chapter in much more detail.

Notes

1   Cipra (1983).
2   We reported early work on tests in Ryan and Williams (2000, 2003) and Williams and Ryan (2000, 2002b), and on the MaLT project recently in Williams *et al.* (2005).
3   Sweller (for example, 1994, 1998, 2004) has shown how significant cognitive load can be for children's performance on tasks, with implications for curriculum and pedagogy.
4   For example, Roth and Bowen (2001).
5   It seems that in low-stakes assessment, low anxiety can be equated with low motivation and adversely affect performance (Petridou and Williams, accepted).
6   Much work has been done at undergraduate level by Schoenfeld (see, for example, 1985, 1994) and by many at secondary level, for example Bell *et al.* (1978, 1993), Burkhardt (1981, 1991). Burton (1984) did the classic work at primary and early secondary school level.
7   Reports in the academic literature, for example, Ryan and Williams (2000, 2003) and Williams *et al.* (2004), have informed professional publications, such as that by Ryan and Williams (2002a, 2002b) for the TTA, in which various arguments have been analysed in the manner of Toulmin (1958).
8   Williams *et al.* (2004) suggest that this shows how errors/claims are backed by reasons/misconceptions.
9   For example, Skemp (1971), and also instrumental and relational understanding (1976).
10   See Ryan and Williams (2003); Hadjidemetriou and Williams (2002b) and Williams *et al.* (2004).
11   The concept of 'voice' is due to Bakhtin (1981, 1986) but developed by Wertsch (1991) and since by many others; see Williams (2005).
12   Hughes (1986).
13   Bernstein (1990), Hasan (1996, 2002), Halliday and Hasan (1985). On Bernstein's legacy, see Hasan (2002).
14   Pirie and Kieren (1994) refer to this effect in problem solving as 'folding back'; typically consolidation during problem solving involves going back from 'formal' to 'concrete' underpinnings before experiencing abstraction and formalization 'again'.

15 There was an extensive debate in the 1960s about uni-model vs multi-model approaches in the literature. This appears to have been resolved; a synthesis suggests that a combination is necessary at different stages of the process of development in relation to a concept and its refinement.

16 Beishuizen (1999) and Anghileri (2001).

17 Lakoff and Nunez (2000). An account of this can be found in Williams and Wake (2007b) and also in Williams, Linchevski and Kutscher (under review) and Linchevski and Williams (1999). See also Chapter 5.

18 Wartosfsky (1979) and Black (1962, 1993) make clear that all these fall on a spectrum of representations.

19 We signal here Vygotsky's zone of proximal development (ZPD): this conception of a learning zone is often too simplistically presented in the literature; we will revisit this conception in Chapter 9.

20 Cooper and Dunne (2000).

21 This disposition/feel for the game is called habitus by Bourdieu (1990, 1997). The symbol-shuffling middle classes develop just this habitus for such games.

22 Bernstein (1971, 1990, 1996). This 'visibility' also relates to 'taken-as-shared' in Cobb *et al.* (2000).

23 Lakoff and Nunez (2000) have an elaborated account of the metaphorical extensions involved in mathematics from elementary school up to university; this is not without its detractors, however (see Goldin, 2001).

24 Lakoff (1987) presents an account of this; also Lakoff and Johnson (1980, 1999).

25 There is a literature indicating that Fibonacci and the golden ratio is implicated in the aesthetics involved – for example, Le Corbusier's Modulor (1948), among others.

26 Though computers, *Star Trek*'s Spock and much science-fiction literature plays on what it might be like if people did reason mathematically and logically 'every day'.

27 We have in mind here the notion of accommodation/development energized by cognitive conflict. See also Ryan and Williams (2003).

28 Dickson *et al.* (1984) on the van Hiele model; see also Chapter 5.

29 A stream of papers on this by Vershaffel and his group (see, for example, de Bock *et al.*, 2002) has developed the notion across the curriculum, and includes *inappropriate* extension of linear prototypes; also see Hadjidemetriou and Williams (2002a); see Chapter 7 for an example.

30 Lakatos discusses such monstrous polygons, and the 'monster-barring' they induce.

31 For instance, the US standards and the latest UK curriculum now postpone written algorithms in favour of informal – by which one might read 'meaningful' – methods.

32 Brown showed how different models of multiplication are appropriated at different ages, as part of the CSMS study in Hart (1981).

33   Misailidou and Williams (2002) showed how additive tendencies are maintained and this has been confirmed to some extent by the data in the MaLT project.

34   Understanding the negative integers is dealt with in some detail in Chapter 5: we show how it is necessary to work with models that represent the identity of the integer with a single 'object', first on the sociocultural plane.

35   The results from CSMS studies (Hart, 1981, 1984) showed this, and our replications and extensions show this has not changed (for example, Misailidou and Williams, 2003).

36   There is an extensive literature in maths education on counting in particular – for example, Resnick and Ford (1981) – and in general on process–object reification, including work by Sfard (1991), Sfard and Linchevski (1994) and also Gray and Tall (1994). It speaks of historical and hierarchical processes of building up mathematics, in which new concepts are built (in part at least) by extensions from the earlier/older mathematical processes. Reification is seen as a sudden ontological shift after sometimes extended periods of condensation. See Linchevski and Williams (1999) for an account of this and Koukkoufis and Williams (2006) for an extension into semiotic theory.

37   Gray and Tall (1994) use the term 'proceptual' thinking implying flexibility – that is, the ability to switch process–object view. This is obviously important when 'opening up the box' of a closed concept to examine its interior workings (usually provoked when the box 'fails' in some sense: Williams and Wake, 2007a).

38   This has been examined in depth since the APU (1991) and SESM projects – for example, Booth (1984).

39   Williams and Wake (2007a) describe the black-boxing of mathematical work, after Latour (1987).

40   The visuo-spatial dimension of mathematics is always in danger of underemphasis in policy and practice: Joseph (1991) refers to the Indian mathematical tradition, in which a visual proof of the misnamed Pythagorean relation is accompanied by one word, 'behold'. There is more on this in Chapter 5.

3　Children's mathematical discussions

I cannot teach anybody anything; I can only make them think (Socrates)

What we want is to see the child in pursuit of knowledge, and not knowledge in pursuit of the child (George Bernard Shaw)

Argument in discussion: persuasion through reasoning

This chapter is predicated on an assumption about teaching and learning mathematics; we can call it a pedagogical hypothesis or even a theory. Our assumption is that significant, intelligent learning takes place through learners interacting with others in discussion about mathematics, in a mathematical dialogue.[1] By a dialogue we mean something substantially more than just a discussion – we mean almost an argument (without the connotation of aggression) in which differences of view are exchanged and explored rationally – that is, logically and mathematically – with a view to persuading with coherent reasoning. We call this *argument in discussion* to highlight the cognitive and collaborative nature of the dialogue. Following Wells, we characterize classrooms developing such inquiry dialogue as communities of inquiry.[2]

In a *community of inquiry* the dialogue combines the characteristics of conversation with the rigours of reason and persuasion. Children are encouraged to talk and listen to each other, they share responsibility for sustaining the dialogue, they make statements of understanding or thinking-in-progress, and they use and consider alternative points of view in order to strengthen or make new connections. The dialogue involves a cycle of articulation, re-formulation, reflection and resolution (see Figure 3.1).

There are several key requirements for such a dialogue to emerge. First, there must be some 'problematic', a shared problem but with some differences of view – that is, something to discuss and argue about. Second, there must be opportunities for the children to communicate, voice a point of view and be

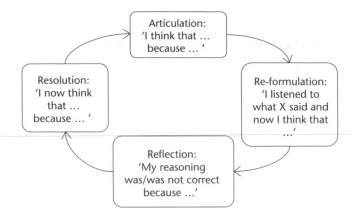

Figure 3.1 A cycle of dialogue.

listened to, seriously. Third, there must be some criteria for evaluating what makes a good argument. In addition, if such a dialogue is to offer mathematical learning opportunities for the children, then 'more advanced' mathematical arguments, ideas and concepts must enter the dialogue and provide resources for the task at hand. Fourth, there must be opportunity for reflection on the discussion: what did we (as a group) think, what do we now think, what made us change our mind (see Figure 3.2)? This is what this chapter is all about.

We are aware that many classrooms and lessons go by apparently without such dialogues. We know that children do seem to learn mathematics often by

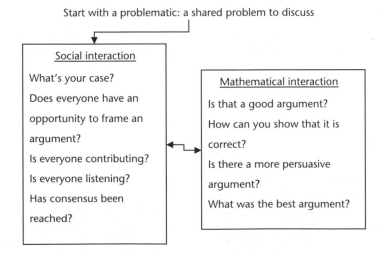

Figure 3.2 Organizing productive group argument-in-discussion.

copying examples and practising routines initially modelled, and later corrected and assessed, by the teacher. We do not claim that dialogical teaching is the only pedagogy through which children can learn. But we do believe that dialogue is necessary for reasoned, 'mathematically intelligent' learning; we also believe that there are some critical points in mathematical development that can most efficiently and effectively be handled in this way.

Towards a dialogic pedagogy

We said a key starting point of a dialogue is a problematic, a difference of opinion of some significant kind. These can erupt by accident at the most unexpected times: for example, when working with a group of primary student-teachers an argument breaks out about the nature of 'nought point nine recurring' (0.999 . . .).

Scenario 1

The group had been asked to suggest the largest number that is less than one, and nought-point-nine-recurring is one suggestion. A student challenges this, saying that it is not less than one, but in fact is equal to one. It is then claimed that it cannot be the same as one, it must be a little bit smaller. But no, it is argued, one-third is the same as nought point three recurring (0.333 . . .), so multiply by three . . . it has to be the same. 'Ah, but however many nines there are in the recurring, you are always less than one, so it *is* a tiny bit less than one,' counters another student. Then support for this view comes from an unexpected place: '. . . and anyway if it was the same as one, why would we give a different name for it?' Shortly, the whole class demands that the lecturer adjudicates, and is infuriated when the lecturer merely rehearses the argument and declines to declare the 'correct' view.

It will be argued that the above discussion was one held by mature adults, who know how to listen, debate, articulate and reflect on the dialogue. Just so, and is this possible with children? The purpose of this chapter is to give examples of children's reasoning and arguments in significant developmental moments, to explore their dynamics and potential for learning, and hence to make inferences for a dialogical pedagogy.

Scenario 2

Let us take you to a reception class where the teacher told us that she likes to teach reception (4- and 5-year-olds) because she feels she can enculturate the class to her way of doing things; her lesson certainly proves unusual. 'I want to develop a new idea I've been thinking of for getting into "odd" numbers,' she tells us. She begins her class by talking about her washing. 'We always end up with some odd socks in our house – sometimes I find a missing sock at the back of the washing machine. It's very annoying to get up and find you have only an odd sock. . . . Look, here is my wash bag and it's got an odd number of socks in it.' She shows the class the bag of socks: there are quite a few socks in there but it is not obvious it is an odd number of socks. Then she asks the children to solve the problem: 'How many socks are there in the bag?' She suggests they take some time, talk about it and maybe draw a picture to show what they think.

The children get materials and work in pairs or small groups. All the while she talks to groups and emphasizes, 'It's *odd*, have you ever had an odd sock?' One boy complains, 'But Miss, I don't understand what you mean.' 'Well, this is problem solving, so think about it,' she replies. Later on one child asks if she can guess. The teacher announces to the class, 'Jodie asks can you guess the number: that's good for problem solving – yes, guessing is good – a good strategy. But having a *reason* is better.'

The teacher judges after about 20 minutes that it is time to gather thoughts: she has noticed some groups have some productive ideas to work with. She gathers the attention of the class and asks for ideas. Many of the class have guessed 'ten'. The answers are collected, with reasons, on the board. One child says 11 – that is a guess, too – and receives no special praise. One child has drawn a picture showing seven socks on a washing line; the teacher asks the child to describe the picture. 'Well, a bird came flying in and took a sock off the line – so there were seven.' A few other children have similar stories with reasons why the number was chosen: several of these account for the 'odd' number by a pair losing one sock! The atmosphere is quite intense and though a bell sounds for playtime there is no movement. Finally, the teacher has elicited some 'reasons' for choosing a number of 'odd' socks, and the children have heard that, though guessing is good, a reason is better: a child tries to count the socks in her wash bag and with help gets 11: the lesson ends.

These reception children were presented with a problematic and were given the opportunity to present their points of view and then to listen to the reasoning of others. Their teacher had set the scene for the next step in learning: children adjusting (or consolidating) their point of view in response to the dialogue. Because the teacher was explicit about 'what makes a good argument' the children are learning what makes for good mathematics. It is not arbitrary, but has to make sense, perhaps through some narrative of mathematics in context.[3]

An analysis of mathematical argumentation

In our research on mathematical discussion we encouraged children to provide a reason for what they thought, to listen to each other, to build on what someone else said, and to ensure that everyone understood. The explicit aim of the discussion was to persuade or be persuaded. In general children find it unnecessary to argue propositions that are taken-as-shared, including the rules of argument in such situations. But conflicting answers and reasoning provide the dialogue with dynamics. We thus categorize *argumentation moves* related to *alternatives, conflict, clarification, press* and so on.[4]

In our research into children's arguments, we established small discussion groups consisting of four 11-year-old children who had previously given a variety of significantly different responses to a diagnostic assessment item of interest (a problematic).[5] The focus of the discussions was on children's own reasoning and argumentation. The researcher-teacher role was primarily to facilitate peer group discussion rather than to 'teach', but also to provide useful representations, referents or models, where these were thought to be necessary to make progress, but were not spontaneously forthcoming from the group.

Here we present part of a transcript of an argument about the ordering of the numbers 185, 73.5, 73.32, 57 and 73.64 from smallest to largest.[6] The children reported their responses to this question on a diagnostic test taken some days earlier. Two of the children, Kim and Natalie, had previously ordered these numbers as 57, 73.5, 73.32, 73.64, 185, which was consistent with the 'decimal point ignored' error, while Elise had the correct ordering.[7] Richard's response had been incoherent.

The teacher-researcher orchestrates the argument in discussion by collecting the different points of view and asking the children to provide reasons for their decimal ordering.[8] The analysis on the right summarizes the argumentation moves in the dialogue – both social and mathematical dimensions.

Transcript 1

Teacher:	A few days ago you all ordered these numbers from smallest to largest: 185, 73.5, 73.32, 57 and 73.64. Do you remember what you did? Can you write it down?	The problematic and response recalled
Kim:	OK. I put 57 there. (.) Then I put 73.5 (.) Then I put 73 point thirty-two, then I put 73 point sixty-four, then I put 185. [57, 73.5, 73.32, 73.64, 185]	Everyday decimal language
Natalie:	Well, I got 57 at the beginning too. And then I got 73.5. Then I got 73 point three-two. Then I got 73 point six-four. Then I got 185. [57, 73.5, 73.32, 73.64, 185]	Mathematical language
Teacher:	Could you explain why you put 73.5 before 73.32 (three, two)?	Seeks backing

Natalie:	Because 73.32 (three, two) has got two digits after the decimal point and 73.5 has only got one.	Decimals as whole numbers
Elise:	I'm not so sure, because 73.5 is basically 73 and a half. 73.64 (six, four) is (.), I'm not sure if it would be over a half or under (.) Actually I think the same as Kim (.) because, like Natalie said, there are two digits there, and two digits there, and only one digit there.	Doubt Introduces fraction referent but not secure – abandons correct answer
Teacher:	What do you think, Richard?	Checks alternatives
Richard:	Same as Elise.	Unhelpful consensus
Teacher:	The same (.) If I had a number line (.) Are you used to seeing a number line? [*Children nod*.] And I had 72, 72 would be back there [*drawing*]. 73 would be there. 74 would be there. Where would you put 73.5?	Introduces new number line activity – drawing with 72, 73 and 74 equally spaced
Teacher:	Do you want to do that Richard?	Elicits response
Richard:	[*Writes 73.5 halfway between 73 and 74.*]	Number line product: 0.5 is *halfway*
Teacher:	Can anybody put any other numbers in between 73 and 74?	Checks alternatives and presses
Kim:	Yeah [*puts 73.64 above 73.5*].	Number line product
Teacher:	Why have you put it bigger than 73.5?	Checks backing
Kim:	Because it's over a half.	Backing: uses fraction equivalence
Teacher:	Any other numbers you could put on that number line? Do you want to have a go Natalie?	Presses
Natalie:	73 point two-five.	Number line shows two decimal place conflict
Teacher:	73 point two-five, where would that go? (.) Could you tell us why you put 73.25 *just* there?	Focuses on 0.25; placed halfway between 73 and 73½
Natalie:	It's a quarter of the number.	Backing: fraction equivalence

Teacher:	Do you agree with that? [*Children nod.*] So, it's gone (.) why has it gone exactly there? Is that because it is halfway towards a half?	Checks backing
Natalie:	Yeah.	Confirmation
Teacher:	Could you put a number on that number line Richard?	Develops number line
Richard:	Erm, 73.45 [*places it between 73.25 and 73.5 . . . and places 73.75 between 73.5 and 74*].	More two-place decimals
Teacher:	73.75, right? That's (.)?	Presses
Richard:	Three-quarters.	Backing: fraction equivalence
Teacher:	So you put that halfway between 73 and a half, and 74 . . . Where do you think 73.32 should go?	Press
Kim:	Before 73.5	
Teacher:	Why?	Elicits backing
Kim:	Because 73.5 is a half and 73.32 is just after a quarter.	Resolution of referents
Teacher:	Could you say why it's just after a quarter?	Checks backing
Kim:	Because a quarter is 73.25 and 73.32 is bigger than 73.25 [*all agree*]. I now think 73.32 is there, and 73.5 is there.	Kim changes mind
Teacher:	You all want to change your minds now? Now why did we go wrong in the first place?	Seeks reflection
Kim:	Because we saw them as two-digit numbers, and we thought that the two-digit numbers were more than a one-digit number.	Makes new knowledge explicit
Elise:	I would say that 73.25 is a quarter, and it's less than 73.5 because that's a half, and 73.32 is just over a quarter, so it would be just under 73.5	Connects fraction and decimal

What can we learn from this argument? First, the children started with different answers and so there was something to discuss. Only Elise had the correct ordering of 0.32 and 0.5 previously, while two of the others had 0.5 < 0.32. When asked for an opinion, despite being doubtful about Natalie's ordering, and citing the connection that 0.5 is the same as a half, Elise came round to Natalie's incorrect view that the two-decimal place numbers should be bigger than the one-decimal place numbers.

This is a common view for which the teacher-researcher was prepared. At a key point when the unhelpful answers emerged, the teacher-researcher, seeking to make use of the 'half is 0.5' mentioned much earlier by Elise, introduces the number line and marks 72, 73 and 74, and the children have the knowledge required to place 73.5 halfway between 73 and 74 and subsequently offer 73.25 and even 73.75 at the quarter and three-quarter positions on the line: they are using their knowledge of fractions like ¼ and ¾ to make the required connections. Mathematically, Natalie's placing of the 73.25 on the line begins the breakthrough (see Figure 3.3) because now a two-decimal place number is appearing to the left of the 73.5 mark (and later another two-decimal place number, 73.75, to the right).

Figure 3.3   Number line: '73.5 is halfway and 73.25 is less than that'.

From here the contradiction between the children's original ordering and their emerging orderings on the number line becomes more and more obvious. Kim spontaneously points to the place where 73.32 should go, and they all agree to 'change their minds'. The last two utterances from Kim and Elise show that they have even gained some knowledge about what they previously thought and where they went wrong, and what they have now learnt: 'We thought that the two-digit numbers were more than the one-digit numbers.'[9] Interestingly, Elise is initially persuaded by others' arguments that 0.5 < 0.32, but comes back to her previous (correct) position and finds articulation and reflection. In terms of our Figure 3.1, we argue she has shown signs of learning the most from this interaction.

The teacher-researcher also supported the social interactional dimension of the children's discussion as a group endeavour: everyone participating, listening to each other and building on what has been said. The video-recording shows intense involvement, puzzlement, and satisfaction with the eventual breakthrough as a group.

The introduction of the number line seemed to be a key pedagogical decision, as it provided for an apt representation, and fortunately the children had enough knowledge of fraction–decimal equivalents to make good use of it. In another group, however, we found that the number line did not quite work in the same way, because one child, Alan, was willing to place 0.5 (point-five) and 0.50 (point-fifty) at two different places on the line, and did not agree with his peers that they were the same number. The argument was based on place value headings showing the redundancy of the 'end' nought, but this did not persuade him: for Alan 'half' was 'point-fifty' and not 'point-five'. His peers persisted in articulating alternative mathematical arguments to persuade him and appeared to strengthen their own understanding at the same time by engaging with his point of view.[10]

Some readers may agree with critics who have told us that many teachers will not have the subject expertise to maintain open discussions like this, and will consequently feel quite threatened in such 'open' contexts. In our view it is not a matter of subject knowledge, or subject knowledge only: it is a matter of knowledge about the best tasks, representations, models, contexts, and so on, to introduce in a given situation: what Shulman called *pedagogical content knowledge*.[11] Again, in our view it is probably correct to suggest that many teachers will not have 'in their heads' the required knowledge for all the domains of knowledge they are likely to meet in such situations. But we believe it might be possible for them to have this knowledge at their 'fingertips', in the curriculum documents, lesson plans, assessment tools, and so on, provided as tools of the trade.[12]

Ignoring the progress of the mathematics for the moment and looking at the argument as a dialogue, the significance of each answer being justified and the focus on the reasons behind answers should be apparent. The most important remarks by Kim and Elise at the close of the dialogue could not have happened without this. We suggest that most lessons avoid argument and reasoning, and that errors are usually straightforwardly *corrected* by the teacher until the children get their own calculations correct. In the above discussion it should be clear that the productive conclusion of this argument would not have happened in such circumstances.

Mathematical dialogue: what makes a good mathematical argument?

By a 'mathematical dialogue' we do not mean to restrict attention to the spoken word, though oracy is for us important and is often undervalued in classrooms. In a mathematical dialogue we certainly include all the calculations, scripts, diagrams, problems and solutions that make up mathematics and mathematical argumentation generally.

When discussing probability with student-teachers a classic problem enjoyed by all involves inviting a student to select one of three cups that contains a prize (for example, a sweet).[13] When a cup is selected, the teacher then reveals one of the remaining two cups to be empty (see Figure 3.4). The student is then invited to change their selection of cup, if they so wish. The question for argument is, 'Is there a good reason to switch? Is there a better chance of winning with the other cup, or doesn't it matter?'

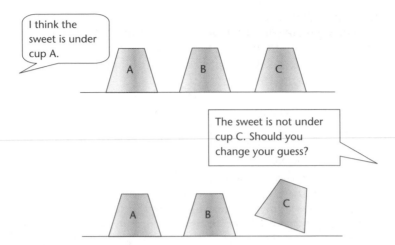

Figure 3.4   Best chance to win: stay with or switch original choice?

This puzzle usually generates at least two conflicting positions. Each must be articulated, understood and justified. Everyone must be brought to understand the key arguments put forward. If necessary, the teacher can introduce an argument that has not been voiced (in classrooms with younger children this might involve a stratagem such as, 'When I asked a child this yesterday, *she* said . . .', and so on). In cases where there is more than one position then the debate shifts to evaluation of the argument: what makes a good mathematical argument in such a case? In the case of the missing sweet, there might be *intuitive* arguments – for example, 'Imagine we replace the problem with a similar one with 1000 cups, and the teacher gradually reveals 998 empty cups – would you then be more inclined to switch?' There might be *empirical* arguments: 'If we try running the task many times with strategy X versus strategy Y then we might find one strategy produces a better rate of success' (this might be simulated with dice or a computer, also, to eliminate the 'teacher' from the game). Then there might be arguments that adopt some form of probability theory. But which arguments are valid?

Thus a good mathematical argument often involves *evaluation* of argumentation, and hence the growth of knowledge about what mathematics *is*: what counts as good mathematics, how we learn or discover new mathematics, and so on. This is metacognitive knowledge and makes for intelligent learning – learning to be a learner of mathematics, or learning to be a mathematician.

Maintaining dialogue in practice: social interaction

In this section we examine another example of children's discussion and ask: how is the dialogue facilitated by the teacher-researcher? Again, there is a social and a mathematical dimension to the discussion.[14]

The 'stamps' problematic (see Figure 3.5) was designed to address the concept of congruence and orientation in the light of a real-life context (that is, the need for rotation in the plane rather than reflection). The main errors found in our data analysis were A and E or E and F (*two* shapes congruent) and A, E and F (*three* shapes congruent). We expected these errors to diagnose lack of consideration of the 'real' context/constraint. The analysis of the transcript highlights the strategies the teacher-researcher uses to maintain the dialogue with the 11-year-olds.[15]

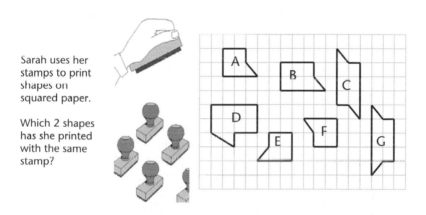

Sarah uses her stamps to print shapes on squared paper.

Which 2 shapes has she printed with the same stamp?

Figure 3.5   Stamps problematic.

Transcript 2

Teacher: . . . And [*to Alan*] you think A and E are the same stamps?

Elicits Alan's backing for A and E

Alan: If you flip that shape over, that bit will be down there and then you put it on there, it will be . . .

'Flip' reason

Teacher: Yeah, Tim would you listen to what Alan is saying because he's saying something interesting here, and we want *one* person at a time – go ahead.

Social rules: Tim should listen to Alan and take turns

Alan:	Actually they're all the same. If you turn that over like that, the arrow thingy will be there and (the) same with that one, so you bring it over there =	Alan now says A, E and F. Mental rotation out of the plane
Teacher:	[*To others*] Are you following this?	Social rules: Listening and engagement
Alan:	= you turn that over there . . .	
Liam:	The arrow's pointing that way . . .	Liam agrees: shows listening
Alan:	Yeah, and then you put that on top – there you go, *voilà!*	
Teacher:	So, if you flip F over that way, same as E, and if you flip A over that way it's the same as E, so they're all three the same? That's Alan's argument. Do you agree with that?	Reformulation of Alan's argument: rotation out of plane. Social involvement: checking
Liam:	I agree with Alan.	Liam agrees
Teacher:	You agree with Alan.	Echo
Alan:	[*With satisfaction*] Yes!	
Teacher:	Do you agree with Alan, Tim?	Checks alternatives
Tim:	No.	Conflict
Teacher:	And Tim disagrees. OK. Tim, what's your argument?	Presses for backing
Tim:	Well, these are *stamps* so you can't like pull it out and then twizzle them about because = Right, if it's A = if you like *turn* it around 90 degrees it would be the same, but like = can I draw on this?	Stamps' context: twizzle means 'flip'. Conflict: 'turn' vs 'flip'. Introduces tool: drawing
Teacher:	Yeah.	Permission
Tim:	Right. So like that, then if you turned it another one, that way, it would be facing like that, that!	A to F by two 90-degree rotations in the plane but not correctly to E
Teacher:	So you can just turn A through 90 degrees?	Checks Tim's backing
Tim:	Yeah, and then if you turn it that way again another 90 it would look like = like that, and if you turn it again it would come back to that.	Series of rotations by 90 degrees in the plane

Teacher:	Can we just all have a look at that a minute? What Tim does is take A = was it A you took?	Focuses on Tim's reason. Seeks clarification
Tim:	Yeah.	
Teacher:	Turn it 90 degrees, another 90 degrees and another 90 degrees, that's what Tim is saying.	Reinforces clarification
Liam:	And then the =	
Teacher:	Tim, can you just finish your argument? So what's that got to do with A?	Cuts Liam off: back to Tim. Presses argument

The analysis shows the teacher-researcher's inputs to the discourse and influence on the discussion in general. Being aware of the diverse responses of the children in advance, the teacher-researcher seeks to ensure that the arguments for any particular response are clearly voiced first; the whole first half of the above transcript is about *listening, clarifying* and ensuring the *whole group understands* Alan's reasoning. This includes Tim, who has the 'right' answer: it is important that even those children who had the 'right' answer listen to and understand the others because the focus is on reasons for changing one's mind or not. Then, in the second half of the above, Tim's reasoning is heard and clarified, and it is important that Alan and Liam listen to this.

Part of this social process may be to reformulate the child's reasoning, in some cases echoing it, so that it is more emphatically voiced in the discourse. Occasionally it involves checking others are listening and following, and sometimes asserting the need for the argument to continue without another point of view distracting.

There are other elements involved here and later in the transcript, such as ensuring that potentially productive tools and referents are introduced at some point even if the children do not raise them spontaneously (as in the previous section for ordering decimals). The reader may be interested to know that a creative construction of the use of the stamp 'from the other side of the paper' was discussed, thus justifying the inclusion of 'flip' shapes suggesting that the response 'A, E and F', which we had taken to be a misconception, could be justified and made 'reasonable'.

We use the term *general pedagogical strategies* to describe actions such as the elicitation of a variety of alternative 'answers' and arguments, asking children to listen and sometimes paraphrase others' views, seeking further clarification of arguments, helping to formulate and encourage a minority point of view, seeking support and dissent, criticizing the reasons and not the individual, and so on, as well as pressing for reasons or 'backing'. Examining the validity of these strategies for the transcript of the ordering decimals item above, for example, we find they have equal relevance there, although the specific mathematical content, concepts, arguments, models, tools and referents are quite different.

These general dialogical strategies tend to forestall closure and encourage constructive conflict. In the final post-resolution stage of discussion, further strategies that encouraged reflection included asking children whether and why they had changed their mind, what the argument or misconception had been, and how they would summarize what they had learnt for others.

Small-group dialogues in classrooms

We have so far outlined how discussion developed in a privileged small-group research environment. We started with diagnostic questions or problematics in order to provoke a range of responses that would promote productive discussion of different points of view. The children were set the task of persuading each other, by explanation and argument, of their positions. The giving of clarifications, reasons, justifications and informal 'proof' was imposed as far as possible by the researcher-teacher as the 'rules' for the discussion. The reflective stage – articulating persuasive argument and perhaps change of mind – helped the children to make new or stronger connections in their knowledge. We now discuss how these ideas can be transferred to the classroom.

The choice of problem or argument-starter is critical, and the crafting of the problematic is not simple. Known misconceptions can be provoked to allow for productive discussion but the problematics must also include some prompts or conflicts suggesting an alternative frame for argument. For example, the ordering decimals question includes 73.5 rather than, say, 73.1 because the 0.5 is a known strong link to the alternative fraction frame for children at this stage of learning. The problematics must also be manageable: with too many different responses the discussion becomes chaotic.

We began researching whole-class pedagogy with a group of teachers in inquiry groups who expressed interest in working with the dialogic method in their primary and secondary school classrooms.[16] We provided resources or teaching 'tools' (diagnostic questions and known common responses, summary maps, argumentation charts, writing frames, and teaching strategies including rules for discussion, transcripts and videos) based on our research to support the teachers in their planning, and then shared discussion of pedagogic strategies and learners' responses grounded in examples of video-taped lesson excerpts.

Collaborative discussion in 'real' classrooms can be facilitated by *deliberate planning*: considering what problems will be worthwhile, what groupings will sustain collaborative discussion, how the social rules will be established and what reporting strategies will focus the group.[17] Other decisions have to be made *in the flow of the moment* – teachers' concerns revolved around questions such as: is everyone involved, is the group on task, how to sustain rather than end the argument, and what mathematical interventions will be fruitful, when should the group be left alone?

Different teachers held different views about how to group children. The discussion can be in pairs, in small groups or whole class. Some teachers used a combination of these at different stages of the lesson. The membership of each group is thought to be critical: who best goes where, who will talk with whom? By deciding how to mix the groups in terms of the range of the children's *already known responses*, the teacher can help shape the interactions and so the development of the learning. Teachers in our inquiry groups have used mixed-response groups where the group immediately responds to conflict; and others have initially used same-response groups where the children first voice a shared position; and a mixture of these. The groups were usually arranged by the teacher in these ways, but additional consideration to the social dynamics of their class was always a consideration; for instance, it may be unhelpful for some children to repeatedly be positioned as being in the wrong in their peer group. Some ready-made discussion prompt sheets for 11- to 14-year-olds outline arguments that children have made in our research settings – these can be used to distance the child from the argument to avoid such social stress or to model reasoning (see Appendix 2).

Some teachers worry about children all agreeing on a misconception together – as in decimal ordering – believing that the misconception may be 'contagious' in some sense. If an incorrect answer is accepted by a group of children a conflict can sometimes be engineered by the teacher presenting a fictional child's position and charging the group with persuading that 'child' why she is wrong. We also usually found that there is teacher anxiety that a misconception should not be left unresolved by the end of the lesson – that a child should not leave the class with an incorrect idea. The following cases show how different teachers resolved this issue.

Case study 1: Rachel's 'unbearable tension'

One teacher in our inquiry group, Rachel, with three years' teaching experience, set up small-group discussions using our problematics with her Year 6 class (11-year-olds). She was initially very nervous about children discussing errors and misconceptions in the classroom, and experienced 'almost unbearable tension' while children's errors were allowed to be considered for a sustained period without being corrected, or even contradicted. However, she subsequently developed lessons based on the method of 'conflict' grouping in terms of the children's answers to the diagnostic items. She used her own

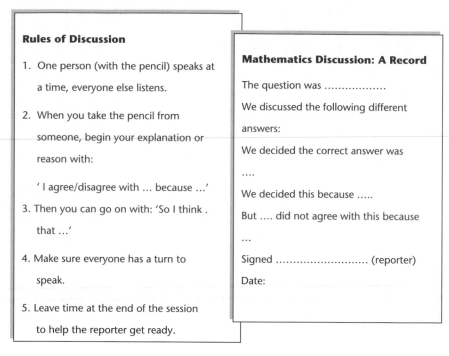

Rules of Discussion

1. One person (with the pencil) speaks at a time, everyone else listens.

2. When you take the pencil from someone, begin your explanation or reason with:

   ' I agree/disagree with ... because ...'

3. Then you can go on with: 'So I think . that ...'

4. Make sure everyone has a turn to speak.

5. Leave time at the end of the session to help the reporter get ready.

Mathematics Discussion: A Record

The question was ....

We discussed the following different answers:

We decided the correct answer was

....

We decided this because .....

But .... did not agree with this because

...

Signed .... (reporter)

Date:

Figure 3.6 Focusing discussion and reporting in classrooms.

rules of discussion document and writing frame to organize the plenary session of group reports to promote listening and group reporting practice (see Figure 3.6).

One group discussing the item 'ordering of decimals' dealt with four different answers (see Figure 3.7) and also wrote down after their discussion whether they had changed their mind or not. The dynamics of the discussion and changes of mind reveal some complete shifts and some partial shifts that significantly inform their teacher about the stage of learning for each child. The social dimensions are also informative (*who* is persuasive). Nicola and Samantha have made a partial shift by ordering the 57, the 73s and the 185 correctly. Claire, Scott and Michael have made complete shifts and report that the argument that '0.5 is ½' has been persuasive, while Andrew has actually reported that the persuasive argument was that '.5 is .50' (*what* is persuasive).

Ultimately Rachel was herself persuaded that it would take time for children to resolve their long-held misconceptions; at least she was sufficiently persuaded to make this point at a subsequent meeting with other teachers where she made such remarks. Had she ultimately 'changed her mind' herself? We cannot be sure.

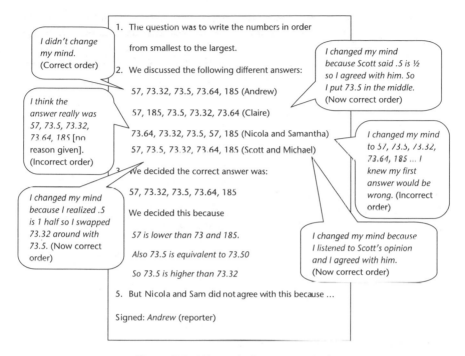

Figure 3.7   Who and what is persuasive?

Case study 2: Megan's unmixed and mixed groupings change their minds

Megan was a teacher with ten years' experience who developed a variant of the 'conflict lesson' for her lower-set Year 9 girls (14-year-olds) who 'enjoy talking'. She also used our diagnostic items but first grouped the children into *same-response* groups on the basis of responses to the diagnostic test item at hand, and after the groups again had written down their reasons, she rearranged the class into *conflict* groups, prompting with 'See if you agree. Can you explain it? See what each of you is thinking?' She was keen to 'slow down' the problem solving and concentrate on thinking and listening.

Her two-stage model for forming groups appeared to be very effective in allowing the girls to formulate their own positions and then consider and argue opposing ideas. She constantly reinforced listening skills throughout the class period. In addition to this difference, however, we also noted that Megan began with a strong belief in discussion, argument and 'not telling them the answers all the time'. 'I am much happier with this kind of teaching, where the pupil's thinking is given precedence. This matches my ideas of interactive teaching.'

Megan was also willing to end the lesson *without* a final, definitive, authoritative answer or explanation – that is, without closure (the class actually went on to discuss the decimal item again the following week), believing that conceptions will not necessarily be changed in the short term. She expected to return to the key ideas over an extended period of time.

One of the problematics used by Megan was the 'ten question quiz' (see Figure 3.8). The responses from her class were: 8 (that is, 5 + 3); 7 (that is, 5 – –2); 18 (that is, 5 × 3 + 3); 10 (that is, 5 – –2 + 3). The incorrect response of 8 is found by adding 3 to Julia's final score (one-step correction). The incorrect response of 7 allows for the readjustment of the 2 points removed (one-step correction) and the incorrect response of 18 is a misinterpretation of the final score as 5 answers being correct.

In a quiz game of 10 questions, points are scored in the following way.

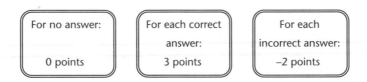

For no answer:	For each correct answer:	For each incorrect answer:
0 points	3 points	–2 points

The winner is the person with the highest total score.
Julia's last answer was incorrect. She finished with a score of 5.

What would her final score have been if her last answer had been correct?

Figure 3.8   Two-step problem: ten-question quiz.

The reflective stage in dialogic pedagogy involves the articulation of a change of mind (or not). In the final stage of the 'ten question quiz' discussion, the 14-year-olds were asked to write individually about any change of mind and what had made them change their mind in the class discussion. Some of the written responses recall the homogeneous grouping followed by heterogeneous grouping. Grouping by same response and then mixed response was clearly productive in generating discussion and conflict. Some girls reported that they were still considering two answers and could express an argument that had persuaded them to change their mind; thus there was evidence that the shift of attention from answers to reasons had impacted differentially on some of these girls.

Anka's dissonance is not as yet resolved:

> I am not going to change my mind about the 8, but in a way, a little bit, I think the 10 is correct too, because now I get the idea where you get the 7 from, and you add it on to 7. I think it is 50/50 that it is 8 and it is 10.

Sharon's change is warranted instrumentally:

> I changed my mind [from] 18 to 8, because it means the final score was 5, and her last question was correct, so that means 5 add 3 = 8.

Talia's reflection reveals processes of argument and backing:

> When I was in my last group, one of the girls got 10 and I strongly disagreed with her, because I thought 'if Julia started with 5', then she would have had just +3 to 5 which is 8, so how could she get 10? But when I came to this group, everyone got 8, so I thought I was right. But then I started to think about how Danielle would have got 10, so I started to work it out: 'Julia's last answer was incorrect, and she finished with 5' (that means she started with 7), but if she got it right, it would have been 7 + 3 and the answer would have been 10. Then I explained my answer to the rest of the table and they agreed.

Reflection on changes of mind (or not) had been a key component of the small-group discussion research environment and transferred effectively to whole-class presentation, with the added requirement that the children in the classroom setting had to write arguments down so that Megan could capture them.

Slowing the pace of the discussion

In Megan's case, the 'two-stage lesson plan' allowed the girls to take time to articulate and listen to at least two different arguments. Megan was happy to aim to 'slow down' the pace of discussion because of her belief in a classroom culture of discourse, and also *essentially* because of her beliefs about the pace of children's learning. It seems to us that this slowing of pace may be a general feature of the transfer of discursive patterns from small groups to larger groups or plenary class sessions: what can be taken for granted in a small group (for example, if an individual does not follow the argument) has to be socially structured and organized in the larger group; this takes time and slows the pace.

In addition, the two-stage lesson and the final reflective record meant that 'change of mind' was made more visible and assessable. We suggest that Megan's lesson plan was a conceptual instrument (not actually visible on paper) through which she crystallized her intention to slow the pace of the lesson; but it also served to mediate this practice, by focusing attention on argumentation and change of mind as opposed to learning specific mathematical content or methods.

Discussion and conclusions

The pedagogical hypothesis for this chapter leads to a particular privileging of discussion of a certain type we called dialogical (after Bakhtin).[18] In this view, learning and teaching are thought of as communication, and mathematical learning as a certain kind of dialogue in which the rationale is mathematical argumentation. Learning is here considered to be expressed as a particular change in argumentation – for example, from one that views decimals as a pair of numbers separated by a point to one where a decimal is represented by a point on a line. Reflective discourse on learning is held in particularly high esteem in this perspective.

We analysed some particular arguments in children's discussions from two distinct points of view. On the one hand we found they have a particular substantive mathematical content, and constructive interventions by a teacher might need to be particular to the mathematics, or mathematical topic, at stake. For instance, the introduction of productive models, tasks or contexts into the discussion might prove critical. This kind of activity relates to what Shulman (1986) called teachers' pedagogical content knowledge, in contrast to general pedagogical knowledge. But we prefer to specify it as content-related classroom *practice*: the introduction of a particular model at a particular point, for a particular purpose for instance.

Then, on the other hand, we examined argumentation in discussion from a more general mathematical point of view. This led to a view of mathematical discussion as being about articulating reasons for different positions or methods, listening and evaluating those reasons, making judgements and drawing conclusions based on 'good mathematical thinking'. Evidently this requires specific mathematically related understandings also, but these blend into good social norms of discussion.

Notes

1   It has long been known that children's errors and misconceptions can be the starting point for effective diagnostically designed mathematics teaching. The key mathematical work on this in the UK was done in the 1980s by the ESRC Diagnostic Teaching Project (Bell *et al.*, 1983, 1985) in which cognitive conflict was seen as a route to developing understanding.

2   Wells (1999). We also draw significantly in our thinking on the work of Mercer (1995, 1996, 2000), Edwards and Mercer (1987) and Mercer *et al.* (1999).

3   More on the need for socio-mathematical norms (after Yackel and Cobb, 1996) and the need for explicit pedagogies (for example, after Hasan, 2002, and

Bernstein, 1990) later: the main point will be argued that these things need to be made explicit if *all* children are going to have access to them.

4 Following Stigler and Hiebert (1999) and Wells (1999).

5 In this study a primary school cohort of 74 Year 6 (11-year-old) children in England was screened with a test that was designed to reveal common errors that had already been identified as relevant to their mathematics curriculum and level (Ryan and Williams, 2000, 2003). Essentially this involved identifying the most important common errors on tests for which we had collected a national sample of data ($N = 1759$) covering the entire mathematics curriculum for Key Stage 2 (Year 6, end of UK primary school). From these errors, which had previously been researched (Ryan *et al.*, 1998), we identified the most interesting errors based on the criteria that they should be: (a) common enough to reward a teacher's attention, (b) relevant to a significant locale of the curriculum being taught at the given age level in focus, and (c) significant in terms of the literature on the psychology of learning. The result was a diagnostic pencil and paper test, of some 30 items, lasting about 30 to 40 minutes and (later) a 20-minute mental test. The test items were drawn from the whole primary mathematics curriculum.

6 Ryan and Williams (2002b, 2003).

7 Widely published research from as long ago as the 1980s (APU, 1982) showed that large numbers of 11- and 15-year-olds respond to simple decimal tasks with two errors: the so-called 'decimal point ignored' error and the 'largest or longest is smallest' error. These signal two important misconceptions about decimals, which are typical in children's development of the decimal number concept. Our diagnostic item also uncovered children who grouped the whole numbers, 57 and 185, and decimal numbers, 73.5, 73.32, 73.64, separately.

8 We have used Jeffersonian notation for the transcription: (.) indicates a short pause, = indicates the break and subsequent continuation of a single interrupted utterance.

9 The appeal to discourse addressing a distant audience is important in supporting articulation. Compare Radford (2002, 2003) addressed in Chapter 6.

10 The particular affordances of the number line are discussed in Williams and Wake (2007b) and in Chapters 5 and 9.

11 Shulman's (1986) three categories of teacher content knowledge – subject matter content knowledge, pedagogical content knowledge and curricular knowledge – are intertwined in practice. *Pedagogical content knowledge* includes 'an understanding of what makes the learning of specific topics easy or difficult: the conceptions and preconceptions that children of different ages and backgrounds bring with them . . . If those preconceptions are misconceptions, which they often are, teachers need knowledge of the strategies most likely to be fruitful in reorganizing the understanding of learners' (pp. 9–10). This knowledge is characterized as including 'the most useful forms of representation of . . . ideas, the most powerful analogies, illustrations, examples,

explanations, and demonstrations – in a word, the ways of representing and formulating the subject that make it comprehensible to others' (p. 9). We call these referents.

12 This idea of 'distributing and socializing' the needed knowledge is an important one we come back to later.

13 This is the well-known 'Monty's Dilemma' problem. Monty Hall was the host of the US television game show *Let's Make a Deal* and the three doors problem was a popular segment. Behind one door was a new car prize, behind the other two doors were goats. The dilemma is, after choosing a door and the game show host opens another door revealing goats, should the contestant *stay* with their original door choice or *switch* in order to be more likely to find the car?

14 Yackel and Cobb (1996) advanced the notion of socio-mathematical norms – that is, what are viewed as acceptable mathematical explanations or justifications in classrooms. In inquiry discourse there are also social norms – that is, the behaviours and responses that support the dialogue.

15 Ryan and Williams (2002b, 2003).

16 Williams and Ryan (2002a).

17 See Boulter and Gilbert (1995) for a report on the use of argument in science classrooms. Ruddock (1979) identifies three commonly held 'environmental' impediments to the use of discussion in classrooms: seating arrangements, traditional teacher authority, and teacher dominance in terms of talk and style of interaction. Haworth (1999) discusses the 'political' qualities: the dialogic features of children's discourse in whole-class interaction and small-group interaction where external authoritative and internal persuasive forces are at play. She argues that it is small-group interaction that enables children to initially 'find their voice' (see also Dunne and Bennett, 1994). Haworth's study has a cautionary message, suggesting that small-group interaction is a bridge to the socio-political genre of whole-class interaction. This notion of a bridge is further suggestive of our own choice of research method.

18 Bakhtin (1981, 1986).

4   Developing number

Introduction

In this chapter we provide examples of some of the most important concepts and common errors with regard to number in general, and 'counting', 'two-digit whole number subtraction' and 'multiplicative concepts' in particular. This selection of topics covers the full age range from 4 to 15 years and allows us to introduce some key ideas for developing diagnostic teaching. We also discuss aspects of early number bonds in the context of spatial embodiment in Chapter 5, and the special case of negative integer conceptions in Chapter 6, where the topic is used to introduce semiotics in a way that helps with the understanding of algebra too.

We will show how significant learning problems can be diagnosed by 'counting troubles' involving errors and whole number misconceptions. We will then present a pedagogy for using 'situated intuitions' and models to construct two-digit subtraction strategies; this is associated with the common 'smaller from larger' errors in subtraction (for example, $35 - 18 = 23$). We then demonstrate how to make and interpret a developmental chart for the 'multiplicative field' using data from Appendix 1, and discuss the pedagogic implications of these results in terms of using 'context and modelling' in 'scaffolding'. A scaffolding pedagogy is described for making use of such developmental hierarchies: this involves appealing to context or model to support, or scaffold, reasoning. Some models are shown to facilitate exploratory talk, and contexts are sometimes found to provide the necessary 'backing' arguments for more advanced multiplicative strategies and conceptions. Finally, we warn that the linear ratio model can become prototypical.

Counting troubles diagnose early problems

When asked to count a small set, or when performing some simple addition and subtraction problems by counting, answers that are 'out' by just one or two can sometimes be explained by a counting error. If their sequence of numerals is faulty, for example, young children may go wrong in counting after a few small numbers ('1, 2, 3, uh, 5'), or they may jump through some of the 'irregular' numerals between 10 and 16, or later still they may jump when 'counting through a ten or a hundred' thus '. . . 37, 38, 39, 41, . . .' or '. . . 98, 99, 101, . . .'.

The linguistic failure of the numeral system in English, especially around the irregular sequence 'eleven, twelve, thirteen, fourteen and fifteen', explains many children's delays in mastery of the sequence of numerals needed for counting; irregular is another way to say they just do not make sense! This is in marked contrast with Welsh, Chinese, Japanese and many other languages in which the linguistic patterns support the mathematical structure with terminology such as 'ten-one', 'ten-two', and so on (see Table 4.1). Furthermore the evidence suggests that this cultural advantage is very helpful to early years Chinese and Japanese children.[1] Other recent studies have shown how different cultures are advantaged or disadvantaged due to the familiarity of certain mathematical practices (such as origami or abacus use in Japan) as well as these linguistic cultural advantages. The sign for a 'square' used by the deaf, for instance, involves drawing a four-sided shape with the finger, making the deaf equivalent of 'How many sides has a square?' as trivial as 'How many sides has a four-sided shape?'

Table 4.1 The -teen numbers supporting the mathematical structure

Number	Welsh (m)	Chinese	Japanese
10	un deg	shi	jū
11	un deg un	shi-yi	jū-ichi
12	un deg dau	shi-er	jū-ni
13	un deg tri	shi-san	jū-san
14	un deg pedwar	shi-si	jū-shi
15	un deg pump	shi-wu	jū-go
16	un deg chwech	shi-liu	jū-roku
17	un deg saith	shi-chi	jū-shichi
18	un deg wyth[2]	shi-ba	jū-hachi
19	un deg naw	shi-jiu	jū-kyū
20	dau ddeg	er shi	ni-jū

One conclusion is that, at least in English, teaching should emphasize counting to 100 rather than counting to 20, since this allows patterns to be established and counting to begin to seem 'reasonable' to children despite some inconsistencies. The trouble with 'counting to 20' is that so much of it is then unreasonable; by comparison, one cannot quite get the counting rhythm going.[3] There is a general point here that mathematics is culturally and historically situated, and we may need to design pedagogical approaches accordingly, selecting and making the most of the 'best' mathematics for teaching.

With very young children counting in order to find 'how many', initially quite naturally goes wrong because of a fault with the one-to-one correspondence principle. The one-to-one correspondence principle for finding the cardinality (the numerosity or numerical size) of a set requires that each object in the set is assigned a counting number (or numeral) on a one-to-one basis. That is, we give one and only one numeral for each object being counted, without repetition of objects or numerals, using the numerals in order: 1, 2, 3, 4, and so on. If, for instance, an object gets counted twice, or a numeral gets skipped, perhaps because the numbers are not coordinated with the finger pointing, then the count is likely to go 'over' by one, or maybe two. On the other hand, if an object is skipped then the count is likely to end up 'under' the correct answer for the set.

Tasks that present the children with a loop of objects, like a necklace of beads, for instance (see Figure 4.1), may be more difficult to count than a set of objects in a clear sequence or horizontal row. So, for instance, MaLT found that 77 per cent of 5-year-olds could correctly circle 5 out of a row

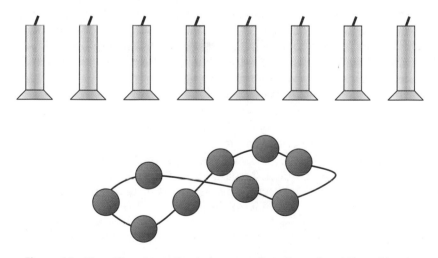

Figure 4.1   Two different counting tasks: a row of candles and a necklace of beads.

of 8 candles and 83 per cent correctly count an array of 7 socks, with about 7 per cent making an error of one on either side of the answers in each case.[4] However, only 69 per cent could correctly count a *necklace* of 9 beads with 17 per cent making the counting error; we think this is probably because there is no clear start and end to the necklace (again, see Figure 4.1) and so children are inclined to 'lose their place' and either skip over or count the beads more than once. For children who make such an error in the necklace context, attention clearly needs to be focused on the start and finish of the counting sequence.

The physical coordination of action (pointing) and speech (saying the numerals) involves developing a rhythm of speech, action and gesture.[5] This takes practice and is probably best done in group chanting, rhyming and the like, making use of the children's experience of rhythms that have been established in nursery rhymes and songs since the cradle. We speculate that the 'language and lore' of the playground might contribute to this skill development in important ways also, and wonder whether social exclusion from this peer activity might account in large part for some children's slow development.

> As I was walking up a scabb't lane, I met a scabb't horse. I one it.
> I two it . . . I three it . . . I four it . . . I five it . . . I six it . . . I seven it.
> I ate it![6]

The actions of counting involve touching or pointing with the fingers: brain research using magnetic resonance imaging (MRI) shows that the same parts of the brain function when the 'fingers are acting/touching' as when counting 'in your head'. This is suggestive of a developmental sequence of internalization of number that starts with actions of touching and pointing, progresses through speech but that eventually is internalized subvocally.[7] Thus combinations of counting on fingers, rhythmic rocking, gesturing with the fingers, and so on, are all likely to be helpful and significant embodiments for children's internalizing of counting. Even when counting is 'fully internalized', it is common to observe children nod, touch fingers, and so on, rhythmically as they count when solving problems.

Recently, some primary schools have begun to wonder if the role of activity with manipulatives and materials is still as important as it once was. (We recently heard of one nursery teacher who discovered that their new classroom had an interactive whiteboard but no sandpit!) There is a general point here: it is emphatically our view that the bases of mathematics are bodily and spatially situated, even if such activity does need to be mediated by language and communication before it becomes fully mature.[8]

In Chapter 2, we described how errors in early arithmetic often arise due to miscounting – for example, when children 'count on' from the first numeral in the count, such as in 5 add 4 thus: '5, 6, 7, 8, so the answer is 8'. Similarly children may count the 'ticks' instead of the 'intervals' on a number line and get a wrong answer, out by exactly one 'over' the correct number (see Chapter 5). Up to 18 per cent of 5-year-olds and 11 per cent of 6-year-olds are 'one out' in single-digit counting (see Appendix 1: M5.18, M6.25b). This also happens when children miss out the 'ten-number' when counting on, as in '. . . 37, 38, 39, 41 . . .'. Such errors are persistent right through the first years of school. A total of 39 per cent of 6-year-olds and 12 per cent of 7-year-olds produce such errors with counting through tens (see Appendix 1: M6.23b, M7.5). Mostly these errors decline with age as children develop more efficient strategies based on knowledge rather than counting: so a computation like 7 + 6 = 13 need not be performed by counting but by using knowledge of doubles and doubling, such as in 'double 6 is 12 and 6 + 7 is one more, so 13' or bridging through ten using number bonds '7 and 3 makes 10, and 3 more is 13'.

This is a general principle for number work with larger numbers, decimals and fractions, and so on: the more basic, 'primitive' methods generate errors that are less likely with more advanced strategies. An example later on in secondary school arises when a calculation like 7 × 99 is carried out by long multiplication, involving many steps that are error prone, instead of using a distributive strategy (7 × 100 − 7).

Consequently, an error may often be diagnosed as the likely, or even inevitable, outcome of relying on primitive methods that make too many demands on 'processing capacity' and memory: such cases suggest children need to move on to *new strategies*, rather than repeatedly practise inefficient methods. Some in particular argue that extended, routine counting activity can be a sign of children's lack of 'normal' development in the early years. Indeed this is often an indicator that children are not developing more efficient strategies, and so may be falling behind. It is also claimed to be diagnostic of dyslexia.[9] For the reader who is keen to look immediately at some means to 'move on', we refer to the discussion of the number line and bead lace in Chapter 5. The idea is to push the children to work with number bonds, so that sums like 18 − 4 would never be tackled by counting down, but rather by observing that 8 − 4 = 4, say. In the next sections we describe other examples of how young children can develop new, more powerful strategies of their own, at later stages of the curriculum.

A new pedagogy for two-digit subtraction: overcoming the 'smaller from larger' error

A very common error in two-digit subtraction arises when children subtract the smaller from larger digits when subtracting two- or three-digit numbers, say 53 − 34 = 21, or 358 − 162 = 216. In previous research we have found that the two-digit subtraction task was one of the hardest for 7-year-old children, with only about 20 per cent answering these correctly. They seem to be particularly difficult if presented in vertical format: it is widely believed that horizontal formats can encourage a more diverse range of solution strategies, while the vertical format is associated with the regular 'vertical' algorithm that seems to encourage this 'bug'.

For the three-digit subtraction '458 − 162 = ?' in vertical format (see Appendix 1: M9.26) only 30 per cent of 9-year-olds answered correctly and 17 per cent still made the smaller from larger error, $458 − 162 = 316$. In a sense, these children 'know' that subtracting the smaller from larger digit is not the right thing to do, as most of them (75 per cent) correctly subtracted $40 − 21 = 19$ in the horizontal format (M9.3). In fact in this case the error $40 − 21 = 29$ was as uncommon (5 per cent) as the smaller from larger error (4 per cent). But the combination of horizontal format and perhaps the unreasonableness of an answer like $40 − 21 = 21$ (when everyone knows that $40 − 20 = 20$), helps them to 'know' it! Note here again how for the 9-year-olds the contrast between formats and sizes of the numbers supports a potentially productive contradiction between the two cases: we will return to this point when we discuss 'cognitive conflict'.

In Chapter 2 we talked of this as an error of *overgeneralization* of 'subtract smaller from larger digits' in one-digit and simpler two-digit tasks, but it is symptomatic of something else as well. The teaching of formal rules for performing arithmetic tasks without an adequate *intuitive or conceptual basis* is doomed to generate an almost endless list of such 'bugs'.[10] Although it is interesting to try to identify the particular bugs that children have created, in some of these cases they are so copious that we doubt that they are individually and separately of any great significance. We argue that they simply reveal the creativity of children's capacity to generate rules without meaning, and hence the importance of teaching for strategies understood by contexts from which they draw sense.

Where are we to turn to establish an intuitive and conceptual basis for computation strategies? Manipulatives like unifix cubes, Cuisenaire rods and Dienes blocks have long been used to help children enact work with number; the use of these materials was justified by Bruner's formulation of three modes of communication in developing understanding: the 'enactive' (involving direct manipulation of materials), the 'iconic' (involving images and pictures of those materials) and the 'symbolic' (words, numbers and signs) modes.[11] Bruner's, and others', approach was inspired by Piaget's theoretical proposition that a mental schema is the result of internalizing an external action on objects. By acting with materials together in a collective, children can engage with actions and images, but also in talk together that later becomes internalized in images and verbal thought.[12] A picture is sometimes worth a thousand words. An 'activity' that engages with materials and pictures and words may provide the basis for new mathematical strategies and conceptions. At any rate that is the claim of this section of the chapter on two-digit subtraction. Let us see if you can be convinced!

Previous research devised a means of extending the usual strategies for adding tens and units with manipulatives that include ten-strips and one-strips.[13] Typically children in Years 1 and 2 (6- and 7-year-olds) can quite quickly develop procedures for adding two-digit numbers with the aid of such strips. (See Figure 4.2 for the addition of 28 and 15.) However, subtraction provides some additional problems for children that the researchers wanted to address.

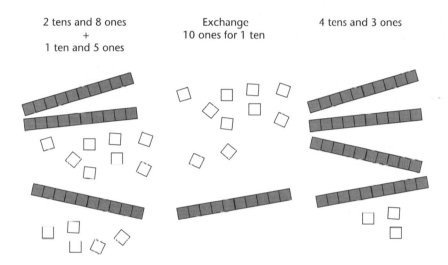

2 tens and 8 ones
+
1 ten and 5 ones

Exchange
10 ones for 1 ten

4 tens and 3 ones

Figure 4.2   28 + 15 = 43: exchange 10 ones for 1 ten.

Typically children find the *inverse strategy* for subtraction less intuitive. The pedagogic approach was to situate subtraction in an activity where the children are buying and selling (embedded in a game of lotto) using ten-strips and one-strips for 'money'. The children in this situation perform payments that can be considered as (and that the teacher later models as) subtractions. For example, you have 63 in your wallet, you pay 21, so you have 42 left.

An interesting problem arises when the children have, say, 63, they want to pay 26, but they do not have 6 ones in their wallet. Classically, the method taught is to *exchange* a ten broken down into ten ones. However, this is not the intuitive strategy in this situation. What would *you* usually do to pay 26 when you do not have the right change? You would pay 30 and expect 4 in change, and so did the children! (See Figure 4.3 for this compensation strategy.)

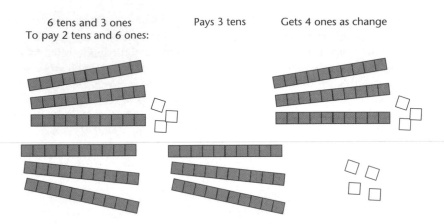

6 tens and 3 ones
To pay 2 tens and 6 ones:

Pays 3 tens

Gets 4 ones as change

Figure 4.3   63 − 26 = 37: child pays 26 of the 63 by paying 30 (leaving 33 in the wallet) and gets 4 change (leaving 37 in the wallet).

Here we present some of the transcript of a group of children with a researcher-teacher when working on such a problem for the first time.[14] The children are buying and selling their picture cards. Barry is interested in buying a sofa card for $47. He removes 4 ten-strips and says:

Barry: I don't have (. . .)
Interviewer: Does anyone have an idea?
Angel: To give one like this. [She points at one of Barry's ten-strips.] Barry removes 1 more ten-strip from his 200-board and gives it to Vy, who hesitates.]
Interviewer: [To Vy, the owner of the sofa card] What will you do?
Vy: I'll give change.
Interviewer: How much change? You were supposed to get 47 and you got 50.
                    [Vy and Angel announce a few numbers: 2, 5, 7.]
Angel: [Shouts] Three!
                    [This answer is approved by all and the game proceeds.]

This is an interesting case, which is quite typical of a group that is tackling this problem for the first time. The resources of the group as a whole are engaged in this joint work, with almost all the group involved in a collective solution. Here it seems to begin with Barry: he knows he cannot pay the full amount exactly, though he has paid 40 and has another ten-strip. We suggest he knows that he has enough money and indicates this by handing over another ten. Perhaps this is a conditional offer; at any rate there is a problem in just handing it over, and Vy hesitates to simply take it.

Then Vy comments that she can give some change, while the others seem to agree but build on this to work out how much change Barry should get. Typically the group collectively evaluates the completed transaction and has to be satisfied before progressing to the next move of the game. The group may simply accept this for the time being because they have no objection, or they may actively concur; at any rate they will have to re-engage with the process subsequently in different roles – for instance, when it is their own turn to make a purchase or sale. The responsibilities in the transactions shift as the roles rotate in the game, involving each player in offering a sum for a purchase or later in working out, perhaps with others' help, the change for a proffered amount.

The fact that this activity is constituted as a game is relevant, and will be discussed at greater length in a similar case in Chapter 6. But the main point here is that the transaction was given meaning as a simulation of a buying–selling activity. Sociologists have studied such social contexts and define them by the set of social obligations they typically impose; thus, in our culture, it is 'understood' that the purchaser can offer more than the price and the seller must provide change. It is 'expected' that the shopkeeper will work out the change; there may even be special counting-on strategies invoked as custom and practice in the marketplace, though this is not evident in this example, and such practices may well have died out in recent times with the ubiquity of electronic devices at the point of sale that record and calculate for the shop-keeper. This understanding or 'intersubjectivity', then, provides a 'situated intuition' that is transferred and revivified in the classroom game.

Because these shared cultural expectations are imported into the class-room with the simulation, they provide a set of social affordances and con-straints just as powerful as those provided by the 'rules of the game' here – that is, that each player must take their turn, that there are fair rules for all, and there has to be a means to decide who wins and how the game ends. The *affordances* allow for the children to construct solutions to the problem and have been carefully crafted to presage two-digit subtraction strategies thought to be productive. The *constraints* help to close down the set of options in a social context that help make it manageable and meaningful, and indeed to avoid certain strategies that might not be so productive for pedagogy.

But what of the affordances and constraints of the *manipulatives* here? These strips provide a useful representation of the numbers, visibly reminding us that they are worth ten. As a manipulative, they allow for or afford non-verbal communicative activity: Barry holds out the ten-strip without having to formally verbalize an offer: 'I offer you this, will you accept it . . . what will you give me back?' Vy even hesitates, and we think we know why without her having to say, and we interpret this as 'but it is too much . . . there is a problem . . .'. As such the manipulative has afforded an action, a gesture – the hesitant offering of the ten-strip – to begin a whole collective 'conversation'. The group takes it as a sign of there being a problem, and seem to grasp to a greater or lesser degree what the problem is. Thus the group can recognize the problem and appeal to the configuration of the shopping context to suggest, 'Yes, because she will give you change.' Then the problem is transformed: it now becomes the problem of the seller to work out the change, though the buyer is still interested![15]

Semioticians (semiotics is the name for the 'science of signs') will say that the manipulative here acts as a *sign,* and does a lot of work in mediating the communication in this collective act of problem solving. It is particularly important in allowing Barry to 'act' before he verbalizes: so much work is done by gestures, by exploratory, heuristic forms of language in problem solving. Manipulatives and other representations (diagrams, graphs, tables, and so on) serve to help learners engage mathematically as such *before* they are fully able to formulate their new ideas in formal language. Indeed by the time the new learning is formulated in proper, formal language, most of the hard work of problem solving has usually already been done. (More examples of this are given in Chapter 6.)

Finally, the actual physical structure of the 'unbreakable' ten-strip is an important constraint here too: the ten-strip embodies its equivalence as a set of ten units (in its length) but it does not afford the breaking up of the ten into ten units. This is important: if we had used a set of unifix cubes stuck together in tens then it would have been too easy for the children to break off the required units as they wanted. The fixed ten pushes new problem-solving, with either a trip to the bank to exchange the ten for ten units or a 'giving change' compensation strategy. The latter strategy was of course our target, because of its potential mathematical value.

The building of this intuitive strategy as an alternative to the 'break a ten' is important in helping children to make a connection between the intuitive mental method they will typically use in their life outside school (and therefore one that is reinforced often) and harder calculations on a number line later. Typically outside school, mental arithmetic is done by handling the larger units first (from the left-hand side), but in school we often teach written algorithms that start from the smaller unit (from the right-hand side); these algorithms often go wrong because they do not make much sense to the children.

Before moving on let us summarize the features of this construction of a new mathematical strategy that helped the children. There was 'enactive' work with manipulatives designed to constrain problem solutions, but it was part also of a social activity that drew on the children's cultural model of buying and selling, tapping into their experiences as consumers. A key intuition from the cultural practice of buying and selling became transformed into an associated strategy for two-digit subtraction. In addition, the designers of the method planned for this intuitive strategy to be consistent with the everyday methods for calculation.[16]

Scaffolding with context and models: multiplicative conceptions and strategies

Researchers have begun to use the term 'multiplicative conceptions' to refer to the whole field of concepts related to multiplication, division, fractions, ratio and proportion.[17] Mastering the 'multiplicative field' provides a major part of the number development of the mid- to late primary and secondary number curriculum. The child's development of these ideas grows from 'additive conceptions' through the development of doubling to repeated additions or 'times-ing'; it then generalizes to multiples, and use of the symbols × and ÷ for multiplication and division; and so proceeds to the beginnings of fraction representations and simple 1:n ratio and proportion tasks, and eventually to 'ratio and proportion' tasks involving fractions. In the remainder of this chapter we will draw on this area of the curriculum to develop pedagogy involving scaffolding (via contextualizing and modelling).

We will discuss the first group of concepts here, particularly relevant to 5- to 8-year-old children. This provides us with the opportunity to discuss a key developmental path that seems in fact already to leave many children behind in mathematics even by the age of 8 years or so. In Table 4.2 the capabilities of 5- to 8-year-old children are presented in a hierarchy as a *developmental map*; this involves grouping the relevant competences by the difficulty of tasks that demand them. Generally children can master tasks in a lower level in the hierarchy earlier than they do in the higher levels, and we interpret this as a hierarchy of the order in which the competences are, on average, mastered (given current curricula and pedagogy as the norm). The assignment of a *scale score* allows us to assign approximate ages on the map, which gives a rough indication of when, on average, children achieve the competences at that level.[18] For the convenience of an international audience we will provide the age at which a scale score is expected by an 'average' child. For example, the scale score of 41 is the average for children aged 5 years 8 months.

Before the first level, children can count only in ones and do not yet have any notion of doubling; for instance, they have to see all the socks in the 7-pairs task so that they can count them all. At level 1, children can now find the double of a small number that does not involve a -teen number, and they can solve simple problems with doubling even when some of the objects are not shown (for example, the wheels on a toy car). At level 2, the children can additionally work out doubles of single-digit numbers that go through ten, and use this in problems like finding the number of objects in two boxes if given the number in one box, and even with four boxes if most of the objects are visible in attached diagrams. At this stage they can also count the number of pairs shown without being distracted by the number of objects (for example,

Table 4.2 Developmental map of children's multiplicative conception (MX.Y = Malt reference, SS = scale score)

Level 0: [up to 5 years 6 months: SS < 40] **Counting by ones only**
Can work out the number of socks in 7 pairs when all the socks are visible (e.g. by counting in ones) (M6.15, SS = 35)

Level 1: [up to 6 years 2 months: SS = 45] **Beginning to double**
Can work out 'doubles of simple numbers' (M6.16, SS = 40)
Can work out how many in a small number of pairs (only some objects are visible) (M5.25, SS = 44)

Level 2: [up to 6 years 6 months, SS = 48] **Doubling and beginning to 'times'**
Can explicitly 'count the number of pairs' when presented with a figure showing some pairs (without becoming lost in the counting of individual items) (M6.19, SS = 45)
Can work out 'doubles of single-digit numbers, including those going through ten' (M6.17, SS = 46)
Can also work out the number of objects in four boxes where each box is visible, and the objects in the boxes are mostly visible (M7.15a, SS = 48)

Level 3: [up to 7 years 4 months, SS = 52] **Solving times problems in context**
Can now double two-digit numbers (e.g. 12, 24: M8.13a, SS = 50) but not 'going through ten' (e.g. 38)
Can now solve 'times' problems/tasks involving numbers of objects like 4 × 5 or 20 ÷ 2 where some of the information (but not all) is visible in the supporting diagrams (e.g. a box of 20 balls is shown to have 2 balls in each row, but the lid obscures the number of rows)
Can solve money problems (e.g. 3 bars at 60p per bar: M8.8, SS = 51)

Level 4: [up to 8 years 6 months, SS = 59] **Symbols, representations and 'times tables', beginning fractions and ratio**
Can identify or select simple 'multiples' from a list (M7.7, SS = 54)
Can now 'double two-digit numbers going through ten' (e.g. 38: M8.13b, SS = 55)
Can recall multiplication facts, and work with symbols like × and ÷ to represent tasks
Can solve some harder 'multiplication problems' including simpler ratios involving 1:n (M7.25, SS = 57)
Can shade ¼ of a circle divided into eight parts: the beginning of fraction representations (M8.4b, SS = 58)

Level 5: **Multiplication, division, fractions and ratio problems**
Can use symbols × and ÷ more flexibly (e.g. nominate numbers for ? ÷ ? = 5: M8.34, SS = 61) including the commutative principle for multiplication (a × b = b × a)
Can use simple fractions in harder cases (e.g. correctly shade ¼ of a shape: M8.10, SS = 62)
Can find a unit fraction of a number or 1:n ratio (e.g. ⅓ of 18; recipe for 10:20, M10.10a, SS = 60; sandwiches 3:6, M12.12a, SS = 62)
But has not yet mastered fraction equivalence ½, ¾ and ⅛ (M8.19, SS = 71, the easiest such fraction set)

---

they correctly answer '7 pairs' rather than '14 mittens' when asked for the number of pairs of mittens).

At level 3, with some visual support, the children can solve problems involving 'times' by counting, including some money problems, and can double two-digit numbers (but not going through ten, thus double 24 but not double 38). At level 4 the children can double two-digit numbers going through ten such as double 38, can recall multiplication facts and can use symbols × and ÷ in the representation of multiplicative problem tasks. They can also solve simple ratio tasks involving 1:n and can shade a quarter of a circle that is divided into eight equal parts. At level 5 the children can use multiplication and division signs more flexibly and use the commutative principle for multiplication. They can also find a unit fraction of a number but have not yet mastered the equivalence of unit fractions.

Here we briefly describe how to build a hierarchy such as this from the database in Appendix 1. Select a group of items with the required theme (for example, counting up and down in 1s, 2s, 5s and 10s), and place them in order of scale score (SS). Where there are significant gaps in the scale score it may be worthwhile looking for items that would appear within these gaps, in case sense can be made of these. Where clusters of items emerge in levels, look for some coherent sense or cause for the development. To convert scale scores to approximate average ages for MaLT5 to MaLT8, the MaLT manuals provide, for instance, conversions of scale scores to (years:months) as follows: SS 40 = (5:7), SS 45 = (6:2), SS 50 = (6:10), SS 55 = (7:9), and SS 60 = (8:11).[19] The use of a 'scale score' as a child's 'score' as well as a test item's difficulty is achieved by the use of the Rasch model; in this model it is expected that a child whose scale score is 40 (average age 5 years and 7 months) will have a 50 per cent chance of getting a test item of that level of difficulty correct (for example, finding the double of 3).

The y-axis on the graph in Figure 1.1 is measured in logits, which is essentially this scale score under a linear transformation (scale score = 61 + 5*logit). The fact that the age intervals between these scores are gradually growing (7 months, 8 months, 11 months, 14 months) is simply a reflection of the curve in the graph in Figure 1.1, which suggests declining rates of progress over the years. (More technical information is available in Appendix 1.)

From this data one can immediately see that mastery of doubling seems to develop slowly over a long period, and certainly is an issue for many children throughout the ages 5 to 8 years. One obvious reason for this is the size of the number to be doubled: at level 1, small digits; at level 2, digits that double up 'through ten' (for example, double 7 is 14); and at level 3, double two-digit numbers (like 12 and 24); but only at level 4 do they achieve doubling 'through a ten' (for example, double 38 is 76). Thus the performance of doubling is strongly dependent on the size of the numbers involved, because the children are mastering the numbers to 100 and place value over this same period. Indeed, mastery of 'doubling' requires mastery of the whole number system to 100 as well as being required by it!

The basic *concept* of doubling per se is essentially secure by level 2, when the children are able to work explicitly with the term 'pair', as in 'How many pairs are there?', and can solve a problem requiring the doubling of any single digit without being shown all the objects in the 'pair'. In this case, 'scaffolding' is provided by the use of supportive diagrams from which some of the objects can be counted, either the number of pairs or the number of objects 'in each pair' is helpfully shown. As this scaffolding is reduced, the child must either visualize the missing objects and count them 'in the mind' or develop strategies for counting them as a group or box – that is, count up in 2s. Progression from level 0 (when a 'How many?' problem is only solvable effectively by counting all the individual, visible objects) to level 4 involves the ability to solve increasingly difficult tasks of this type with only partially visible information in diagrams.

Presented with a task with only partial information visible in the figure, such as to find the number of wheels on two cars, the child at level 1 may count the visible wheels (and so get the answer '4' or even '2' or '6' for the wheels visible on one car, or the whole 3). Such children clearly have no 'doubling' conception that having 2 cars means they should add 4 and 4. On the other hand, those at level 1 who know how to double simple digits but do not know their number bonds are likely to go wrong on doubling 9 and say 19, miscounting using a number line, for instance (see Figure 4.4).

A similar progression can be seen with regard to problems involving multiplication and division in context, such as when asked 'How many balls are there in 4 boxes?' with each box holding 3 balls. In such problems, solutions are generally achieved at level 2 if all the information is visible and at

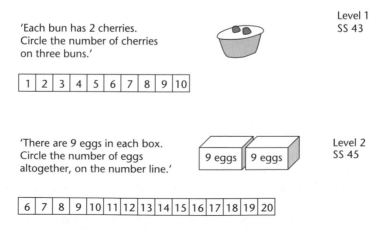

Figure 4.4   Scaffolding for progression in 'doubling'.

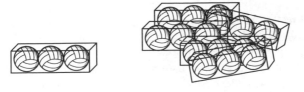

Level 3
SS 48

In 4 boxes there are _ balls.

Figure 4.5 Scaffolding with progressively fewer visible cues.

level 3 when much of or most of the information is not visible. Finally, at level 4, children succeed at problems with no such visible information, including simple cases with only symbolic presentations (see Figure 4.5).

The general point is that these diagrams offer contextual support for children developing the concept; they are a kind of 'scaffold' for the concept. That is, a figure showing 3 balls in each of several boxes may help the learner to see that they are required to count in threes: '3, 6, 9, . . .', say. Teaching with these scaffolds over a long period of time may be necessary to the learner's development of the concept. The pedagogical principle is to flexibly remove and replace these scaffoldings appropriately; so a child who is stuck without the diagram or context is offered a diagram or context, or eventually is reminded 'You could draw a diagram', 'Can you think of a context?' The scaffolding can be reintroduced by the teacher and increasingly by the learner themselves as and when they feel the need; indirect 'verbal' references can be made so that these then come to replace the original scaffold itself. The appropriate teaching strategy involves practice of tasks typical of the *next* stage of development with this flexibility of scaffolding. The idea is that learning involves the learner internalizing the '3, 6, 9 . . .', eventually subvocally, into inner speech, to verbalized thought.

Thus, a child who is working on a problem to find how many cherries are needed for 7 cakes with only one 'cake with two cherries' visible, may be helped by suggesting successively that they (i) imagine the 7 cakes and count up 2 at a time in their head seven times, 2, 4, 6, . . .; (ii) use seven of their fingers to model the drawings of the cakes, each knuckle being a cherry; (iii) draw the 7 cakes and associated cherries. Pedagogy then involves the art of knowing how to do this so that the learner comes to take over this scaffolding role themselves, to 'regulate themselves' rather than depend on the teacher or other external mediator to do so. The use of a hierarchy of 'lower level' and 'higher level' questioning would seem necessary: 'Could you use this specific model/context, for example, draw a figure, table, . . .?' to 'Would some kind of model or context help?', perhaps to 'What strategies do I usually suggest in this type of problem?'

Modelling fractions

In Table 4.2, we saw that the concept of ¼ was developing only at level 4, at about 7½ to 8½ years old on average, when the children become able to shade correctly a quarter of a cake sliced into 8 parts (that is, they correctly shade 2 parts). Children at level 2 correctly shade ¼ (one slice) when the cake is sliced into 4 equal slices, but this is indicative of a still primitive under-standing of the fraction as a single slice, and one finds that the same children may shade ⅛ for ¼ (that is, one slice rather than two) if the same cake is cut into 8 slices (see Figure 4.6). The shading of one slice in the first part of the question in fact gives a quite false view of the children's understanding of fraction.

However, the children who shaded 2 slices in the second part of the ques-tion, while they may be said to be able to focus on the part–whole relationship here, may not have generalized this understanding. Examining a harder ques-tion at level 5 shows the concept is by no means completed at this level. Only 7 per cent of 8-year-olds recognize that ½, ¾ and ⅛ represent the same shaded fraction of a circle (see Appendix 1: M8.19, SS 71).

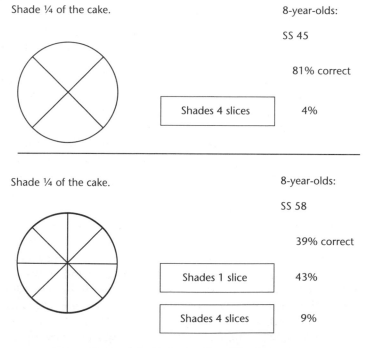

Figure 4.6 Understanding of fractions.

Many of those who can grasp the part–whole relationship in the case of a cake may be baffled when the whole is a rectangle cut into parts in different ways. This is quite consistent with the literature that suggests that part–whole relations are most obvious when the whole is a circle (pie or cake); and it is important not to be misled into thinking that children have developed the general conception based on this one particular context. An understanding of the equivalence of fractions generally requires flexibility of the view of the unit involved, typically only managed with multiple representations using rectangle models. The fact that 75 per cent of 9-year-olds thought that a circle cut into 4 unequal parts by parallel lines gave a shaded part representing ¼ is a salutary reminder: this makes for one of the most difficult fractions items in primary tests (see Appendix 1: M9.27).

In conclusion, concepts such as that of the fraction ½ and ¼ continue to develop over a prolonged period of schooling and 'having the concept' is often a slippery idea: concept acquisition is always a work in progress, and a lot depends on the context of the concept, the model or representation, and the mode of assessment of the task. Indeed conceptions of fractions continue to develop with that of proportions right through secondary school, as we will see shortly.

Context: internal as well as external

Context provides mathematics with 'meaning' and 'sense' because it connects the mathematics 'with other text', con-text, even if that 'other text' is sometimes another, more familiar part of mathematics. Consider the second task in Figure 4.4. This use of egg boxes in MaLT 6.22 can be, and usually is, said to be a context for the mathematics 'add 9 and 9', 'double 9', or maybe even '2 × 9'. And we agree these different formulations involve at least a change of context. In the data cited previously, we showed how in fact these different problems make quite different demands on children, but the data do not in themselves explain why. Certainly the word-problem involving eggs and a picture of egg boxes allows a different meaning from '2 × 9 = ?'; indeed some children might try to solve the context problem by counting on, or even counting all the eggs.[20]

For those children who already have symbolic knowledge – that is, those who can do formal 'sums' like 'double 9' or '2 × 9' – the problem may well be solved by application of these number-facts to the problem. What Table 4.2 tells us is that such children are generally quite a bit more advanced than those who can solve the contextual problem by some other means: the context provides support – potential scaffolding – for those who are not yet confident with more formal approaches to 'applying number-facts to problems'.

In the above examples we have drawn attention to features of the tasks that made them easier or harder; clearly, the more complicated the numbers the harder the task. Indeed, even when the structure of the question is identical, the larger, less familiar numbers can obscure the solution path. For instance, to notice that '$27 + 27 + 27 + 27 + 27 + \ldots = 270$' is the same as '$? \times ? = 270$' turns out to be significantly harder than recognizing the structurally equivalent equality '$3 + 3 + 3 + \ldots = 33$ is the same as '$? \times ? = 33$'. Note that here the numbers appear as a context for examining algebraic structure, and the point is that a correct response can be obtained either thinking numerically with the numbers themselves, or thinking algebraically about the structure of multiplication. The former route is easier if the numbers are familiar and the arithmetic modest. This effect of *number as a context* is important throughout the primary and middle school years at least, and is sometimes explained by arguing that younger children do not think 'structurally' or formally, but prefer to reason within the context. Their familiarity with the particular numbers here is pertinent to the perception of the task, and this is a general property of 'concrete' thinking.

The notion that the actual numbers involved define a context is somewhat counterintuitive: is not the whole idea that 'pure number' questions are essentially context free? There are indeed two different conceptions of 'context' here that should be clarified. The 'real world' of egg boxes does provide an *external context* for the task – one can imagine that particular knowledge about such egg boxes (which unfortunately used to contain, and sometimes still do, 12 to a box instead of 10) can be utilized as a resource for the problem $9 + 9$: after all we are one short of a box of 10 in each case, so 'two short of 2 boxes, that's 2 short of 20, so 18'. But additionally the child's own knowledge provides an important context, a world of number that provides an *internal context* for their strategic reasoning and problem solving. Greeno suggested that the way one 'knows number' is analogous to the way one knows a landscape/streetscape.[21] If you are asked to direct someone to the local rail station, no doubt you will say, 'You turn left at St Dominic's, straight on until you reach the library, then two blocks to your right.' On the other hand, others might say 'Head for the Fancy Firkin, take a right and keep on until you get to the Red Lion, then over past the Frog and Bucket . . .'. Thus problem solutions are constructed in large part from the knowledge resources the solver has available.

The point is that problem-solving strategies are constrained by this internal context, the knowledge base that the child brings to the problem, just as much as by the external environment. There are many solutions to a problem, and the way an individual structures their solutions is characterized by their knowledge of and disposition towards their internal 'number environment'.[22] If you want to subtract 37 from 201 you might say 'From 37 to 100 is 63, then 101 is 164' but another person might prefer '201 down to 41 is 160 then 4 to 37, so that's 164'. The way we end up at a solution to a problem is constructed from our particular knowledge resource; this knowledge resource is, in a sense, the 'internal context' for our work towards a solution.

These solution strategies can be diagnostic of the learner's various knowledge bases, and this applies to correct solutions as well as errors. Making these strategies visible, such as through the number line representations of those in Figure 4.7, can help children themselves as well as a teacher share these strategies and expose the state of knowledge of the learners.

We emphasized above the importance of providing the 'times-ing' task with a context and a diagram with certain keys features visible or partially visible (see also, for example, Table 4.2 – a level 3 item showing that a box has 2 balls in each row, and asking for the number of rows that make a box of 20). This is of course a key factor in the context that makes children's existing strategic resources employable in more demanding tasks. Similarly we have argued that a manipulative model or representation and a simulation of a situation such as shopping can provide resources for developing more advanced procedures, concepts and strategies. We argued that contexts can be pedagogically useful as scaffolding, and this applies to internal context too. Thus, if a strategy works for small numbers, such as counting the knuckles for doubling, this can be extended to larger numbers, counting the 3 bones on each finger to generate multiples of three, or hands for five.

The astute reader will have noticed how, in certain tasks we have cited, the task is provided not only with a 'context', but also with a model such as a number line. The use of a model is particularly important in helping children build solutions. Of course we want children to use such models independently in their reasoning (the above argument about 201 – 37 is a case in point), but one assumes they will develop such independence from experiencing repeated, guided use when necessary: the idea is that later on a child

Two solutions for 201 – 37 = _

(i)

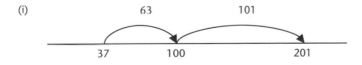

(ii)

Figure 4.7 Preferred connections: (i) bonds to 100, (ii) counting down in 100s and 10s.

solving a problem without the provision of a number line may be prompted to consider with questions or prompts: 'Would a number line help?' or even 'Can I think of a model that would help?'

Conflict pedagogy using models: multiplicative versus additive strategies

We now consider the next stages of multiplication, extending Table 4.2 with Table 4.3.[23] The key to this phase is the completion of the conception of

Table 4.3   Multiplicative structures up to age 15 years

Multiplication, division, fractions and ratio problems (SS < 64)
Can use symbols × and ÷ more flexibly (e.g. nominate numbers for ? ÷ ? = 5: M8.34, SS = 61) including the commutative principle for multiplication (a × b = b × a)
Can use simple fractions in harder cases (e.g. correctly shade ¼ of a shape: M8.10, SS = 62)
Can find a unit fraction of a number or 1:n ratio (e.g. ⅓ of 18; recipe for 10:20, M10.10a, SS = 60; sandwiches 3:6, M12.12a, SS = 62)

Beginnings of ratio and fraction equivalence (SS < 68)
Can solve harder ×, ÷ number sentence problems (e.g. ? ÷ 5 = 5; 6 × 0.5 = ? 100 × 8.2 = ?; M10.28, M11.6: SS = 65; M12.26, SS = 66; M12.26, SS = 68)
Can shade ⅔ of a rectangle split into 6 (M10.9, SS = 67) and recognize some other equivalent fractions (e.g. ¹²⁄₂₀ = ?; M13.33, SS = 67; ⅔ = ⁴⁄₆, M10.9, SS = 67; M9.34, SS = 71)
Can solve ratio tasks (e.g. recipes, costs) involving halving and adding (50% of ? = 16, M10.5b, SS = 66; 8:12 = £4:?, M11.17, SS = 67)

Ratio and fraction equivalence and problems (SS < 77)
Can solve number sentences with fractions (e.g. ¼ of ? = 16; M10.5b, SS = 68)
Can use the fraction equivalence ½, ²⁄₄ and ⁴⁄₈ (M8.19, SS = 71)
Can add fractions with common denominator (M11.29, SS = 72)
Can solve harder division problems and 'short multiplication' (e.g. remainder, M11.9, SS = 69; measures: M13.2, SS = 68; average: M12.3, SS = 70), and
Can solve harder ratio problems (e.g. applied to speed; M10.19, SS = 74), or using a ratio of 4:6, 10:15 (M10.10b, SS = 70; M12.12b, SS = 76)

Fraction and ratio equivalence (SS ≥ 77; only a small minority of 11- to 15-year-olds can do these)
Fully grasp the concept of a quarter in the part-whole context (M9.27, SS = 79)
Calculate using a ratio of 100:120, 30:100, 4:6 = 6:? = ?:15 etc. (M12.10a, M13.39a: SS = 77, M13.39b, SS = 78)
⅜ − ¼ = ?; ¼ + ⅜ = ? (M12.36, SS = 77; M14.35, SS = 77)
Calculate 0.2 × 0.4 (M11.28, SS = 82)

---

equivalent fractions and ratios in simple cases; the main error emerging in this phase is that commonly known as the *additive tendency*, which is the tendency to respond with an addition, subtraction or difference when a multiplicative relation is required.

We will focus on ratio and proportion in relation to the additive tendency, drawing in particular on the way performance varies with context, how this affects additive versus multiplicative strategies and on the role of models and representations in argumentation and hence in the scaffolding of learning.[24]

Recent findings cited here are entirely consistent with the work of the 1970s and 1980s, though the more recent studies are larger in scale and, of course, up to date.[25] The pattern of development for 11- to 14-year-olds shows that (i) there is a big difference between solving ratio and proportion in the numerical cases of 1:2 or 1:*n* on the one hand – that is, those that can be solved 'additively' by repeated addition – and the general solving of problems involving any ratio *m:n* on the other (almost all the children in secondary school can do the former and almost none the latter!); (ii) there are stages in between that involve successful 'building up' strategies using 1:*n* and halving-and-adding, as in cases such as 8:12 or 4:6 where the extra part to be added is a half of the whole; (iii) throughout all this development many children prefer to 'add' or 'subtract' numbers in the problem, and avoid multiplication, division, fractions (especially 'unfriendly' fractions). This additive tendency accounts for a large proportion (in some research over a third) of the variation in performance on these ratio tasks; and (iv) there are very significant differences in strategy adopted according to context, which is suggestive for curriculum development and pedagogy.

Beyond this, however, new research has investigated the effect of 'models' and representations (diagrams, ratio tables and the double number line) on children's performance and argumentation. In one study in the UK, effects on the ease of items when a model was provided were found in a few cases, but in general there was no effect on performance under test conditions.[26] This is an interesting result, as it seems to be contrary to the research from Dutch schools and to the main argument in this book! They find not only significant differences in performance by children who use models in general but in the context of ratio and proportion in particular.

The explanation for the difference is probably that the mass of the population in the UK have not been taught to use such models in the way the Dutch samples have. What was interesting, however, was how the introduction of a model – in this case a simple picture – into small-group discussions, made a big difference to the quality of the group discussion. Qualitative analyses of children's talk in this context showed how the picture enabled productive problem-solving talk, what Barnes originally called exploratory talk.[27] Even having a simple picture to refer to allows the children to point to elements of the problem and its context informally, in ways that help the communication of ideas between children, and between a teacher and children. In one fairly typical group discussion, for instance, the 'contextually referenced' utterances in the talk increased after the introduction of a diagram from 7 per cent to 39 per cent; the difference was entirely accounted for by the referencing of the picture to signify elements of the context.

The significance of references to the *external context*, rather than just to the numbers in the task, is regarded as essential to the shift from additive to multiplicative reasoning in a task. Justifications for 'additive' procedures are almost always purely numerical. That is, when a student suggests that $3:10 = 4:11$ and is asked 'Why?' children almost always refer to the numerical relationship alone: 'Because the difference here was 7, so it should be the same here.' On the contrary, if multiplicative reasons are to be justified, an appeal to the context is necessary; this is a necessary but not sufficient condition.

Thus, for instance, if one asks, '3 tins of red and 6 tins of yellow makes the same colour paint as 7 tins of red and how many tins of yellow?' (one of the hardest contexts studied in the literature, as it calls for a functional or 'intensive' ratio), one finds that many children argue with the numbers to get an additive answer, '3 and 4 makes 7 so you add 4, and the answer is 10.' (We will notate this argument, after Toulmin: the *claim* is $(3,6) = (7,10)$; and the *backing* is 'because you add 4'.) The actual context of mixing paint does not enter this argument.

The chain of reasoning that most successfully led the 'adders' to change their mind involved the extended use of their additive strategy to suggest that logically, to be consistent, $(3,6)$ would have to be the same as $(1,4)$ and even $(0,3)$, implying that 0 tins of red paint and 3 tins of yellow paint would give the same colour of orange paint as the 3 tins of yellow and 6 tins of red did – an absurd contradiction that causes most students cognitive conflict![28]

However, such arguments assume that the numeric task is linked to the context of the problem and thence to knowledge and common sense from outside the mathematical world – for example, to that of mixing paint (the relative inexperience of children with such contexts perhaps being a factor in their difficulty with this problem, but it is also an example of an intensive, 'between qualities' relation, and as such known to cause more difficulty). Thus the claim that $(3,6)$ is the same as $(7,10)$ typically appeals simply to the relations between the numbers: 'Because it's the same difference', or 'You add 3.' But how is the addition justified? There is usually no backing argument for addition in the context (though if you want only to 'cover the walls' and don't care about the colour, another 'constant sum' strategy is suggested, perhaps $(3,6)$ is the same as $(7,2)$!). Thus a pedagogy that supports dialogue and reasoning related to the context, drawing on 'common sense' about or, better, 'a sense of structure' from the context, is the most likely source of reasons that can undermine additivity.

A model found elsewhere, mostly in the Dutch RME tradition, involves

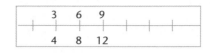

Figure 4.8   Table and double number line models for the ratio 3:4.

the use of a *table* or *double number line*. Figure 4.8 shows a table and double number line representing 3 loaves shared between 4 people, a (3,4) ratio.

The literature internationally suggests that this representation has a number of important affordances for multiplicative reasoning.[29] First it is accessible to early modelling of ratio problems because it is constructed from additive processes (thus 3, 6, 9, . . . and 4, 8, 12, . . .) that the children find 'intuitive'. However, on reflection the table itself – and the equivalent double number line – can come to constitute the ratio and fraction (in this example, 3:4 or ¾) and so can be used as a model for ratios and fractions that contradicts the additive strategy, as (3,4) = (6,8) and not (6,7). (Note the shift through reflection from a 'model of' a problem context – 3 loaves for 4 people – to a 'model for' the new mathematics of ratio 3:4.)[30]

Another model that has been found useful extends the double number line dynamically: it involves the use of a piece of *elastic* that stretches to yield equivalent ratios. That is, its parts remain in the same proportions even as the stretching changes the values of the parts in the ratio. In Figure 4.9 the elastic is marked out in the ratio 3.7 and is used to divide the line of length 20 in the ratio 3:7. The advantage of the elastic over the table or pictorial models is that its structure constrains one to a multiplicative model by virtue of the elastic property that ensures the tension is constant throughout, and so enlarged in the same ratio throughout the length of the elastic. While the children could conceivably use the table to record an additive relation (thus, 5, 7, 9, 11, . . .), one cannot envisage this for the elastic.

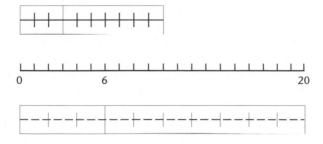

Figure 4.9   Stretched elastic dynamically shows the ratio 3:7, ³⁄₁₀ or 30%.

We finish with a comment on the 'linear prototype', which describes how many children tend to use the linear, ratio method even when a task demands something else – for example, addition. The point is that the tendency to overgeneralize to inappropriate cases is ever present; the only solution is in coming to understand how mathematics comes to be applied as a model to a limited range of situations and cases. This knowledge about one's mathematical knowledge, or metacognition, is an essential aspect that attaches to all learning. A widely used example is: 'A student gets $^5/_{10}$ on part A of a test and $^5/_{10}$ on the second half. They claim that $^5/_{10} + {}^5/_{10} = {}^{10}/_{10}$ and that they should therefore be awarded 100 per cent.' But there are even more absurd questions that have been used to show how lacking in meaning children's mathematics can be. Every class test should include one like this: 'A driver is 19 and his passenger is 15. How old is the car?'

Conclusion

In general, we conclude that sense and meaning come from contextualized problems that connect with common sense from outside mathematics, or from familiar mathematics previously mastered, to be attached to the new mathematics. The most successful contexts allow intuitions to be imported into mathematics from familiar situations. The more familiar the situation may be, as in buying and selling, the more intuitive the children's response is likely to be. We refer to intuitions about such situations as these as 'situated intuitions', and suggest that this is a field of research much in need of development; there is little known as yet.[31] Then there are less familiar situations, like mixing paint, that might be used precisely because they are demanding, or even that provoke inappropriate mathematics; these can press the learner to analyse the model to be introduced. This begins to invoke the idea that mathematics is itself a 'model' that can be applied appropriately and inappropriately to situations; this is characteristic of the next, post-15, stage of mathematics.

Finally, we also note the significance of the models, representations and manipulatives in the mediation of problem solving and group communication in learning mathematics. At the least these should provide enhanced communication, allowing heuristic forms of discussion in which less than fully articulated thoughts can be communicated by actions, gestures and informal talk. At best, they may offer a structure that constrains while affording productive strategies, as in the ten-strips or the ratio elastic. While it is true that there is still a lot of research to be done on these, the research that has been done is not well known outside the academic community.[32]

Notes

1   See Nunes (1996) and also Hatano (1982). Though we can be thankful we do not learn to count in French in which eight-tens is 'four-twenty', and so on.
2   In Welsh there are also alternatives for 18: 'tri ar bymtheg' means 'three on fifteen' and 'deunaw' means 'two nines'.
3   Ginsburg (2002) makes this point.
4   MaLT (2005). standardized diagnostic assessment and error analysis for moni toring and teaching.
5   Gelman and Gallistel (1986).
6   Scottish playground rhyme from Opie and Opie (1959).
7   Butterworth (1999).
8   There is more comment on embodiment, gesture and internalization in Chapter 5.
9   Gray *et al.* (1999). Also Yeo (2003) on dyslexia.
10 A precious book by Ashlock (2005) now in its ninth edition is devoted to cataloguing these bugs in computation.
11 Bruner (1966) originated the use of enactive, iconic and symbolic modes.
12 We appeal to Piaget's notion for the genesis of schema here, but also to Vygotsky because of the importance of semiotic mediation through language. For Vygotsky, the word-sign is inseparable from the verbal-thought to which it is attached.
13 This work was initiated by Williams and Linchesvski, and empirically researched by Kutscher *et al.* (2002); a summary is in Williams *et al.* (under review).
14 Williams *et al.* (under review).
15 Hasan's 'contextual configuration' in Halliday and Hasan (1985).
16 No one has yet quite worked out how to extend this to three digits, so a research project beckons!
17 The first was Vergnaud (1983) on multiplicative structures.
18 But we do not necessarily claim that these stages are longitudinal, that children progress necessarily or ideally from one level to the next. Additionally, it should be borne in mind that the spread of scores over a specific age is very great, as Figure 1.1 indicates. Thus the central 50 per cent of the population might be spread over 10 scale score points, which is indicative of at least 15 months of development, but this ratio grows with age, of course.
19 MaLT (2005).
20 We suspect these strategies explain why so many children get the answer 19, or give up. It seems that these counting strategies involve prodigious amounts of memory and concentration, which explains why many mistakes that we say

are due to 'overload' of working memory can also be attributed to 'primitive strategies'.

21 Greeno (1991).

22 There may be more involved than just this: Greeno's cognitive approach might well be supplemented here by a social approach to 'habitus'. No doubt there is much involved in the 'internal environment' that is social, cultural, classed, gendered, and so on. More on this in Chapter 9.

23 In the UK this is Key Stage 2 and 3; the levels we have so far described above in Table 4.2 correspond approximately to levels 0 through to 4.

24 The ZPD (zone of proximal development) and the learning zone: Vygotsky surely had a conception of 'development' that goes beyond simply 'learning', in fact his whole point was that learning should always be in advance of development. We will therefore follow Tanner and Jones's (1999) use of the 'learning zone' if we simply mean the zone of new learning being scaffolded.

25 Some of the best work of the CSMS and SESM studies of the 1970s and 1980s involved ratio (Hart, 1981, 1984); and the data analysed by MaLT and by Misailidou and Williams (2003).

26 Misailidou and Williams (2003).

27 Barnes (1976); Barnes and Todd (1995).

28 Gorard (1999) used the same technique, critiquing quantitative research errors.

29 Streefland (1991).

30 Treffers (1987).

31 Linchevski and Williams (1999); also Williams *et al.* (under review).

32 Work on the arithmetic rack is still not widely known in the UK, and we know of no research on the use of elastic in developing ratio strategies to this day.

5 Shape, space and measurement

Introduction

In this chapter we will reassert the significance of shape and space for understanding measurement and number in particular, and for envisioning mathematics in general. There are several reasons why this aspect of mathematics should be regarded as an essential part of the mathematics education of all children, and we argue that devaluing this aspect can be seriously debilitating for children's learning. We will outline the van Hiele developmental model and show how this can help make sense of learners' errors and the curriculum for geometry, and we will suggest some alternative pedagogies for development and the need for new lines of research. We then adopt a similar approach to errors and misconceptions in measurement, and conclude that the curriculum needs to find new ways of engaging children in *re-inventing* measurement.

The importance of visualization in shape, space and measurement

In a trite and obvious sense, space is all around us, and representing the essential 'spatial' worlds of science, technology, construction, art and sport involves understanding shape and space, and their representations in diagrams, figures and so on. If you want to understand tides or the paths of the planets, the behaviour of chemicals, how machines move, how buildings stand up, perspective, or sports match strategy, the first objects you are likely to encounter will be spatial. Learning to read often highly conventionalized figural representations of such phenomena is not trivial and requires a well-developed sense of visualization and the graphic use of space, as Tufte has shown.[1]

This practical argument is only the beginning, however, and perhaps the least persuasive argument for the prominence of spatial representations and their ubiquity in mathematics and mathematics education. We will appeal to the notion that all cognition has a visuo-spatial dimension, indeed that our minds and cognition are always essentially *embodied* and hence spatially mediated.[2] Even the most abstract cognitions involving language and language-like sign systems, such as mathematics, betray their embodied roots in the use of spatial metaphors.[3] Take, for instance, time. Time is embodied in terms of travelling along a path, as in 'going forwards/backwards in time': the past is 'behind us' but we always have much in the future to 'look forward to'. We conclude that this spatial aspect is therefore essential to our culture's concept of time.

Even our memory seems to be spatially accessed: psychologists studying gesture have shown how the movements of eyes and hands seem to search for, reach out and 'get hold' of the word we are struggling for in heuristic (problem-solving) talk, for instance.[4] Some mnemonists consciously organize their memory spatially, inventing a memorable, striking journey through the objects to be recalled. So it is in mathematics; every mathematical idea is organized in, and through, space and the body. Our fingers embody the digits to ten, the ordering of number is achieved in the number line, and so mathematics proceeds eventually to relativity, envisioned by Einstein as he imagined himself travelling through the universe on a beam of light.

Visuo-spatial embodiment

Thus visualization allows one to access spatial, embodied intuitions, and these are essential to almost all mathematical thinking, especially in number and algebra. Some argue that there is a visuo-spatial style of thinker and problem-solver, or a visuo-spatial intelligence that contrasts with verbal-logical styles or intelligences,[5] but we believe that language and mathematics, and so every act of communication and hence thought, has (in *normal* brain functioning) a visuo-spatial, embodied aspect that involves the 'holistic', imaginative, left-hemisphere element even while it is also written into the right-hemisphere through language and culture.[6]

Figure 5.1 shows that two odd numbers always sum to an even number because the 'odd bits' 'even' themselves out, and Figure 5.2 shows that the sum of the first 10 numbers equals half of 10 by 11 because the rectangle measures 10 by 11 and this is twice $1 + 2 + 3 + 4 + \ldots + 10$ (after Gauss).

We have already argued the importance of models and metaphorical entailments, for instance in the number line, the double abacus, and so on, in previous chapters (Chapters 2, 3 and 4). Such artefacts are all around us in mathematics: the table as a means of spatially organizing number pairs representing functions; the Venn diagram spatially organizing set union and intersection; the graph dynamically representing fractions, and so on. These are essential in marshalling visual and spatial knowledge and intuitions to

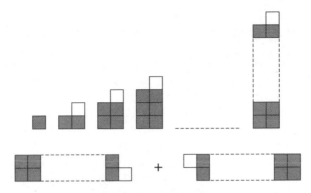

Figure 5.1   Odd plus odd equals even.

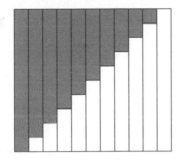

Figure 5.2 $1 + 2 + 3 + \ldots + 10 = \frac{1}{2}(10 \times 11); 1 + 2 + 3 + \ldots + n = \frac{1}{2} n (n +1)$.

one's understanding of mathematics. Effective connection-building when learning mathematics or problem solving with mathematics almost always involves a spatial aspect.

Geometrical argumentation

As one might expect from the historical account, geometry offers us some of our first experiences of mathematical argumentation at every level, from the most informal justifications to the most formal proof. The justifications for the earliest algebraic formalism in 'odd plus odd equals even' or 'the sum of the first 10 integers is half of 10 times 11', for instance, have a vital visual component as expressed in Figures 5.1 and 5.2. On the other hand, Euclidean geometry offers the development of a non-trivial experience of a deductive system based on simple shapes. This provides experience of important elements of logic at quite early levels. For example, knowing that 'every A is a B' is not equivalent to and does not imply 'every B is an A' can emerge from the

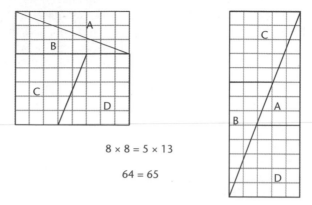

$$8 \times 8 = 5 \times 13$$

$$64 = 65$$

Figure 5.3 Dissection paradox: a fallacious visual proof.

reflection that 'every square is a rectangle' does not imply 'every rectangle is a square'. Figural representation does not make thinking immune from errors, however. It is known that proofs based in erroneous diagrams can be very hard to detect, particularly as the figure is so intuitively persuasive; for example, in Figure 5.3 it is visually 'proved' that 64 = 65.

Unfortunately, some curricula, especially for those of lower attainment, do not value geometry, seeming to regard it as relatively less 'vital' than number and algebra. By this means the learner may be deprived of the very experiences and resources they need to 'catch up' intellectually. This error of judgement is perhaps due to the lack of a coherent approach to shape and space in the curriculum. In many curricula, it is often not obvious what the necessary path of development or learning trajectory is supposed to be. One coherent approach to this for geometry is the van Hiele model.

The van Hiele model of concept development in geometry

What is needed, in our view, is a systematic approach to the development of geometric ideas and ways of thinking such as that provided by the van Hiele model (but not manifest in many curricula).[7] In addition, the van Hiele model can help us to understand the significance and value of many errors that learners make in relation to shape and space, and prototyping in particular.

Level 1: visualization – recognition, naming and the mathematical voice

In many early-years classrooms children are exposed to a universe of plastic shapes, of many colours and sizes, thicknesses, and so on. They learn to *name* these shapes, based on holistic perceptions of them, and tacitly on certain features of their appearance pointed out to them as salient: the pyramids are the ones with a pointed head and that do not roll; you use the cylindrical stamp to print a circle, which is curved like a face (with eyes and mouth put on); the rectangular block prints a rectangle useful for drawing a house, and so on.

This level of activity is associated with establishing the founding concepts of shape and van Hiele regarded this as the *first level* of geometrical concept development. But we know that very young children have a lot of work to do to master this level of expertise with shapes: we mentioned in Chapter 2 the puzzle of the 'mathematical voice', and this is most important here. The terminologies of 'square', 'face', 'edge', 'line', and so on, all have their own special meaning in the mathematics classroom and this in general conflicts with the meanings the child has learnt elsewhere: the town square is not 'square', a person's 'face' is not usually flat, the edge of the stream is not usually straight, the railway line has two lines of rail, and so on. The *mathematical* voice comes to be recognized as an element of a new 'game' of 'doing mathematics' or, better, 'talking mathematics' that takes place in the mathematics lesson.

Leakage of knowledge and language from other practices is a necessary part of connection-making between mathematics and the child's 'real world', but inevitably this causes contradictions in the meanings. Thus shape recognition and 'naming' are error prone (sometimes for quite sound, logical reasons) and pedagogy can exploit these by making them explicit. So we have a 'mathematical literacy' approach, recognizing that mathematical ways of speaking reveal just one more language or genre that learners need to pick up:

Q: 'How many times can you subtract 7 from 83, and what is left afterwards?'

A: 'I can subtract it as many times as I want, and it leaves 76 every time.'

For more advanced mathematicians: 'There are 10 types of people in this world – those that understand the binary system and those that don't.'

Level 2: analysis – naming properties

At the *second level*, children begin to name the features or properties of shapes and so classify them. Thus the circle will be 'curving all the way around' and this may be accompanied by a gesture with a finger tracing around the edge of the circle; the square may have 'four straight sides' or the rectangle may have 'four sides', 'four right angles', pairs of sides that are 'parallel', and so on.

Of course at the first stages of development each concept is prone to prototyping: perception and naming takes place naturally in this way, and cannot simply be 'blamed' on the necessarily limited set of examples provided by the teacher. But psychologists have argued that concepts can be taught most efficiently through a combination of providing a 'rational set' of examples and counterexamples ('exemplification moves' in the literature) and explanations of the relevance of these for the conception ('definition moves'). This approach, though somewhat formal and abstract, does make sense; thus a rational set of examples of the concept of 'triangle' will include some that are not 'the right way up', some that are 'oblique-angled', some large and small, perhaps some on the side of three-dimensional solids, and so on. Rational counterexamples will include not only those with more than three sides/angles, but also some with three curved sides, and so on.

However, what makes a set of examples 'rational' is the way their properties relate to the definition of the concept, which invokes reasoning mastered at the next van Hiele level, and so is not obviously accessible to children working at a purely perceptual level. Indeed it is just this kind of reasoning that serves to help the learner to acquire the next level of concept formation.

Level 3: abstraction and informal definitions

In the *third level* the learner's focus shifts from recognition and description (from the perception and naming of the whole and its features) to an articulation of how the distinction is made to classify or name the shape through informal arguments. So the triangle is justified as a triangle through a typical definition move related to geometrical properties – for example, 'This is a triangle *because* it has three sides and three angles.' Likewise a circle is recognized as such because it is curved, a rectangle is recognized because it has four straight sides and its angles are all right-angled, and so on. Then the definition move becomes more refined: the shape with three curved sides is not a triangle *because* the sides of a triangle must also be straight; the shape is a circle *because* it is a constant distance from its centre point; and any triangle continues to be a triangle even when rotated, reflected or enlarged, and so on (see Figure 5.4).

In a sense the concept becomes finally stable or 'concrete', in Piaget's terms, at this level, because its invariance (unchanging character) under different transformations is recognized. Clearly all this takes some time and experience with a rational set of tasks designed to draw attention to just these transformations, and activities aimed at developing this level of conception can be best thought of in this way.

At the third level attention therefore shifts to the relations between the properties of objects and the relations between objects such as class inclusion and transformations: the square is a type of rectangle, the rhombus is a type of parallelogram, and so on. The relations or translations now themselves become the objects of contemplation, which is the focus of this level of

Tick all the triangles.

8-year-olds:

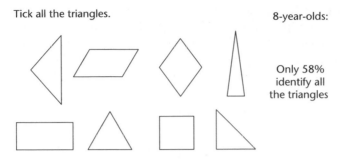

Only 58% identify all the triangles

Figure 5.4 Concept of triangle.

development. An example of this might be the observation that a combination of two rotations is always a single rotation, or the properties of 'being a rhombus' and also 'being a rectangle' imply 'being a square'.

In moving from the second to the third level, a wide experience and discussion of different examples of shapes with relevant and irrelevant properties may help children to appreciate relevant and irrelevant properties of shapes, helping to lay the foundation for reasoned rejection of common stereotypes or prototypes (see Figure 5.5). For instance, it is important to have the experience of drawing around triangular and rectangular shapes or stamping blocks in many orientations in space, so that these shapes might be recognized in a variety of orientations.

The pedagogical point to be noted about moving learners on from level 2 to level 3 is the increasing focus on reasoning and arguing about 'properties' of shapes. Some of these are more demanding than others, the simplest being numbers of sides and angles, and the more sophisticated including symmetries and transformations, sizes of angles, parallelism, and so on. Prototyping will not generally be finally resolved until level 3, when the properties themselves

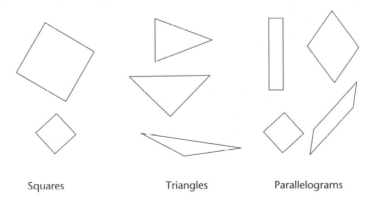

Squares   Triangles   Parallelograms

Figure 5.5 'Rational' sets highlighting non-prototypical aspects.

become the object of discussion. When these are articulated, brought to conscious attention and controlled to a degree independently of the contexts to which they refer, then a shape-name becomes more than a class of objects (for example, a set of all types of squares), and is rather its definition (for example, a rectangle with equal sides). At this level the child is *beginning* to formulate definitions and is able to discuss properties themselves and the relationships between them.

Level 4: deduction – formal definitions and constructing proof

The ultimate abstraction of the property from the set of shapes to which it refers finally occurs with more formal statements such as 'A reflection in the x-axis followed by a positive (anti-clockwise) 90-degree rotation is equivalent to a reflection in the line $y = x$.' At level 4 the child focuses on the properties themselves formally. So a child will now argue that a square has all the properties required of a rectangle, and so *is* a rectangle, without question. Prior to this argument, the child might believe this to be true because an authority says so, but at this level the child's authority comes from their own logic and reasoning. They now understand the necessary and sufficient conditions to define any shape as a rectangle.

At level 4 properties like 'having a line of symmetry' and 'having equal sides' become the object of discussion and analysis in themselves and not merely properties of some particular shape or shapes. While one can discuss whether 'having a line of symmetry' implies 'there must be some equal angles' in the context of polygons; this stage is complete only when the properties come to be objects of manipulation and thought in their own right. This 'objectification' is facilitated (as with number and algebra) through symbolizations and representations that allow them to be acted on as objects. The use of arrows and vectors for translations, matrices and other representations for transformations such as reflections and rotations is consistent with the semiotic objectification of relations and properties of shape and space. Matrices later on in the curriculum are excellent representations for exploring and discovering such relations as that above.

Level 5: rigour – comparing mathematical systems

The final van Hiele level of concept development in geometry involves understanding the formal aspects of deduction, the use of proof and non-Euclidean systems.

Progression from one level to another

Notice that, in the van Hiele model, each level emerges from the previous one; the model helps to understand pedagogy as a matter of offering tasks and representations that help facilitate advances in learning from one level to the next.[8] The *processes* that were implicit in the activity at one level thereby become the very *objects* on which the learner acts at the next. This cycle of activity is typical of many developmental models, including that of Piaget.[9] The process of moving up from one stage to the next involves a reflection on one's processes and objectifications (including, critically, the naming of them).[10] We introduced this idea in Chapter 2 and developed it in the case of number in Chapter 4, where we argued that good pedagogy helps object formation by providing contexts and especially models that represent processes as objects to be worked on.

Research indicates that most 12- to 15-year-old children actually remain at the second van Hiele level of competence with spatial concepts: there is only a generalization of level 3 thinking across a wider range of experience.[11] In our research we found significant numbers of children using prototypes based on perceptual response and evidence that many children had not moved to a property focus (see Table 5.1 and Appendix 1 for further detail).

Table 5.1 Some common Shape and Space errors and misconceptions

Age	Percentage	Error
5-year-olds	33%	Select only prototypical shapes
5-year-olds	12%	Identify a rectangle as a square
7-year-olds	30%	Name a cube as a square
8-year-olds	27%	Confuse half and quarter turns
9-year-olds	21%	Say a parallelogram has a line of symmetry
9-year-olds	69%	Fail to identify a zero coordinate
10-year-olds	13%	Use a half-turn prototype
11-year-olds	63%	Incorrectly model a rotation as a reflection
11-year-olds	10%	Reverse Cartesian coordinates
11-year-olds	23%	Match angle size by distance between arm endpoints
12-year-olds	20%	Count only the visible edges on a 2D drawing of a tetrahedron
12-year-olds	21%	Say parallel lines have same length
13-year-olds	39%	Fail to recognize a diagonal line of symmetry
13-year-olds	33%	Fail to imagine the correct net of a cube
14-year-olds	30%	Fail to use parallel lines to calculate a missing angle in a figure

Alternative routes to higher-level thinking

We began this account by describing the commonplace activity of the early years classroom, where shapes are sorted, compared or grouped by surface features. The concept of a circle, for instance, emerges from experience with a collection of shapes called 'circles', with varying sizes, colours, and so on, but all with the 'same' curved edge. At the next level of activity, then, its properties will be studied closely, and articulated explicitly; this will eventually include the fundamental property of the circle, which defines it as such in Euclidean geometry. Eventually the curriculum may introduce problems involving loci (but this is generally at GCSE level – for example, 'A town is to be placed within one hour's drive of an airport. Show all the places where it could be located').

However, compare this experience of the circle concept with a lesson in a Japanese classroom for 6- to 7-year-olds.[12] The teacher has a hoopla set, lines up the children along a line and asks each child to throw the hoop at the stick. Clearly the child at the end of the line has a hard time throwing the hoop at the stick and complains, 'It isn't fair.' The teacher asks how to make the game fair for everybody, and the children begin to organize themselves in a curve around the stick. Each child wants to get nearer, but the only fair solution is to measure in some way, perhaps using a piece of string, so that each child is *equally distant* from the target. From there the teacher asks the children to construct a circle in their workbooks using whatever they have to hand (for example, string and rulers). The *concept* of the circle thus emerges from a problem-solving activity as a locus of points equidistant from a central, focal point, and is defined by its mode of construction as well as this quintessential property.

In terms of van Hiele these children are arguably at least working at level 2, as they are conscious of the *property* of the circle from the start. This approach has them starting with the essential property of the shape required to solve the problem and ending up with the perception of the shape as such. There has been no obviously 'vertical' progression in mathematical demand from level 1 to level 2 here, as expected by the van Hiele model for children at this age, but rather an immersion in the quite natural emergence of a circle conception as a solution to a problem. This approach seems at first sight vastly superior to a van Hiele-type approach that seems to argue for a vertical, multi-stage route to developing concepts that might more readily be developed through a direct attack on a problem requiring the construction of the targeted conception. In this sense it seems to parallel the attempts we made to avoid the algebraic route when learning of integer arithmetic (see Chapter 6).

Freudenthal spoke of school mathematics as being a process of guided re-invention. Understanding the historical evolution of a concept may be helpful in constructing a learning trajectory, but it will not necessarily provide the best route now, when we can perhaps more clearly see the mathematical landscape than did the original explorers. For a start, we now have new technologies that can make the ascent, possibly by new routes, that the historical explorers did not have: new machines allow us for example to quickly calculate with numbers, to construct figures, sketch graphs, to solve equations and build formulae.

New entry technologies: 'constructing' the properties

The use of a geometry package (for example, LOGO) can provide the key experiences of construction of shapes from rules: a rectangle is *constructed* by a short program of simple instructions involving right-angle turns in much the way that the circle was described as being constructed to solve a problem above. As such one can see that the rectangle can be represented as an object (a program) whose internal structure represents an essential set of defining properties of the shape. In this (micro)world, the instructions relate to the properties of the shape and become the subject of discussion and manipulation per se.

In the LOGO program for the rectangle, then, we see how van Hiele levels 2 and 3 are bridged. The action of the program draws the rectangle, the program itself is the set of defining elements that relates to its essential properties. For instance, in the initial construction of a rectangle, fd 20 rt 90 fd 30 rt 90 fd 20 rt 90 fd 30 rt 90, one may notice that the rectangle does not 'work' unless the forward steps are of the right lengths with opposite 'sides' equal. In Figure 5.6

To Rectangle :length :width

fd :length rt 90 fd :width rt 90 fd :length rt 90 fd :width rt 90

End

> Rectangle 50 50

Figure 5.6 LOGO 'Rectangle' program with length and width the same.

the program 'To Rectangle' uses variables, and the case where the length and width values are the same becomes pertinent.

The use of LOGO-based Roamers or Bee-bots to construct paths and shapes using instructions involving vector motion, length and angle can also be an early route to an appreciation of the fact that *angle* is essentially a measure of turn, helping to avoid the prototypical error made by many children, who appear to believe that the 'size of an angle' is a measure of the 'gap' between the 'arms'. In the MaLT survey, 23 per cent of 11-year-old children used the length between the end-points of the angle arms as the measure of the size of the angle (see Appendix 1, M11.18b). We do not think this could happen if the children situated their understanding of angle in the context of such experiences; these prototypes can be viewed as the result of a lack of an intuitive, situated context with which to 'make sense' of the mathematics.

This 'situated intuition' approach demands analysis and research about pedagogy and learning of mathematics, but may provide value in opening the door to 'higher levels' of mathematics for the children through 'horizontal' modelling (that is, building the mathematics to organize the real-world phenomena intuitively).[13]

Measurement and its conceptual development

Measurement is justifiably seen as important because it provides the main route to the application of mathematics to quantities in all daily life, science and technology practice. As Lord Kelvin said, 'To measure is to know' and 'If you cannot measure it, you cannot improve it.' Perhaps equally important, though less widely recognized, measures and measurement (as with shape and space) also provide a route for learners *into* mathematics. For example, measurement can provide models through which sense can be made of number work, as discussed later in this chapter where length is an essential entry point to arithmetic on the number line.

The child's early understandings of a measure are essentially perceptual ('this looks longer than that', 'this feels heavier than that', and so on). As with the van Hiele levels for geometry, the early stage involves perceptual errors at least until about the age of 6 and 7 years, and later for more 'indirect' measures such as weight.

The early stage of measurement was characterized by Piaget as 'conservation' of the measure, and involves the shaping of the concept in such a way that irrelevant distractors begin to be ignored. Thus in conserving the *number* of a set of discrete objects, the length of the set must be ignored. In our research on number, 14 per cent of 5-year-olds had the 'longer is more' misconception (see Figure 5.7 and Appendix 1, M5.16).

'Who has more toys?'   5-year-olds:

83%

14%

Figure 5.7 The 'longer is more' misconception.

In conserving *length*, however, both the beginning and end of the length must be coordinated. In the next stage, the number of units must be coordinated with the size of the unit when measuring. The classic Piagetian task involves children recognizing that the measure of a quantity must be independent of the unit being used to measure it.[14] For example, the *length* of an object does not change with a change of unit. The Vygotskyan school views this as an awareness to be cultivated rather than a natural stage of development, and a number of researchers have shown that 'measurement training' does actually improve children's performance on conservation-type tasks.[15] In fact Davydov and Galperin (following in Vygotsky's and Leont'ev's footsteps) created the early number curriculum from measurement where number properties emerge as the result of solving important measurement tasks and problems, ensuring that the mathematics of number is seen as rational from the start.[16]

Measurement, the number line, number and length

Consider what the spatial structure of the number line offers number and measurement. First of all, the number line is thought of as a set of points that one can pass through, as in the journey along a path (space/length) or a journey through life (time/days). In this model, a number represents a discrete number of units of length or time (metres, days) which can be structured into *subsets* of length (usually 5s or 10s of metres) or time (for example, 7 days). Adding is represented by putting two lengths or times together end to end, as in the union of two sets. But even the simplest pedagogical models of the number line involve potentially helpful mathematical structure.

Figure 5.8 shows the laced bead string with 5 white and 5 black beads alternating. Here 4 white beads and 5 black beads and 1 more white bead shows 10. This basic structuring provides opportunities for manipulation of units and 5s, like an abacus, and hence for building strategies based on bonds

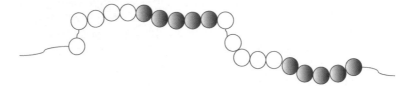

Figure 5.8 The bead string based on bonds to 5 showing $4 + 6 = 10$.

to 5 (so $4 + 6 = 5 + 5$, because you take a white from one side and add a white to the other side and still have 10, and so on). Note the significance of this spatial modelling for the acquisition of number properties and addition strategies; these number properties do not intuitively arise from the putting together of two sets of objects, 4 beads and 6 beads, and then counting. Rather they emerge from the spatial structure of this bead string or number line. We therefore argue that the number bonds are here actually derived from spatial relations, and should properly be justified through such manipulations and strategies. Essentially, we would say that to justify $4 + 6 = 10$ just because it works by counting is a poor argument compared to the intuitive, enactive, spatial one. In fact $4 + 6 = 10$ can be argued to be an intuitive property of measurement, and measures become the context for situating number bonds and number facts intuitively.

But the number line has an additional property, that between any two points there is a *line segment* or stick whose length represents another number; so we have the 'number-stick' model (see Figure 5.9).[17] This, in combination with the 'set of points' model, now provides for a complete model for addition, subtraction, and 'times' and division, and hence of rational number, while it may be introduced at first simply as a model for the whole number. Why is this? It is because of the spatial arrangement of the number line and its measurement properties.

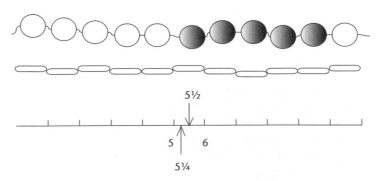

Figure 5.9 From point model to number-stick model to number line: from $5 + 6 = 11$, to half of 11 is $5\frac{1}{2}$.

So we can begin with addition and subtraction as with the string of beads. But the spatial arrangement of the line (that is, its *continuity*) allows us to put 5 and a half and 5 and a quarter between 5 and 6 in the appropriate places: halfway and a quarter of the way along the path or journey. Historically, mathematicians have argued, the placing of new numbers on the number line (or in the number plane) has been a crucial inventive leap forward in mathematics, and we argue that this is reflected in the importance of such models for learners 'reinventing' mathematics.

A feature of the spatial drawings or figures that we use to represent mathematical objects is that they allow actions and gestures and, so, when internalized, mental visualizations that reflect them. Some research indicates that initially gestures appear in communication before the words are recalled; this is reflected in mathematical communication, where gestures and informal language are used before the formal mathematics has been conceptualized by the learner.[18]

In conclusion, the place of spatially organized models is central in developing mathematical communication, and hence mathematical concepts. This is especially true of measurement and number, but it will also be shown in algebra and graphs.

Standard tools: end-points of measurement scales

To measure a quantity we need to conceive of it as segmented, and recognize that segmentation is usefully done in comparison to some standard unit.[19] In Chapter 2 we pointed out how confusion between 'the ticks' and 'the intervals' on a standard scale was a common error identified by us in our analyses of test errors in the measurement of length or indeed of any quantity using a scale in which length is the *proxy* for the quantity being measured, such as temperature, weight/mass, capacity, angles (see Figure 5.10).[20] We understand this to be due to the disconnection of measurement from the underpinning mathematical idea that a series of segments or units is being counted. In the case of length, the units are the intervals or gaps, or sticks between the 'tick marks': the numerals on a ruler indicate the end of the thing being measured and the zero marks the beginning. In terms of 'process–object' linkage, it seems that the ticks mark the end of a process of measuring along the ruler, but that this process has typically been 'lost' to the child using the ruler/measurer, who then takes 4 (ticks) from 18 and gets to 15.

In the first case in Figure 5.11 the length being measured is read as '9', but the error is quite consistent with thinking that 'measurement is counting', as the counting numbers start from 1! In the second case, the error is aligning the beginning end-point of the ruler without checking that it is the zero mark.

$18 - 4 = ?$

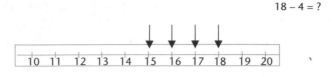

Counting the 'ticks' or numerals: 18, 17, 16, 15

Instead of ...

Counting the 'gaps' or numbers: 17, 16, 15, 14

Figure 5.10 $18 - 4 = 15$: 'counting the numerals' error for scale or counting.

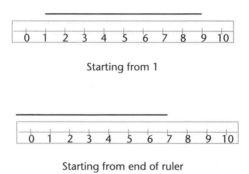

Starting from 1

Starting from end of ruler

Figure 5.11   Misconceptions about the end-points of the ruler or scale.

Looking at the data in Figure 5.12 from a large sample of 6-year-olds, we see that although 91 per cent correctly measure the toothbrush to be 7 paper-clips when the paperclips are aligned to the ends of the toothbrush being measured, only 50 per cent are correct for the comb when the paperclips are not exactly aligned with the beginning and end of the length. The difference between 91 per cent and 50 per cent is accounted for by two errors: 36 per cent of 6-year-olds just count all the paperclips shown and get 7 again, and another 4 per cent count 6, perhaps ending but not beginning in the right place.

The third task of comparing the lengths of the toothbrush and the comb was dramatically more difficult for the 6-year-old children, with only 18 per cent of the sample being correct. Most errors were giving the measure of one of the objects only. At this level children find the two-step complexity of the task overwhelming.

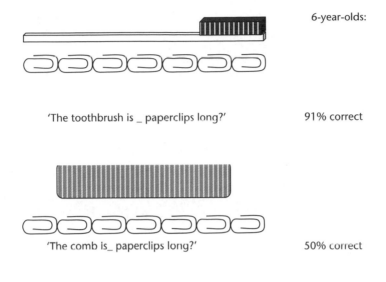

6-year-olds:

'The toothbrush is _ paperclips long?'   91% correct

'The comb is_ paperclips long?'   50% correct

'The toothbrush is _ paperclips longer than the comb?'

18% correct

Figure 5.12   Measuring and comparing lengths.

Scale prototypes and scale intervals: a conflict pedagogy

Previously, in Chapter 2, we described a 'unit scale prototype' where children think that each interval or division on a scale is one unit. This kind of error is very common in all measurement situations. The unit scale prototype also involves thinking a scale increases by a unit of 10, 100 or 0.1, say, but the same problem arises right through to 15-year-olds. When the scale is in units of 2, 4 or 5, say, the difficulty for children increases significantly. Similarly if there are non-prototypical numbers of scale *markings* (see the section on 'competition' below, where there are 6 divisions per unit) the children also have increased difficulty finding the scale.

Our research found that only 32 per cent of 8-year-olds could correctly read the ruler in Figure 5.13, with 17 per cent of them having a unit scale prototype and 27 per cent of them estimating the reading (see Appendix 1, M8.23).

For 9- and 10-year-old children, 50 per cent of 9-year-olds mark the 2.4 kg mark on a scale incorrectly by counting the intervals as 0.1, 0.2, 0.3, 0.4, . . . instead of 0.2, 0.4, 0.6, 0.8. . . . Similar results were found for 10-year-olds, with 35 per cent reading a scale as 2.2 instead of 2.4 kg, and a further

The picture shows a 30-centimetre ruler.
Write down the measurement shown, in
centimetres.

8-year-olds:

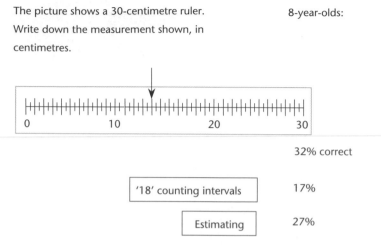

32% correct

'18' counting intervals   17%

Estimating   27%

Figure 5.13   Unit scale prototype (unit of 1).

15 per cent reading it as 2½ kg, either estimating the point as roughly halfway along the scale from 2 to 3, or counting the position as half of the number of 'inner' tick marks, or simply avoiding decimal notation (see Figure 5.14 and Appendix 1, M9.21 and M10.18).

Similar errors arose with older children when readings were taken from measuring cylinders, so this is probably an issue for development right through school. The unit scale prototype arises in many situations and is worthy of discussion: one successful strategy that children use to check the scale is to count backwards and forwards in the scale to check that it 'fits' with both ends of the larger unit. For the problem shown in Figure 5.14 counting forwards to the 3 kg unit (. . ., 2.4, 2.5) would create a cognitive conflict requiring adjustment of the smaller interval unit.

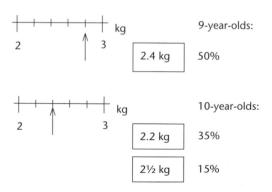

Figure 5.14   Unit scale prototype (unit of 0.1).

In a competition children get points for how quickly

they can type 10 words. Michael took 50 seconds. Put

a cross to show his 50 seconds.

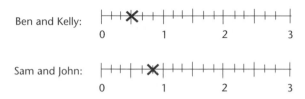

Figure 5.15   Competition: marking 50 seconds on a minute scale.

In our previous research of the 'competition' problem (see Figure 5.15) we found the common error made by 11-year-olds was to mark 50 seconds halfway along a minute scale marked in 6 intervals. This response is associated with the '100 seconds in a minute' conversion error but the transcript of the discussion also shows the problems children have with working out the scale interval.[21] The children had previously answered the question and were recalling what their response had been.

Teacher: What are you going to do there? '50 seconds', where are you going to mark your 50 seconds? (.) So you put your mark in the middle of the 0 to 1 there?
Ben: Yeah.
Teacher: Can you explain why you did that?
Ben: Well, I just thought because it's the middle, (.) and it's the biggest line, it would be 50.
Teacher: So you thought it was the biggest line and it's in the middle. So this big line here, what does that mean on the scale?
Ben: It's one minute, so I went half.
Teacher: One minute, so you went halfway. Is that the way you thought as well Kelly?
Kelly: Yeah.
Teacher: Can you remember what you did Sam?
Sam: I think I put it the same as John, because I realized it was a *minute* so it's *60*, and then I dropped (.) and then I went back ten (.) half of it's 30 so I put it at 50 because (.)
Teacher: OK, so your argument is that a minute is 60 seconds so John says halfway would be 30 seconds, right?
Sam: Yeah.
Teacher: Now tell us again Kelly, what's your reasoning for putting 50 seconds in the middle?

Kelly: Erm, because it was like, the biggest line's in the middle (.) I don't know really, I did it because of (.) the same as Ben.

Teacher: Yeah. It's a very normal thing to think 50 is halfway. When would 50 be halfway? Why would you think 50 was halfway?

Kelly: A hundred.

Teacher: Up to 100. Do you think that's right here?

Kelly: No, I don't because it's 60 seconds in a minute.

Teacher: 60 seconds. So what length of time would that represent, if this is a minute?

Kelly: 30.

           [Later]

Teacher: . . . Now, what I didn't quite follow John is (.) I understand why you didn't put [your cross] there, but what made you put it there, on that particular (.)

John: Well, each line (.) between one line and another line, is 10 seconds and so I went one second, I mean 10 seconds, 20 seconds, 30 seconds, that's halfway. And then 40 seconds and 50 seconds and then I got to there which is 50 seconds and there's another 10 left so 10 from 60 is 50.

Teacher: Did you follow that? Where did he get the 10 seconds from?

Ben: Erm (.)

Teacher: He said, to start with (.) he said, this first bit's 10 seconds. Where did he get the 10 seconds from do you think?

Ben: Erm, (.) I don't know.

Teacher: Can you help Kelly?

Kelly: Erm, (.) that one would be 10 but (.) so it's 10, 20, that's 30, that's half, so that one to that would be 30, 40, 50 and then (.)

Teacher: (.) 60. So it works, 10 seconds for each bit. Can you think John, where did the 10 seconds, (.) how did that occur to you in your head?

John: Because, erm (.) there's 6, (.) gaps, well (.) and there's 60 seconds in a minute, so I divided 6 into 10 and then I got, erm (.) I mean, it's like 10 seconds there, because there's like 60 seconds in a minute and I just divide it by 6 and I got 10.

The other children found it difficult to explain how to get the interval value and after some more discussion the teacher pressed Kelly.

Teacher: Kelly, did you follow that? . . . Can you put it into your own words for me?

Kelly: Erm, well, if that's like 60, erm, seconds, erm, to get 10 you'd need to do like them 10, 20, 30 and it just sort of follows on. You can say it's ten because of all the little things there, and half is 30 and then there's one, two, three, four, five, six . . .

Counting forwards and backwards was the most persuasive strategy for this group in discussion. This suggests a general pedagogic strategy for handling unit intervals in measurement problems: the 'guess the interval, check for conflict, then improve'. Reflection on this trial-and-improve method may offer a 'vertical' mathematization – that is, the leap to division that Kelly, despite apparently hearing John's argument, does not achieve.

Measuring and reading time: scales and non-decimal units

Measuring time causes problems for children right through primary school.[22] The historical timepiece, like the analogue clock, still prevalent in everyday experience and the source of common language, involves rotational scales and a conscious switching for quarter and half turns in relation to either the hour *past* or the hour *approaching*. Later these common fractions of a turn are converted to 15-, 30- and 45-minute intervals and eventually to a minute unit to give more precise measurement. We also need to be able to read clockwise and counter-clockwise, such as '6 minutes past' or '6 minutes to', after gauging which hour is the focus. The added complexity of non-decimal scales of course adds another layer of difficulty for the novice. Traditionally only the hour scale is enumerated on the clock face and both minute scales for quarters, halves and unit minutes must eventually form part of the mental image of the minutes scale. The analogue clock therefore is a complex scale; in fact there are two scales, they are circular and have indicators for hours and minutes (or fractions of an hour), which must be identified and read separately and then coordinated.

So what are the initial problems for children? Consider the reading of a clock face showing the time 2:45 or a quarter to 3 (see Figure 5.16 and

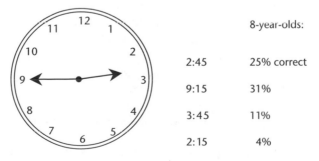

	8-year-olds:
2:45	25% correct
9:15	31%
3:45	11%
2:15	4%

Figure 5.16 Reading the time.

Appendix 1, M8.30). The national sample of 8-year-olds was asked to select the correct time from a list containing 3:45, 2:45; 9:23; 2:40; 3:30; 9:15 and 2:15. The most common errors are 9:15 and 3:45 and have sensible reasoning behind them. Nearly one-third of the 8-year-old children confuse the hour and minute hands on this clock and another 11 per cent of the children confuse the hour involved. The children who read this time as 9:15 have mastered the invisible quarters (or units of 15 minutes) but not the convention for the 'big hand' and the 'little hand'. The children who read this time as 3:45 have similarly mastered the invisible quarters and think that the little hand should point *to* the hours, but have not mastered the subtlety of the fractional position the hour hand holds between the 2 and the 3 here. The third erroneous reading of 2:15 made by 4 per cent of the 8-year-olds may be a sensible connection with earlier concentration on 'quarter to' and 'quarter past' the hour clock readings.

For 9-year-olds there is a dramatic drop in calculating time differences when midday or midnight must be bridged: 73 per cent can correctly work out the number of hours between 2 pm and 5 pm but only 57 per cent can correctly calculate from 9 am to 5 pm. Only 28 per cent of 10-year-olds can correctly calculate the time difference in minutes between 11:15 and 12:45 shown on two analogue clocks: 19 per cent of them have a decimal time prototype or use '100 minutes in an hour' conversion. By the age of 13 we expect mastery of the analogue clock, but 41 per cent of 13-year-olds say the *hour* hand turns through 360° in an hour. This may of course be a concentration issue under test conditions or simply two-step task complexity, but it is a very large percentage.

The non-decimal nature of hours and minutes is also a problem for children. Another time task that proved equally difficult for 8-year-olds was: 'Samantha puts a cake in the oven at this time: 09:20. The cake was taken out of the oven 50 minutes later. At what time did the cake come out of the oven?' In this case 16 per cent of the 8-year-olds made the expected error of 9:70, involving the treatment of the hours and minutes as separate entities, or as a decimal. Answers treating hours and minutes as decimals, or involving the incorrect conversion '100 minutes = 1 hour', occur commonly right up to age 11 years, when 13 per cent of children, of approximately median ability for their age group, provided an answer indicating that 5:15 – 70 minutes = 4:45 (about 40 per cent of the 11-year-olds answered correctly, and most of the rest made other errors). By age 13 and 14 years, high rates of success are recorded on such questions (80 per cent and 89 per cent respectively), but there are still error rates of around 10 to 20 per cent (see Appendix 1).

Area and perimeter: concept and units of measure

Area and perimeter call for practical application, and the best way to develop these concepts is from realistic situations and problem-solving settings. It is often impractical and artificial to assess measuring skills in pen-and-paper formats – even virtual environments for measurement lack the tactile and three-dimensional element that brings measurement activity to life. However, we report here on pen-and-paper responses to very specific tasks that aimed to uncover concept development and attainment of particular calculating skills.

Children have problems with area and perimeter, and it is more than simply a question of remembering which is which! In our research we found that only 20 per cent of 9-year-olds could correctly count the 'distance round the outside of the shape' (see Figure 5.17 and Appendix 1, M9.10). The most significant error, made by 26 per cent of the children, was to count the grid *squares* around the outside of the compound shape rather than the grid square length. (Appendix 2 provides the discussion prompt sheet 'Houses' for peer-group consideration of the typical errors found in classrooms.) The background grid may in fact prompt such an error but it is useful in exposing a shaky perimeter concept and we believe that classroom discussion can help to draw attention to this so that the child's concept becomes stable.

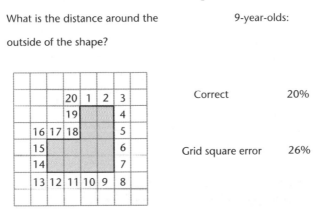

What is the distance around the outside of the shape?

9-year-olds:

Correct   20%

Grid square error   26%

Figure 5.17   'Grid square' error for perimeter.

Later problems do arise where there is simply confusion over the terms 'area' and 'perimeter' when children are asked to match shapes with the 'same perimeter'. We found that 36 per cent of 11-year-olds made such an error by matching by area. Measuring the perimeter of shapes with 'diagonal' sides is also a problem: 13 per cent of 11-year-olds counted the diagonal of a unit square as the same length as the side of the square (see Appendix 1, M11.15).

By the age of 13 years it is expected that children can find the area of rectangles using a formula, but almost one-third of 13-year-olds use the perimeter formula instead of the area formula when finding a missing dimension (see Figure 5.18 and Appendix 1, M13.29). While 60 per cent of 14-year-olds could calculate the 'distance a referee ran around a rugby pitch 90 m long and

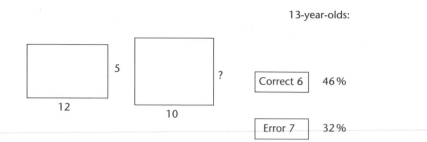

These two rectangles have the same area.

What is the missing dimension?

Figure 5.18 Area–perimeter confusion.

60 m wide', 14 per cent of them calculated the area, and another 12 per cent simply added 90 and 60.

As children start to calculate with units of area measure, conversion between square units becomes *very* difficult. Only 3 per cent of 13-year-olds could find the area in square metres of an A4 sheet measuring 210 mm by 297 mm (using a calculator); 12 per cent used a conversion factor of 1000:1 and 31 per cent made other decimal errors. It seems in this case also, then, that children's errors are indicating that their concept of measurement does not include a recognition of the importance of identifying the 'unit of measure'.

Conclusions

We suggested before that most children seem to be working up to van Hiele level 2 in geometry; that this was indicated by the prevalence of prototypical thinking where each new concept is simply a relationship between particular instances. We pointed to a genetic approach that might allow for more access-ible horizontal mathematizations of 'shape and space'. Something similar might be concluded about children's work in measurement. The maintenance of protypical errors right through primary and early secondary school indi-cates that mathematical thinking about measures remains typically tied to each measure in itself. There is a lack of transcendence in thinking about what is involved in the act of measurement as such; to go beyond this stage might involve some means of gaining access to the way in which measurements are constructed. Perhaps the approach we cited taken by Galperin and Davydov with respect to length will be fruitful: for instance, children might be required to go through a process of building 'measurers' to solve the problem of com-paring lengths of objects that cannot easily be aligned. We have some practical experience of engaging students in the construction of 'measurers' such as 'timers', 'weighing machines', and so on, but have not researched these.[23] We agree anyway that the most useful context is probably length. This is, we suggest, a fruitful field for classroom research and development.

Notes

1   Tufte (1983).
2   Lakoff and Nunez (2000); Nunez *et al.* (1999); Lave (1988); Lave and Wenger (1991).
3   Lakoff and Johnson (2003).
4   As with eye movement and memory, see later in this chapter and Chapter 9: McNeill (1992, 2000, 2005); also Barnes (1976) and Barnes and Todd (1995).
5   Gardner (1983) on multiple intelligences.
6   Butterworth (1999) on left and right hemisphericity of the brain.
7   Van Hiele (1986) and Fuys *et al.* (1988) provide more details on van Hiele.
8   The van Hiele model also provides a template of five phases of learning within each level: information, guided orientation, explicitation, free orientation and integration.
9   Piaget (1970).
10 Treffers (1987, 1993). We argue the term 'vertical mathematization' in *Realistic Mathematics Education* is used in rather this hierarchical sense.
11 Usiskin (1982).
12 Japanese classroom described in Groves and Doig (2002).
13 This apparent contradiction in terms relates to Freudenthal's (1991) suspicion of the terms 'horizontal' and 'vertical': from the mathematical standpoint he insists they are essentially the same, though from the learner's point of view they seem different.
14 Piaget asked children to build a tower with the same height as his tower using different units of building blocks, at some distance from the original tower so that direct comparison was not possible, however a ruler and three sticks were available. The eventual use of the stick was described as a manifestation of *transitive reasoning* by the child – that is, by marking both heights on the stick by direct comparison, the child then deduces that when both towers have the same mark on the stick, the towers have the same height. Then Piaget asked children to compare the height of the two towers by using a small block. When children have developed the logic of *unit iteration* they will use the smaller block to mark out continuous exact parts on the tower, thus achieving exact measurement.
15 Galperin, Davydov and others (see Stetsenko and Arievitch, 2002) proposed that measurement be taught through a series of challenges in which the children have to re-invent the units of measurement for the purpose and

recognize that different units will involve different numbers for the same quantity.

16 Davydov (1982). See also Renshaw (1996) and Stetsenko and Arievitch (2002).

17 Lakoff and Nunez (2000) call the number-stick model a metaphor.

18 McNeill (1992, 2000); Seitz (2000). Roth and Bowen (2001) on graphs and Williams and Wake (2007b) on number lines.

19 Piaget and also Steffe (1991).

20 Indeed the measurement of other quantities such as weight and angle uses length by virtue of a tool that ensures the quantities are proportional. This is helpful to us in this chapter in that many measurement problems are the same as that for length. But it involves something deeper: it can give rise to problems of confusion – the child's use of a protractor can encourage the misconception that the 'size of the gap' between the lines that it measures *is* the angle. This confusion between an object and the entity that reveals its size involves a semiotic problem that Skemp referred to as surface and deep structure.

21 We have used Jeffersonian notation for the transcription: (.) indicates a short pause.

22 Doig *et al.* (2006).

23 In Cherouvim *et al.* (1991) and in Cross *et al.* (1991) we had children devise weighing instruments (primary children) and force-meters and timers (secondary children) but these always involved reference to length as a proxy. Galperin and Davydov worked directly with length itself, which Freudenthal (1991) suggests is the most intuitive.

6   From number to algebra

Introduction

In this chapter we examine the key features, including errors and misconceptions, of the development of a child's number conceptions into algebra conceptions. Algebra is notorious for disengaging children from mathematics and we think that the problem springs from an increasing disconnection between mathematics and the child's common sense. If the pedagogy is inappropriate, children learn to have their intelligence insulted and their sensible questions unanswered – they learn to simply follow meaningless routines. We find that this is often what lies beneath their errors.

We therefore situate the learning and teaching of algebra here in *sense-making*, essentially connection-making between algebra, number, shape and space and contexts that connect algebra with the child's world, and so begin to make 'common sense'. A central idea in algebra is the learner's construction of different conceptions of 'letters' and symbols – moving from the concrete operational stages to symbolic or structural stages of understanding. Again this chapter is grounded in some examples, drawing on our own and others' original research data.

What is algebra?

The study of algebra is often equated with that of manipulating letters and numbers in a symbolic game – for example, finding a general term or the rule, collecting like terms, simplifying expressions, solving equations, finding x, substituting for x. This is the subject of algebra in secondary schools, and perhaps its main thrust. Interestingly, the first great text usually taken as the historical beginning work of algebra, whose title contained the term 'al-jabr', was essentially a text about solving equations.[1] However, *algebraic thinking* truly starts in the early years of primary school, and develops with arithmetic thinking throughout the primary and middle school stages of the curriculum. The foundations of algebra lie in the study of number and arithmetic, and particularly in the mastery of its structure. Some will call this pre-algebra; it is the central subject of this chapter.

An idea and its symbol in algebra are subject to separation. This detachment is a powerful achievement of symbolic algebra, yet it is a trap for the learner. That the ubiquitous x has flexible meaning causes confusion too for the beginner. Is it a number, any number, a set of numbers, or all numbers? Can we work with it when we do not know its value? Once x becomes an entity in itself, detached from known number, the learner has algebraic power of compression of representation, and can manipulate the mental and written objects according to accepted algebraic rules, and can then reason and attach reality once again within the context of the problem in order to check for reasonableness of solution. To think algebraically is distinctly different to thinking arithmetically, yet in the transition to algebraic thinking the use of the arithmetic frame and generalization from arithmetic behaviour is intuitive and sensible.[2]

The concept of generality is a significant stepping stone from arithmetic to algebra. Generalization is seen to be the defining characteristic in the shift from an arithmetic perspective to an algebraic perspective, and generalizing pattern is at the heart of early algebra.[3] Consideration of numerical patterning in arithmetic and shape and space is often seen as an intuitive bridge for the beginning algebra student and current curriculum statements are drawn to such patterning as suitable starting points. A notion of variability is also a significant stepping stone essential for algebraic understanding. These two concepts, generality and variability, embody the structural perspective that is the essence of algebra.

Pre-algebra: patterns and structure of early arithmetic

Let us look at some work on patterns and structure of early arithmetic. The odd and even numbers are notable and interesting precisely because they alternate. The counting numbers '1, 2, 3, 4, 5 . . .' go 'odd, even, odd, even, odd, even, . . .'. What can we say about the number after/before an odd number? What can we say about the number after/before an even number? *Is this always true?* This pattern leads us to notice that odd + 1 = even, even + 1 = odd, and so on. We can then move on to the so-called algebra of numbers modulo 2: odd + odd = even, odd + even and even + odd = odd, and even + even = even; and perhaps later to noticing the patterns in regard to multiplication.

This pattern of odd and even is similarly *generalizable* to patterns involving multiples of 5: odd and even multiples of 5 end in 5 and 0 respectively, so 5 + 5 = 10, 15 + 15 = 30, and so on, generalizes to odd- + odd- = even- multiples of 5, and then to 'odd times 5 always ends in 5', while 'even times 5 always ends in zero'. All these generalizations are testable, and finding just one exception is enough to prove the generalization wrong – an important introduction to algebraic argumentation and proof.

Later, when observing the patterns of digits in the 9-times table, '9, 18, 27, 36, 45, 54, 63, 72, 81, 90', the young algebraist notices (a) the units digit goes down by one each time up to 90, and (b) the tens digit increases by one each time until you get to 90, then skips one. The observation that the digit sum is always 9 (again up to 90) generalizes in an interesting way.[4] These observations about *the rules of arithmetic and how they work* are important to the actual learning of arithmetic itself. One child we interviewed said she knew that $9 \times 4 = 36$ because 'you take one from the 4, that's 3 in the tens column, and then 3 from 9 is 6, so 36'. We thought it remarkable that she had learnt this from her mother at home; but perhaps we should rather wonder why she had not learnt it at school! We think this is because many primary teachers do not believe they are teaching algebra or should be teaching algebra in their curriculum, which they think of as essentially arithmetic.

Pre-algebra is not only preparation for learning algebra later. We think that expertise in arithmetic develops in part through the development of knowledge of the pattern and structure of arithmetic. Thus, an expert in arithmetic 'feels' that $8 \times 7 = 55$ is wrong, because the answer should be even, or because only the 5-times table ends in a 5, or because the answer is only 6 more than 7-squared. All these concerns arise out of awareness of the structure of number – that is, from a pre-algebraic number pattern awareness.

Objects of algebra, metaphors and representations

Notice that in pre-algebra, the structure of arithmetic is described in general, using everyday language. Occasionally, and increasingly with age and learning, language is then abbreviated with formulations such as 'odd' to stand for 'any odd number' or 'you add two to the figure to get the next figure'. The move from describing pattern and structure in ordinary language to describing it in abbreviated language is a subtle but significant shift in algebraic thinking.[5]

The objects of algebra are 'numbers in general'. Similarly, arithmetic processes such as 'times-ing by 9' are also abbreviated and become 'objects' in their own right: they need names and other representations. So, for example, the process of 'multiplying by nine' is discussed in terms of its table representation, or maybe by a function machine ($\times$ 9), or by a graph ($y = 9x$). These objectifications establish the process of multiplication by 9 as a mathematical 'function', which is the object that the table, graph and formula represent.[6]

Tables of numbers, as in times tables, are usually the first representation of the function concept that children meet. It is worth reflecting on such representations as we suggested in Chapter 2 – they never provide a 'complete' representation or view of the mathematics. Like similes and metaphors, representations always have properties that restrict or limit the mathematics they represent in some way. In thinking of the child's 'times table' as a representation of the process of multiplying by 9, and as an 'object' that can now be named and can become an 'object of algebraic reflection', we notice that the table begins at 1, stops at 10, say, and in fact is thus limited to the numbers 1 to 10. What does this suggest? First, that a child is therefore likely to have difficulty with '9 times 0'; perhaps, then, the common errors made with zero. Second, we notice that patterns like the digit sums for the 9-times table may not be so easily extensible to numbers greater than 10. So sums like 9×11 may need to be calculated algorithmically instead of becoming part of the mental landscape.[7]

What about other metaphors and representations for 'times-ing'? The function machine is helpful in allowing operations to become chains, thus the numerical output from one 'machine' is fed into another, and we observe that 'times by 3 and again times by 3' is the same as 'times by 9'. But even this representation, or model, has limitations too. The metaphor of 'function as machine' may make no sense to the child whose experience of machines may have no connection with the mathematician's 'machine' where, say, 'times-ing' is said to be analogous to stretching – unstretching (reversibility) may make no sense for the child in terms of real machines.

Formal symbols: what is *x*?

With the introduction of formal symbols in algebra, children may ask, 'Yes, but what *is x*?' Many teachers probably ignore this plea as an irritation, but we feel this is a good question and worth some discussion and thought. The Greeks used letters as names for numbers to count with instead of the Hindu-Arabic numerals we use today, and it may be natural for children to do the same. Thus it is not uncommon for children to think that $m + 1$ should be n, because n comes after m in the alphabet. We think this error may also be prototypical, having been encouraged by the prevalence of substitution exercises where children may have been given $a = 1$, $b = 2$, $c = 3$, and so on, to substitute into formulae when practising 'substitution'.[8]

It is a pity in some ways that mathematicians do use the letter x, instead of y, say. The predominant use of x in arithmetic as 'times' or 'multiplied by' leads to a lot of unnecessary confusion; thus $5x$ may be read as '5 times' and with good reason, as that is indeed the process that is involved in $5x$. Probably we would be a lot better off using a, b, n, y, z – anything except x. Many years ago, Skemp pointed to several infelicities in mathematical notation (what he refers to as the surface structure) and showed how these symbolizations caused problems at the conceptual level (the deep structure) for learners; unfortunately the cultural inertia in mathematics precludes innovations of this kind from pedagogues, for much the same reason as we are stuck with the QWERTY keyboard on our computers.[9]

School algebra encourages two meanings for the letter x (or any letter when used algebraically). First, it is the name for a specific unknown number or set of unknown numbers.[10] (The term pronumeral is sometimes used to express 'letter as placeholder' for a temporarily unknown number.) Second, it is the name for a generalized number or variable.

x is a number or set of numbers

The first school meaning for x is the number or set of numbers that we have yet to find – for example, the number of socks in the bag, the number I first thought of, the answer to a difficult problem of calculation, a range of possible answers, and so on. We recall the class of first-year children in Japan described by Easley and Easley.[11] Sensei sets the class a puzzle – 'A boy invites two friends to play at his house, and then two more friends come to play, how many are playing altogether?' The class are stuck, they say 'four', but Sensei looks doubtful. Eventually Sensei and the class 'model' the problem. A boy is selected and comes to the front of the class, he invites two friends to play, then two more: aha, five! In a way the answer to the puzzle, that which is not immediately present, may be called x, the unknown, anonymous number that has yet to be found. Arithmetic should often be about such problems; in the beginning we do not know the answer, we have to do some thinking and working, and in the end the answer becomes known – this is x – the name for the thing we want to find, and eventually we have the answer '$x = 5$'.

The 'think of a number' game, where a child or teacher 'thinks of a number' then operates on it in various ways and the children have to find the number, fits well with this. 'I think of a number, I add one, the answer is ten, what was the number?' or 'I think of a number, divide it by 4, the answer is ¾, what is the number?'

An important context for supporting this work is in geometry or space and shape. Historically, many algebra problems were related to practical problems, such as to find a given length or area. So we have a problem like 'The area of a rectangle is to be 400, its perimeter is to be 100, what should the length of its base be?' The base to be found is x, and so the other side is $^{400}/x$, and then half the perimeter is $(x + {}^{400}/x)$, which must equal 50. (Note that x here has two answers: the base could be 10 or 40.)

x is any number

The second meaning for *x* is as the name for 'any number' (or, in the spatial context, any length, say). More accurately, *x* is the name for the typical member of a set of numbers: a 'variable'. So we express arithmetic rules by saying 'add two then multiply by three is the same as multiplying by three and adding six, symbolically written as $3(x + 2) = 3x + 6$. Because this rule is supposed to be true for *all numbers*, then if we attempt to solve this 'equation' we find only that *x* can be any number (children usually solve such an equation to obtain $x = x$, which is of course true for any number).

Important contexts for visualizing such generalizations, or *identities*, such as $3(n + 2) = 3n + 6$ then may be geometric where $3(n + 2)$ is represented by a rectangle 3 by $(n + 2)$, and $3n$ and 6 are represented by rectangles 3 by *n* and 3 by 2 with total area $3n$ and 6. Similarly, identities like $(n + 3)(n + 5) = n^2 + 8n + 15$ can be visualized. Figure 6.1 shows why these identities are obvious.

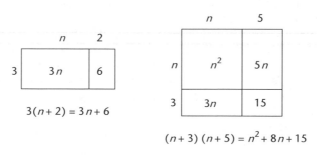

$$3(n + 2) = 3n + 6$$

$$(n + 3)(n + 5) = n^2 + 8n + 15$$

Figure 6.1 Visualization of identities: true for all *n*.

If such uses of algebraic identity are understood as being about what is generally true for number and arithmetic, children should be expected to see the sense in checking any such identity with some values for the variable: putting $n = 10$ into the identities above gives $3 \times 12 = 36$ and $13 \times 15 = 195$. Noticing this arithmetic structure can help a child to perform apparent feats of arithmetic mentally, like the 'vertically and crosswise' rule, originally the Urdhva Tiryak Sutra,[12] which in this simple case is just to add the digits to get the tens digit ($2 + 1$ gives 3 in the tens column) and multiply the 3 and 2 to get the digit column, though if the tens columns are not just one then this involves the 'crosswise' multiplication first, and there may be a need to carry here, as in $13 \times 15 = 1(8,1)5 = 195$, and $14 \times 15 = 1(9,2)0 = 210$.

The context of rectangles for the visualization of number and arithmetic applies only when the lengths are positive, of course. New contexts and visualizations become necessary to make concrete connections with the negative numbers. How can we model negative numbers so that they make sense to children?

Learning and teaching integers/negative numbers or 'minus times minus is plus, the reason why we need not discuss!'

The negative numbers present learners with many problems when they are introduced, and continue to be a problem for children who think mathematics ought to be sensible. Many a teacher has difficulty dealing with questions such as the following: 'When I take away a minus number from a number, such as ı5 take away ‑1, I get ı6, an answer that is bigger than the one I started with. How can you take something away from something and get a bigger answer?' or 'How can you take away something from nothing, as in for instance $0 - (-1) = +1$?' Or, finally, 'Why does minus times minus make a plus?'

Perhaps because the young learner of mathematics fails to get answers to such questions that satisfy their common sense and intuition, they learn that the negative numbers are eccentric and capricious. In such circumstances, mastery requires them to obey the rules without reasons, and as we have seen before humans are very ineffective at performing rules without reasons, hence the common errors with negative numbers mentioned in Chapter 2.

There is an essentially algebraic answer to these questions – that is, that the negative numbers are an extension of the positive numbers, and the rules of operations of arithmetic extend logically and consistently from arithmetic with the 'usual numbers'. Fischbein argued this approach, suggesting that a sound pedagogy must show how the multiplication table pattern from the positive quadrant must logically, algebraically extend to the other quadrants in such a way as to support the rules that 'minus times plus is minus', and 'minus times minus is plus'.[13] So in Figure 6.2 following the +3 times table down from $(+3) \times (+4) = (+12)$, $(+3) \times (+3) = (+9)$, $(+3) \times (+2) = (+6)$, $(+3) \times (+1) = (+1)$, $(+3) \times (0) = 0$, the *decreasing* pattern +12, +9, +6, +3, 0 extends to −3, −6, −9, −12, and so on (formally because of the distributive law), thus providing $(+) \times (-) = (-)$. Extending the argument from right to left, the pattern for the −3 times table $(-3) \times (+3) = (-9)$, $(-3) \times (+2) = (-6)$, $(-3) \times (+1) = (-3)$, $(-3) \times (0) = 0$, one concludes that the *increasing* pattern −9, −6, −3, 0 extends to +3, +6, +9, . . . and therefore $(-) \times (-)$ must be $(+)$.

However, this argument is quite sophisticated, and researchers have argued that if concrete models and representations can establish intuitive support for the rules of integers then these should precede such an approach as that above proposed by Freudenthal (1973). So, many textbooks use the directive nature (up/down) of the integers to model them as vector movements along a number line that extends back to the negative numbers from the positive ones. Figure 6.3 shows the performance for the calculation $(+5) + (-7) = (-2)$: that is, (move 5 up) and then (move 7 down) gives the same as (move 2 down).

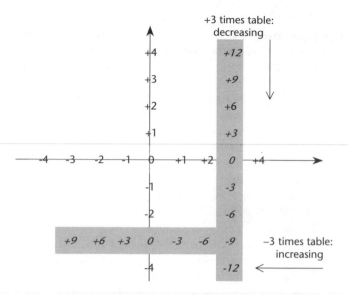

Figure 6.2 The patterning of integers in the times tables, after Fischbein (1987).

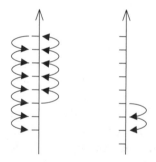

Figure 6.3 $(+5) + (-7) = (-2)$.

Intuitive models for integers as process

This model implements the integer as a *process* (move up/down so far) and the addition process as 'and then'. The model does not readily extend however to 'subtraction' except by a trick that is essentially algebraic/structural (the inverse of addition) and so not concretely intuitive. Therefore some teachers advocate situating the integers in contexts where each number has one of two qualities that cancel out (heaps and holes, protons and electrons, and so on). In one experiment the researchers compared two such contexts in which the integers cancel out. In one context positive and negative are modelled as the number of people going into or out of a building, and in the other context by points for and points against a team.[14] The contexts allowed the children to make connections that helped make working with negative numbers intuitive.

For example, a dice game was presented in which points scored are of two kinds: points 'for' and points 'against'. The children learn that these points cancel down, so if I throw '3 for' and '4 against' this is the same as '1 against' (or eventually in a later version of the game 'minus 1', actually written on the dice as –1). The introduction of the idea of a team score being 'less than 0' was not a problem, due to the implementation of the scoring on a double abacus: clearly your 'score' is the *directed* difference between the two abacus columns (see Figure 6.4).[15]

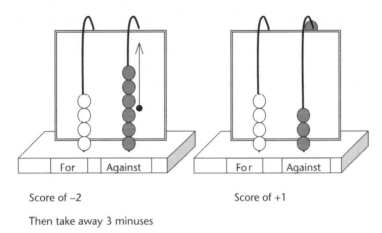

Score of –2   Score of +1

Then take away 3 minuses

Figure 6.4   Double abacus showing (–2) – (–3) = (+1).

There are situations that arise in the game when the abacus is full, and at this point children might 'cancel down' the 'for and against' points on their abacus. In practice, however, it seems to be more intuitive for them to 'compensate' – that is, they recognize that it is 'fair to each team' to take beads from the 'points against' column instead of adding to the 'points for' column, and vice versa. This compensation seems to be quite intuitive, and is the precondition and precursor to subtraction being the same as 'adding the opposite' later.

Indeed the introduction of adding and subtracting 'plus points' and 'minus points' became 'obvious' too: subtracting '4 against' became the same as adding '4 for' your team when you work out the score on your abacus. Finally, the calculation of sums like (–2) – (–3) = +1 can be modelled on the abacus by setting up the double abacus with a score of –2, and taking away 3 of the minuses. In the event that the double abacus does not have 3 minuses to take away, then the compensation strategy is used. The adding of plus points being the same as the taking away of minus points is now formalized in a mathematical voice and the symbolic calculations can be practised.

We believe this is a breakthrough as far as integers go. Later adults might, on this basis, argue that it is 'fair' to remove a bank debt by making a deposit. As far as we know this was the true cultural origin of the integers: Chinese bankers kept records using red and black rods, and the cancellation of debts was executed with these rods just as the cancellation took place on the double abacus. The notion of 'fairness' does seem very powerful in the context of a team game, which was played by the children in the experiments with real dice and in a real competitive spirit.

So what was pedagogically significant in these models for integers? In the development of methods of calculation involving the 'new numbers and arithmetic operations', we had (a) a context in which the positive numbers made sense, but also in which the new numbers could be meaningfully introduced, (b) intuitions from the context of 'fair games' that would support the active construction of productive strategies, and (c) a model (the double abacus) that represented the numbers in ways that allowed modelling of the points scoring, to begin with, and modelling for the symbolic integers operations later (what Realistic Mathematics Education (RME) calls 'model of' and 'model for' where the model of an initial context/situation is generalized over other contexts/situations to eventually become a model for the mathematics).[16]

While we have some evidence that this approach can be successful with children, we are aware of dangers that the use of any context or model brings. This is illustrated by an example of some children who argued that −8 is bigger than −5 because the minus column was filled higher for −8 (represented by eight beads on the minus column) than −5. The fact that an intuitive learning trajectory (to use another RME term) is possible, or even likely, using the method we described does not guarantee it.

It is also doubtless the case that the understanding of integers is not completed until children learn algebra and solve equations systematically. Historically mathematicians achieved a fully formal understanding of the integers only when they began to believe that they truly were numbers, and this happened only through algebra. But it must be remembered that this occurred about the same time that complex numbers became credible, and only quite recently. Perhaps many children will not achieve this for some time after they have learnt to use them in quite intuitive ways with restricted understandings, and perhaps some will never grasp their mathematical reality, much as adults still have difficulty with believing the reality of the 'imaginary' numbers.

Some recent work has started to study the connections that need to be made by the children while they play these games in order to ensure success. 'Connections' is our very loose term for what semiotics refers to as a 'chain of signs'. What typically happens when mathematical connections are built is that each link in the chain needs to be practised until it begins to disappear from consciousness: '*a* squiggle *b*' and '*b* squiggle *c*' becomes elided as '*a* squiggle *c*'. So the chain that links the scoring of a team game involving points for and against to a calculation like (+3) – (–2) = (+5) involves many such elisions that occur only with practice. Once one has been through the process successfully, one often forgets even why 'subtracting the minus' was the same as 'adding the plus'. Some even argue that 'forgetting' is the most important part of the abstraction and hence the learning process!

Indeed this is a tremendously difficult problem for teaching and teachers: we have forgotten everything we need our learners to know except the *end-point* of learning; hence the old saying 'minus times minus is plus' and, for teachers, 'the reason why we need not discuss'. The danger is that all the links in the chain that learners need to be exposed to (and practised before they disappear) are lost to the teacher precisely because they effectively forgot them.

The more elementary the mathematics the more obvious this problem becomes: how did you learn that '7 and 8 makes 15'? This is a tough question to address. It might be that double 7 is 14 and one more makes 15, or maybe that 7 to 10 is 3, and 5 more is 15 . . . But it may have been something quite different: if you claim it was by repeatedly counting sets of 8 and then counting on 7 more to get 15, or by learning 'rote' that 8 + 7 = 15, who can disbelieve you? We will return to this issue in Chapter 9 when we discuss what makes a 'connectionist' teacher.

Algebra proper: from words to symbols

We have discussed the need for sense making by children in the development of algebraic thinking and the use of intuitive models of arithmetic structure. So we now look at the evidence for the type of difficulties children have with school algebra. The difficulties that 12- to 15-year-olds have in beginning algebra were well documented in the 1980s by the Assessment of Performance Unit (APU), the Concepts in Secondary Mathematics and Science (CSMS) study and other projects. These difficulties are confirmed by the recent Mathematics Assessment for Learning and Teaching (MaLT) data (see Appendix 1 for more detail).

The use of a geometric pattern (for example, the number of matchsticks for increasing number of squares in the pattern) as a model for algebraic generalization is tested in MaLT12 and 14. Success in using the pattern to find a value in the table is quite good (35 per cent and 65 per cent respectively, but with about 10 per cent in each case giving just the next term), and suggests that this is a skill that improves between 12 and 14 years. Writing down an expression for the *n*th term in a table also improves dramatically (from 3 per cent to 43 per cent): 12-year-olds' main error is simply to write a number for the requested 'expression'; the 14-year-olds rather produce an incorrect formula (45 per cent provide a formula describing the iteration, or a formula that fits the first term only).

Context-free questions show that only 38 per cent of 12-year-olds and 49 per cent of 13-year-olds can write a correct algebraic expression involving a number and a variable (see Figure 6.5). The main error here made by 30 per cent of both age groups is to 'close' the expression to give $8n$, or even a number like 8 or 9. Even smaller percentages (19 per cent and 36 per cent, respectively) manage a slightly more complex example, where a number has to be added to an expression that simplifies further (for example, add 5 to $3 + n$), with similar percentages making the same sorts of closure errors (see Appendix 1). In the case of the 13-year-olds, a new error emerges: when asked to add 6 to $x + 3$, 11 per cent responded with $6x + 3$. Previous researchers have described these conceptions as being 'letter not used', 'letter as specific unknown', and 'non-acceptance of lack of closure'. These are, in our view, akin to Ashlock's bugs, discussed in Chapter 4: almost anything can happen and children's creativity for invention is boundless when the manipulations of the letters are *disconnected* from an underlying meaning-making context, model or metaphor.

Quite high proportions of 12- and 14-year-olds could use a function machine in reverse to perform the intended calculation – for example, converting Celsius to Fahrenheit (41 per cent of 12-year-olds and 56 per cent of 13-year-olds). However, the facilities can collapse as soon as a complicated

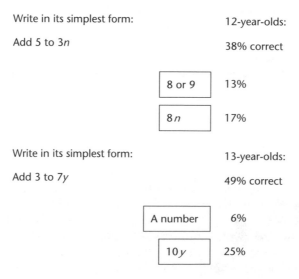

Figure 6.5 Algebraic expressions: 'closing' errors.

literal formula is involved and no function machine model is provided. For example, only 12 per cent of 13-year-olds could correctly find d when $t = 3$ for $d = 5t^2$, with 21 per cent making errors due to the square function. This suggests that the function machine is a helpful metaphor, but perhaps it is not used spontaneously when not provided in the question.

In contextualized problem situations, there is a large gap between the percentage of the 14-year-old population that can write a simple expression for the problem ($20 - n$ pens: 85 per cent), those who can write a formula for a matchstick pattern ($3n + 1$: 43 per cent) and those who can select the correct formula to fit a graph ($V = T - 2$: 20 per cent). This is bad news for the use of algebra in applied subjects at GCSE level (14- to 16-year-olds), and suggests that either (a) science and other applied subjects need to drop their dependence on algebra, (b) they need to teach algebra with their applied subjects, or both.

Where to next? Contexts, models and metaphors as scaffolding

A common conclusion drawn from such research findings for 12- to 14-year-olds is that they need contexts, models and metaphors as scaffolding or support for algebraic competence to develop throughout this period. Less well known, however, is how to *use and withdraw* these models effectively. This would seem to require a better understanding of the function of such scaffolds. The best research to date on this – and the work is by no means complete so these are partially inconclusive remarks – comes from the work of Luis Radford, whose research into children learning to generalize from 'toothpick-type' patterning tasks is very suggestive of a new way of understanding and researching pedagogy. Radford uses semiotic (science of signs) analyses of classroom interactions.[17]

There is one particularly poignant moment when the formulations of the children Radford researched shift from being essentially deictic ('indexical' or 'pointing to') and contextualized by the stick diagram in front of them – as in 'this added to that gives this one' – to a more general formulation involving a semiotic contraction, thus 'the first figure and the number gives the next figure'. Radford notes that one key element in pushing the students from one to the other is the need to address a distant audience, such as the rest of the class. So long as the argumentation is being addressed to the local, small-group audience around the figure, it is not necessary to begin to articulate the pattern more explicitly. The local, contextualized signs remain deictic; this is very supportive for exploratory talk in the small group, as we argued in Chapter 3. Yet the 'press' or demand of a distanced communication that is released from the figural context seems essential in order to generate the need for more symbolic, algebraic language. Radford appeals to a Peircean analysis of the shifting role of signs in different communicative contexts. This work seems to hold significant implications for mathematics learning and pedagogy considered as communication.

Another important aspect in need of more research is in the role of the models involved. The implications, the various affordances and constraints of algebraic expressions and equations represented in function machines, in patterns, in tables, in graphs and in shapes, are not well understood. We know that it is vital that students should be able to visualize expressions like $3x + 1$ in at least these different ways (for example, a numerical, geometrical or symbolic metaphor), but how these visualizations should be developed and used is not fully known.[18]

Notes

1   Muhammad ibn Musa al-Khwarizmi (AD 790–840) was an Arabic mathematician. His *Hisab al-jabr w'al-muqabala* is considered to be the first book written on algebra; it is commonly referred to in its shortened form *Al-jabr*. It was a practical set of rules for solving equations.
2   Ryan and Williams (1998).
3   Sfard (1995).
4   The digit sum is always a multiple of nine.
5   In the historical development of algebra as a symbol system the first stage of *rhetorical* algebra involved ordinary language descriptions for solving particular types of problems and lacked the use of symbols or signs to represent the 'unknown'. It was followed in the sixteenth century by *syncopated* algebra involving the use of abbreviations for unknown quantities. The third stage, *symbolic* algebra, was initiated by Viète, who was the first to use literal symbols in equations, enabling classes of equations to be solved. Viète's symbolic algebra thereby enabled the writing of rules governing numerical relations and the expression of general solutions. However, Viète's generality was restricted as he was unable to accept negative numbers (or imaginary numbers). It is both Viète and Descartes who led algebra away from a dependence on arithmetic and geometry in the seventeenth century. It is here that we have a 'rupture' – a significant change in thinking – constituting the birth of algebra as we know it.
6   Kaput (1998).
7   Greeno (1991, 1998).
8   Much better to use 'real' or 'realistic' formulae like $S = 3T$, where the number of sides $(S) = 3 \times (T)$ number of triangles. See also Hart (1981).
9   Diamond (1997).
10 Kuchemann, in Hart (1981), made these separate categories: letter as specific unknown and letter as generalized number.

11 Easley and Easley (1992).

12 This is described at greater length by Joseph (1991) and Nelson *et al.* (1993). Vedic mathematics has an important feature that underpins these rules: in the Indian tradition the visualization of number is involved.

13 Fischbein (1987) refers to Freudenthal (1973) as the source of the necessity to develop integers formally, and for the 'inductive extrapolation method' we describe here.

14 Linchevski and Williams (1996, 1998, 1999).

15 The game described here was in fact developed from the ideas of Linchevski and Williams by Koukkoufis and Williams (2006).

16 Linchevski and Williams (1999); Treffers (1987).

17 Radford (2002).

18 In one abortive research pilot a research student interviewed some 14- to 16-year-old students about what they visualized, or what they could 'see in their head' when they were presented with various mathematical objects. Expressions like $3(x + 1)$ produced nothing except for the expression itself!

7 Data-handling, graphicacy, probability and statistics

Introduction

This chapter considers and develops the notions of context and culture explored in previous chapters in relation to some errors and misconceptions in data handling, graphicacy, probability and statistics. It also aims to develop some starting points for a teacher's own classroom research.

In the first section, *data handling* is examined. We outline the main findings of MaLT research into tasks assessing the UK curriculum that involve extracting information from tables, charts and graphs, and using the information to solve some more or less complex problems. We reveal patterns and links between these and other areas of the curriculum previously discussed. We also use the data to begin to explore the problem of context in regard to prototype errors in mathematics education. In addition, we illustrate how the MaLT database can be used to build a simple hierarchy of such tasks and interpret them (using Appendix 1).

In the second section we report the errors and misconceptions most commonly identified in relation to *graphicacy* in the secondary school curriculum. New prototypes are described in relation to mathematical graphs, and it is suggested that research on such graphs is still in its infancy compared to number, and shape, space and measures.

In the third section, on *probability*, we examine some tendencies in children's (and adults') probabilistic thinking and discuss the effect of context again. The case of 'representativeness' (including the gambler's fallacy) is discussed in some detail. In the final section, on *statistics*, we provide some starting points for new research into children's probabilistic and statistical thinking.

Handling data: graphs, charts and problem solving

The MaLT tasks involving the extraction of data from tables and charts (including pictograms and other charts) to solve some problems were analysed into a developmental hierarchy in the usual way, and the result could be described and interpreted at four levels.[1] At the lowest level of achievement (say, level 1), children could read a table or chart to find one piece of information but they tended always to read the value of the most popular item, whatever the question. This is interpreted as a proto-typing response based on early 'favourite colour' and 'favourite pet' type data-handling activity.

At the next level (say, level 2), children could use a table or chart to solve two-step problems involving key conversion or interpretation of context (for example, in a simple time context) but a common error was to ignore any key (that is, always to treat the 'unit of representation' in a chart, pictogram or bar chart as one). Again this can be interpreted as prototypical: the children presumably simply assume that each picture or unit square in the chart counts as one vote/person/thing. We think this is the basic prototypical activity in early years classrooms where the children themselves are each represented by one unit in a voting activity, for instance.

In addition, however, at this level of difficulty, errors were found that involved children ignoring terms like 'more' and 'less' in a task. Thus children would correctly answer, 'How many did Katie get?' but incorrectly answer, 'How many more did John get than Fred?' This finding applies equally to arithmetic tasks with young children; for instance, 5-year-old children who could perfectly well count to ten, incorrectly counted all the brushes when they were asked to find 'How many more brushes?' This can be accounted for either by lack of task comprehension (misunderstanding what 'more' and 'less' mean) or cognitive load (that is, the extra task involved above and beyond reading the chart causes 'overload').

At the next level (say, level 3), children could coordinate the task and the data to solve multi-step problems involving harder arithmetic or time conversions. The common error in such multi-step problems was to attend to only one criterion, or make arithmetic or measurement errors. At the final level (say, level 4), children could transform the data in multi-step problems that presented one extra conceptual demand compared to level 3, usually involving comprehension of harder or unusual contexts – for example, data-handling problems using inequalities and time.

As one progresses up the task hierarchy, the increasing difficulty can be explained by a combination of (a) the increasing cognitive load (the tasks involving increasing numbers of steps to a solution), (b) the extra demand and difficulty of the arithmetic or measurement involved, and (c) the introduction of new difficulties due to context (and so often provoking prototyping or overgeneralization).

The cognitive load is generally assumed to increase by one for each additional step or condition required; we pointed out in Chapter 2, for instance, how children may select the middle value in a set of numbers when finding the median, whether the set of values are ordered or not. One can interpret this as a failure to *attend to* the two required conditions in a procedure or concept – that is, (i) order the numbers, and then (ii) pick the middle one. On the other hand, this might also be interpreted as a *misconception*: if the child involved justifies this response by arguing that 'the median is the middle of the set' without awareness of order, then this error may be interpreted as an incomplete conception.

A typical question for 11-year-olds is shown in Figure 7.1, with parts (a), (b) and (c). The first part requires (i) 'train' and 'cost per person' to be coordinated from the task and connected with the table, and (ii) the interpretation of the question to add the three costs (this arithmetic does not place great demands on 11-year-olds). This task sits well within our level 2.

In general, however, a task may require more than just the two actions to be coordinated, such as in the second part: 'George goes on a boat trip. He leaves at 3:15 pm. What time does he come back?' This task is at level 3. Here, the information 'boat trip' and 'time' has to be coordinated from the task and connected with the table, to retrieve the 'time' for the 'boat' of 50 minutes;

Lisa, George and Ali want to go on a trip.   11-year-olds:
There are three trips to choose from.

	Lasts for ...	Cost per person
Train	30 minutes	£4.00
Boat	50 minutes	£6.25
Coach	70 minutes	£8.50

(a) How much does it cost for all three of them to go on the train trip?

SS 57
82% correct

(b) George goes on the boat trip.
He leaves at 3:15 pm.
What time does he come back?

SS 63
64% correct

(c) Ali and Lisa went on the coach trip.
They all came back at 5:15 pm.
What time did the coach leave?

SS 70
40% correct

Figure 7.1   Increasing difficulty for reading and using charts (M11.12).

then this time has to be added to 3:15 (because he 'leaves' at '3:15'). Failure to correctly attend to and appropriately select 'boat trip', 'time', '50 minutes', 'leaves' and '3:15' will lead to an error. In addition, we have the demand of the 'time' measurement context and the arithmetic involved in adding 3:15 and 50 minutes. This latter task causes significant problems for children at level 2, who tend to add 3:15 + 50 to get 3:65 pm.

In general, the advance from one level to the next involves the coordination of one extra demand of any type – for example, one more step, or a significant additional arithmetical difficulty or contextual difficulty. The MaLT scale scores (SSs) for M11.12 (see Appendix 1) shown in Figure 7.1 indicate (scaled) increasing difficulty of the parts of the question.

The third part of the question falls into the hardest level (level 4) because it involves an extra arithmetic demand (subtraction instead of addition): although the question involves the word 'and' (which some children tend to interpret as a command to transform into an 'add' in any task without attending to the meaning of the task) and also involves the same word, 'leave', as in part (b), so this new task has to be transformed into a subtraction. As before, the subtraction 5:15 – 70 minutes is likely to generate a similar error to that in part (b), giving 4:45 pm.

Finally, it is worth mentioning that many of the most difficult data-handling items involve children making use of an *unusual context* when interpreting tables, charts and graphs. In Figure 7.2 we illustrate this with a task requiring children to 'read the small print'. Abby, being a 6-year-old,

Mr and Mrs Jackson are going to an exhibition with their two children, Abby and Ben. They see this price list:

12-year-olds:

SS 73

Ticket type	Cost
Children (under 6)	Free
Children (under 18)	£2.25
Adults	£5.25
Family ticket	£12
(up to 2 children and 2 adults)	

Abby is 6 years old and Ben is 12 years old. Calculate how much the family saves by buying a family ticket instead of separate tickets.

33% correct

'Abby gets in free' error   31%

Figure 7.2 Context: 'reading the small print' (M12.4).

does not go in free to the exhibition because she does not count as 'under 6'. Thirty-one per cent of the 12-year-olds interpreted 'under 6' as including 6.

The competition task discussed in Chapter 2 (see page 14) was of this type also: the task requires the table to be understood in connection with a competition context. Yet, it must be appreciated that this 'context' is not really the context of the question. In a very real sense for the children the *context or situation is the test*; it can be argued that if the children were really in a competition context (or on the family outing) they would not make the mistakes that the school context encourages them to make.

Context difficulties

What, in general, can teachers do, given the academic or school context?[2] The Newman classification has been used by researchers to categorize children's errors with word problems and is appropriate for these types of data-handling problems too, in our view.[3] These are:

(i)   misreading

(ii) miscomprehension (missing the meaning of the task)

(iii) transformation errors (applying the incorrect mathematics – for example, 'add' instead of 'times')

(iv) incorrect processing (incorrect performance of the mathematics – for example, arithmetic process)

(v)   incorrect encoding (misinterpretation of the solution in the problem context).

In the original 1970's research many errors made by immature learners and older low attainers arose in the first three categories – especially the first two. A clear conclusion is that it would be a mistake to address an error in problem solving by directing attention immediately to the 'mathematics' – to the processes of arithmetic. So, in response to a child's plea 'Just tell me, Miss, is it an add or a times?', the teacher may be missing the point if they 'just tell'. Rather, effective pedagogy should try to find the source of the problem from the problem solver's point of view; the first question is 'At which point does the error arise?'

A strategy for isolating the problem might be to encourage the child making an error to go through each of the steps: 'Read the question aloud' (check reading); 'What does it mean/what do these terms mean?' (check comprehension); 'What are we being asked to do? What kind of task/sum is this?' (check transformation); 'How do you do mathematics like this, how do you check this answer by another method?' (check processing); and, finally, 'Does the answer make sense?' (check encoding).[4]

Prototyping from context and curriculum exposure

Prototyping errors in data handling arose chiefly at the lower levels of performance, while the higher-level errors were characterized more by the multi-parts of the task as well. We think this suggests that children are more likely to fall back on a prototype when they have difficulties in reading and comprehending the question – that is, they make an attempt to identify the task with one they have done before, possibly an easier one than is required (for example, ignoring the term 'more', ignoring the key, and so on). What is required is a longer or deeper contemplation of the nature of the task, discriminating the *significant features of the particular problem*.

We suggest context is likely to be the explanation for prototyping in general and again we argue that this is an intelligent act deserving of exposure in discussion. The attempt to connect with a task done before makes excellent sense, and indeed is a key problem-solving heuristic of Polya's classic model.[5]

The particular prototype adopted by children at any given stage might be predictable to some extent by examining the development of the concepts and their curriculum implementation. Block graphs are tackled first with every picture/block representing a unit of one. Similarly, initially diagrams are met with no need of a key, and the number line first used is the prototype where each bead is one object, and then each division on the line counts as one unit, and so on.

In our discussion so far not much attention has been drawn to whether the data are presented in a bar chart, a table or a pictogram. In the research literature we find very little of interest in these differences, and the difference in difficulty between the reading of the table, chart or pictogram itself seems to have little significance once the convention is accepted. This remains true for conventional cases up to the introduction of graphs at Year 10/11 (14- and 15-year-olds), when new problems in interpretation arise.

Graphicacy

In this section we will present some recent research on errors and misconceptions arising when children read mathematical graphs. The study we draw on is based on 14- and 15-year-old children in the UK (assessed as working at levels 5–8 in the National Curriculum).[6] The tasks, using a methodology similar to that in Chapter 2, were interpreted at five 'levels' according to how the tasks demanded (i) use of scales, coordinates and calculations, and (ii) interpretation of global features of the graph. Typical errors and misconceptions associated with these are shown in Table 7.1.

Table 7.1 Graphical performance and errors (14- and 15-year-olds)[7]

Level	Points, scale and calculations	Global features and interpretation	Typical misconceptions/ prototypes/errors
1	Reading off and interpretation of coordinates	Understanding simple travel graphs, change or no change	Reverse coordinates
2	Scales, interpolation and extrapolation	Covariance, distinction between straight-line graphs and curves	Confuse the axes Misinterpreting origin
3	Compare y-ordinates	Mastered concept of 'slope' same speed ≡ same slope ≡ parallelism varying slope	$y = x$ prototype Graph-as-picture Slope–height confusion
4	Harder interpolation Point-wise interpretation	Sketching linear graph Partial global interpretation Constant rate of change	Sketch linear graphs Misreading the scale Origin prototype
5	Calculation of the gradient	Interpret and sketch graphs of linear and non-linear form	Inverse gradient

The study drew on previous research that identified the main errors and misconceptions in graphs as follows.

- *Graphical prototypes*, such as all graphs are 'linear' (linear prototype), they always 'go through zero', they tend to the '$y = x$' prototype, they must be 'continuous', and others. Thus, when asked to sketch a graph, children will tend to draw straight lines, often through the origin, incorrectly for the situation or context. Figure 7.3 gives two examples of this graph prototype – these are answers by teachers when asked to draw a graph showing the height of a growing child/person.
- *Graph as picture misconception*, where the graph is read or drawn as if it is a picture. This could involve misinterpreting specific features of the graph or the figure of the graph as a whole.[8] A classic example is in sketching a speed–time graph for motion of a body rolling up an incline as having increasing speed (positive slope as the incline).
- *Slope–height confusion*, where children misinterpret the slope as the height/y-ordinate in the graph.[9] Thus, in Figure 7.4, a child with this misconception will select graph A (with greater height in the shaded region) as the graph having the greater slope.

As well as these, errors also arise from number (misreading the scale), measurement (presuming a key or scale of one unit), and context aspects of the graphical task (for example, mishandling time as if 1 hour = 100 minutes). The

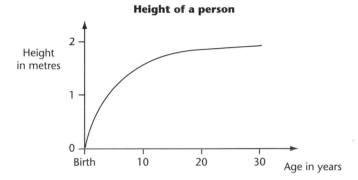

Teacher A:
'Rapid early growth settling off at late teens to a constant height'

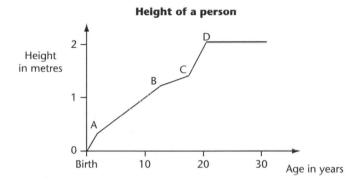

Teacher B:
'Birth to A: quite rapid growth
A to B: growth slows slightly but is steady
B to C: growth slows more 10 yrs–14 yrs
C to D: Puberty – rapid growth (boys)
D: full height – doesn't grow any more'

Figure 7.3 Two teachers' graphs for height of a person from birth starting at zero.[10]

conventions of mathematical school graphs and the nature of early exposure create particular difficulties for children – for example, some children do not recognize points on a graph that are not on grid intersections, some reverse Cartesian coordinates, some have a prototypical view of axes as simply frames or borders capturing a picture and so do not recognize points on the axes, and some draw scales unevenly (for example, 0, 1, 3, 5, . . .) giving special 'non-number' status to zero.

The MaLT graph task in Figure 7.5 (M14.36, SS 81) showed significant problems for 14-year-olds in identifying a linear function from its graph in the

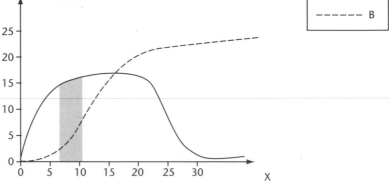

Figure 7.4 Which curve has the greater rate of change in the shaded interval?[11]

Look at this graph: 14-year-olds:

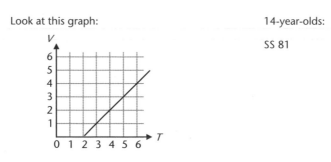

SS 81

Circle the formula that gives the relationship between V and T:

$V = T + 2$ 30%

$V = 2 - T$

$V = 2T + 1$ 11%

$V = T$

$V = T - 2$ 20% correct

Figure 7.5 Intercept error and gradient–intercept confusion (M14.36).

form $y = mx + c$. Only 20 per cent of the children matched graph and formula correctly, 30 per cent read the x-intercept for c, and 11 per cent confused the gradient and the intercept (see Appendix 1).

Research into mathematical graphicacy is still in its infancy and will remain so as long as new graphing technologies and formats keep arising:

there is a major gap in the research literature at present. New graphing technologies and different graph formats do present opportunities for children and their teachers to investigate the hidden dynamic nature of the static graphical image and modelling of real and simulated data.

Probability and chance

We have argued for the importance of data handling on grounds of its significance in everyday and scientific decision making. The case for probability and chance is similar and its importance is increasingly recognized. In almost all practical decision making involving data, some element of doubt is involved, or a judgement has to be made on the balance of likelihoods, or a risk has to be assessed, and so on. Very often, however, psychological research suggests that decision makers are ill-equipped with the necessary understanding of probability and statistics, and serious errors can result.[12]

Not long ago in the UK there was a court case where it was claimed by an 'expert' that the chance of two cot deaths in one family was equal to the chance of one cot death squared, and so the chance was something like one in a billion. However, this entirely spurious judgement made an assumption: that the occurrence of 'innocent' cot deaths happening in the same family are independent, thus effectively assuming that there is no environmental, genetic or other factor clustering such deaths. Similar cases of innumeracy are widely cited. A basic understanding of probability, then, is powerfully argued to be essential to adult life and good citizenship, never mind just for technical work.[13]

And yet probability is still a relatively new field, with controversies over the foundations being only a few hundred years old. Indeed, gambling provided the impetus for early mathematical work in probability, and gamblers are still learning from probability theory today. The best-known misconception in probability is known as the *gambler's fallacy*, where likelihood is based on the pattern of recent events. So in successive throws of a fair coin, if heads have appeared more often than tails, then the belief is that you should bet on a tail – that is, the chance of the next throw of a coin being a tail is now higher because the outcomes should 'even up' to give half and half. A MaLT question with the spinner shown said, 'Ranjit spins a spinner coloured green and white in equal parts. He records the results of four spins as follows: white, green, white, green. What can you say about the fifth spin?' For the fifth spin, 18 per cent of 11-year-olds said, 'White is certain' (see Appendix 1: M11.30, SS 62).

The gambler's fallacy is one example of a tendency called the 'recency effect'; in the gambler's situation above the effect is 'negative recency' because the appearance of many recent heads acts to make the likelihood of a head less – hence a negative effect on the chance (see Figure 7.6). An alternative is the 'positive recency' effect, which implies exactly the opposite: that the chances

1. A fair coin is flipped four times, each time landing with heads up: HHHH. What is the moist liekly outcome if the coin is flipped a fifth time?

Please circle one of the answers.

(a) A head

(b) A tail

(c) A head and a tail are equally likely.

Explain why: _Because a head has been Fliped 4 times and oft the Fith time the liKley ner has increased For a tail._

Figure 7.6 Representativeness tendency: 'negative recency' effect[14].

of a head should be greater after a long run of heads (perhaps justified on the grounds that heads appear to be more likely).

These effects are part of a wider class we call the 'representativeness tendency', so called because it assumes that a sample should properly 'represent' its population in various ways. This 'tendency' is believed to commonly influence everyday decision-making strategies, or heuristics. Indeed, much of the time it makes 'good common sense' and in some situations works quite adequately in making appropriate decisions.

Apart from the recency effects, representativeness tendencies relevant to academic probability have been found to include the following.[15]

- *The random similarity effect*, which leads one to believe that a sample should reflect the population from which it is drawn, and the random way it was drawn from the population. Thus, when throwing a coin a number of times, one might believe that HTHTH is more likely than HHHHT because (3:2) is more similar to the 50:50 proportion expected in this experiment, and HTTHT might seem more likely than HHTTT because the heads and tails are more 'randomized', in the sense of appearing mixed up.
- *The base rate effect*, where relevant evidence about the base rate of the population sampled is overridden by irrelevant information that interferes with 'sound' probability judgements. For instance, there is evidence that even university students' judgement of a probability (for example, that a randomly drawn person is more likely to be a librarian rather than a secretary – much more common in the population) is disturbed by irrelevant information about the person's appearance, whether they wear glasses, and so on.
- *The sample size effect*, whereby the likelihood of a sampling proportion

is held not to approach that of the population as the sample size gets larger. The classic example found to upset medical students is of the proportion of male to female babies in a small clinic compared to that of a large hospital: students often argue the proportions are equally likely to be far from the expected value.

The research into primary and early secondary school age children's thinking reveals that these effects are alive and kicking among children in school. The MaLT project shows that 29 per cent of 13-year-olds responded with just such a misconception (see Appendix 1. M13.26, SS 67). Among a recent survey of schoolchildren in north-west England (Year 6 and 7; 10-, 11- and 12-year-olds) the recency effect and random similarity were found to be relatively easy to overcome (with at least half of 10- and 11-year-olds overcoming most of these effects). However, between 50 and 90 per cent of the sample had difficulty overcoming most of the base rate and the sample size effects.[16]

Intriguingly, when investigating these effects in games designed to provoke the use of the recency effects, the research found that children's behaviour proved generally inconsistent – that is, their use of a strategy was inconsistent within the games, and inconsistent between the game and their paper test result. Quite a few children switch strategies, use strategies to make decisions but do justify them as expected, and some use strategies that they did not give evidence of in the written test (and vice versa). The idea that children come to 'hold' the representativeness strategy in some consistent sense across situations and times then seems doubtful. The notion that decision-making behaviour is strongly influenced by context seems useful here: the contextual influences may even be so variable and dynamic that the children's decision making could appear 'chaotic'.

Nevertheless this tendency to respond to tasks in this way is statistically shown to be common, as indeed are other 'strategies' or 'tendencies': children are known to say that the chance of a six coming up on a die is rarer than other numbers (because you have to wait for a long time for it to come up when you want it), or it comes up more often for other people (for example, 'My mum always wins: she can throw a six more than me'). Here the *'availability' heuristic* is thought to be at work – that is, one estimates chances based on easily accessible memories for events and their frequencies.[17]

Another heuristic that is thought to be influenced by the teaching of probability (especially of sample spaces) is called the *equiprobability intuition*, when events are believed to be, subject to contrary evidence, equally probable.[18] Thus, unless there is strong evidence to the contrary, children are likely to believe that the scores (sum total) obtained from a pair of dice (2, 3, 4, 5, 6, 7, 8, 9, 10, 11, 12) are all equally likely, or that a spinner with unequal sides, or with sides 'unequally' labelled, will give equal probabilities.

In many situations these heuristics seem reasonable: in fact evolutionary psychologists have argued that they have (or at least had when human genes were being selected for intellectual qualities like these) conferred advantages for selection on those that adopted them.[19] A major question for pedagogical research, then, is to discover contexts in which intuitively reasonable heuristics shift and provide possibilities of conflict through inconsistency.

Statistical thinking

In this section we briefly introduce some literature on statistics – more to provoke some as yet unanswered questions than to try to provide comprehensiveness.

Most teachers would claim that the 'average' is the simplest and most accessible statistical concept to teach. Yet we note that the concept of average is often very badly and instrumentally taught as a 'routine' to be learnt, almost by rote: 'Add them up and divide by the number of them.' Indeed, statistics as a topic is rather often taught as being not really about anything, which is a travesty!

This may help to explain the low performance and errors made by children. Inspecting these in Appendix 1, we find that only 24 per cent of 11-year-olds could find the average of a set of decimal times with a calculator (M11.11a, SS 76); 39 per cent of 12-year-olds could average a set of seven rolls of a die: 3, 3, 4, 2, 5, 6, 5 (M12.27a, SS 72); 58 per cent of 13-year-olds and 80 per cent of 14-year-olds could work out the total from the average and the number (M13.9, SS 68; M14.3, SS 63) but only 14 per cent of the 14-year-olds could give numbers that satisfy a given mean and range (M14.26, SS 83).

The 'answer' to learners' problems here must surely be to find a situated intuition that supports the emergence of 'averaging' as intuitive mathematics. In the literature one finds two principal contexts in which statistics can be introduced: scientific experimentation and social science. It makes sense to look to these, then, to find a context from which 'averaging' might emerge in a human, problem-solving activity.[20]

Interestingly, however, some authors criticize this approach as being too focused instrumentally on the mean as an approach to the 'average'. It is argued that a historical analysis of the conception of average leads to a number of observations, and so hypotheses about how humane teaching might be developed. For instance, historically, one of the earliest recorded uses of averaging is in a Fermi problem: 'There are so many men on the average ship, and so many ships, so therefore so how many men involved in the invasion?'[21] Historically also there is some reason to believe that the 'mid-range' is likely to be an 'average' likely to emerge from problem solving.

In 'scientific' contexts in classrooms, however, extremes of data often relate to malfunctioning instruments or otherwise anomalous events: children naturally want to discard data extremes and the mid-range would be quite unnatural – for instance, when asked to find the height to which a ball rebounds when dropped from 1 metre. This context is more likely to lead to a truncated mean average, though a median-type average (for example, the mid-range of the upper and lower quartile) might also seem sensible. The point is that this needs classroom research: what contexts and situations can be transformed into classroom activities that can support the *emergence* of 'averaging' in problem-solving activity?

We close with some results that we have yet to explain, and invite teachers and researchers to engage with these results. Figure 7.7 shows a MaLT question on correlation (Appendix 1: M14.32a, SS 72; M14.32b, SS 75). For part (a) 49 per cent of the 14-year-old children correctly identified a positive correlation. For part (b) 37 per cent correctly identified a negative correlation, but 13 per cent selected 'no correlation'. We suggest there may be a dichotomous

The scatter diagrams show the scores given by different reviewers of three new films.   14-year-olds:

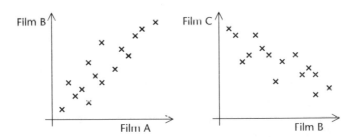

Look at the scatter diagrams. Tick the statement that most closely describes the relationship between the film reviews.

	Film A and Film B				
(a)	Perfect negative correlation	Negative correlation	No correlation	Positive correlation	Perfect positive correlation

	Film A and Film C				
(b)	Perfect negative correlation	Negative correlation	No correlation	Positive correlation	Perfect positive correlation

Figure 7.7 Understanding of correlation.

intuition here ('data are correlated or not') or two-step complexity as the root of the error, but we have not interviewed any children about this. The correct answer can be achieved simply by not noticing that the second graph is for Film B and Film C rather than Film A and Film C, but we think the error is what is interesting here.

Our general methodology in making interpretations of errors has always been to interview children about their responses in some informal way in groups, or in whole classes if there is a sufficiently relaxed dialogic atmosphere.[22] We suggest these might open up some new lines of research for teachers into children's understandings of statistics.

Conclusion

In this chapter we suggested that children's difficulties with data-handling tasks in school can be explained by a combination of (a) the increasing cognitive load (increasing numbers of steps to a solution), (b) the extra demand and difficulty of the arithmetic or measurement involved, and (c) the introduction of new difficulties due to context. These contexts often provoked prototyping or overgeneralization. We suggested that strategies for reading and comprehension of written tasks, together with problem-solving strategies, may serve the children well in such academic contexts.

We argued the importance of data handling and statistics in connection to real-life decision making. However, much data handling and statistics in schools seems to be an empty exercise for many children when the 'decisions' to be drawn from the provided data seem trivial. More important (and sensible) steps surely preceded the data collection. A more realistic and logical sequence would be: 'What (big) question are we seeking to answer? What data should we collect? How could we best organize or display it? How will we best analyse the data to make a sensible decision?' Such wider considerations of motivation, collection, organization and analysis may provide a more satisfying and intellectually engaging context for children as they develop statistical literacy. A cultural historical analysis was also suggested as a source of hypotheses about how to construct such a guided reinvention of concepts. Graphic display of information also calls for some creativity, and the work of Tufte in particular provides us with a range of historical and novel presentations of data relating to social and political contexts.[23]

We argued the case for probability and chance in the curriculum in terms of the social context of decision making, and we outlined heuristics and intuitions that children and adults have been found to commonly use – the inconsistencies of some of these in particular offer opportunities for fruitful 'conflict' dialogic inquiry as outlined in Chapter 3. There is much here for the teacher-researcher to pursue.

We also reported on the performance and some errors and misconceptions of 14- and 15-year-olds related to mathematical graphicacy; many of these errors also arose from prototyping. Interestingly some secondary mathematics teachers were also operating with such prototyping and we see this as another opportunity for developing pedagogical content knowledge. Our next chapter explores pre-service primary teacher subject knowledge, and presents some novel feedback that allows teachers to explore their own understanding and errors.

Notes

1   See Davis *et al.* (2006), who analysed the data handling MaLT subscale items separately.
2   Some, such as Roth and Bowen (2001), argue that the academic context *is* the problem here.
3   Clements and Ellerton (1996); DeCorte *et al.* (1996); Lean *et al.* (1990).
4   Clement (1985).
5   Polya (1945). See also problem-solving heuristics developed by Burton (1984) and the Shell Centre UK: simplify the problem, make a table, look back at the question, and so on.
6   Hadjidemetriou and Williams (2002a).
7   Hadjidemetriou and Williams (2002a). The 'levels' in this table relate to task-demand, not the National Curriculum.
8   These are called 'feature correspondence error' and 'global correspondence error' respectively (Clement, 1985).
9   Janvier (1981); Clement (1985).
10 Hadjidemetriou and Williams (2002a, 2002b).
11 Hadjidemetriou and Williams (2002a, 2002b).
12 We draw on Kahneman *et al.* (1982), whose research has dealt with the representativeness and other heuristics in decision making by professionals and others.
13 Paulos (2001) among others.
14 From Afantiti-Lamprianou's (2006) unpublished thesis on the representativeness heuristic.
15 Afantiti-Lamprianou and Williams (2003); Afantiti-Lamprianou *et al.* (2005).
16 Afantiti-Lamprianou's (2006) unpublished PhD thesis.
17 Kahneman *et al.* (1982): the effect was first studied in relation to the task 'Is it more common to have a word with "the third letter *r*" or "starting with the letter *r*?" Many adults will intuitively estimate that there is a better chance of the latter, presumably because it is easier to recall words beginning with '*r*'. Amir and Williams (1994, 1998) used this term to describe the effect with the die cited here.

18 Lecoutre (1992).
19 There is an interesting, if not entirely convincing, post hoc argument along these lines from Pinker (1998).
20 In an effort to do so one might look to social processes of sharing equally, of equity in social relations in terms of what a fair share of a national cake might be (Nelson *et al.*, 1993).
21 Homer's account in Thucydides' History of the Peloponnesian war in Bakker and Gravemeijer (2006).
22 Hadjidemetriou and Williams (2003); Ryan and Williams (2000, 2002a); Williams and Ryan (2002b).
23 For example, Tufte (1983); his web page is a mine of interesting historical and contemporary material.

8   Pre-service teachers' mathematics subject matter knowledge

Introduction

In preceding chapters we outlined children's errors and misconceptions across the mathematics curriculum in order to inform teacher pedagogical content knowledge – in particular, children's thinking is expected to inform dialogical teaching strategies that can enable the children to reorganize their conceptions.[1] In this chapter we go further by considering teacher's own mathematics knowledge, what errors they make themselves and what misconceptions might be inferred from their mathematical errors. It would be surprising indeed if all teachers and student teachers were misconception-free after their own schooling experience!

We have found that pre-service *primary* teachers often make the same errors that children make – this is not surprising as generalist teachers need to have a broad knowledge base and do not claim to be expert in every curriculum area. Primary and pre-service primary teachers sometimes suffer, too, from a lack of confidence in mathematics and not uncommonly report a history of 'trouble with maths'.

Surprisingly, *secondary* specialist mathematics teachers can also exhibit the same misconceptions as their pupils. For the secondary mathematics teacher the challenge is to confront their own knowledge weaknesses as it is not uncommon for the specialist to find that their own constructions are faulty or overgeneralized. Students in initial teacher training who want to become mathematics teacher specialists usually arrive with a successful record of passing school tests; unfortunately their understanding is sometimes mainly instrumental, and consequently the anxiety for these pre-service mathematics teachers is that they may be found wanting when a child asks them, 'Why?' – a 'tricky' question in the classroom[2] (Why is a square also a rectangle? Why does a 'minus times a minus equal a plus'? Why do you multiply the numerators and denominators?). The teacher's propositional and conceptual knowledge, as opposed to their purely procedural or instrumental knowledge is at stake. Good explanations demand that connections across mathematics, and between mathematics and models and supporting contexts, need to be strong to answer such questions. Indeed, research studies have reported that the most effective teachers of mathematics are 'connectionist' – that is, they make rich (and correct) connections across the subject domain, and can use a variety of representations and models in discussions with children.[3] We suggest that connectionist teachers can be forged through examination of their own knowledge base: awareness and understanding of one's own thought processes (meta-cognitive knowledge) is vital for a teacher, and we argue this is essential to support more constructive, 'connected' and dialogical teaching.

Initial teacher education courses usually screen applicants for their mathematics subject knowledge at selection and then seek to strengthen that knowledge during training, alongside pedagogical content knowledge development, as it is thought that secure mathematics knowledge is related to successful classroom teaching.[4] Another concern is that it is possible that some errors and misconceptions could actually be transferred to children by their teachers unless they are exposed and addressed productively.

In this chapter we discuss errors and misconceptions of pre-service teachers in several mathematical topics. We suggest that the errors have been constructed for good reasons and that the teacher-learner can gain enormously from examining where they came from. We then show how a personalized diagnostic map of achievement and error profile can be used by pre-service teachers to support the development of their own mathematics subject knowledge. Finally, we illustrate how teachers' pedagogical knowledge can be engaged in research studies, by comparing the teachers' perceptions of the difficulties and likely errors of their pupils with the actual research data on pupil performance.

Subject matter and pedagogical content knowledge

Subject matter knowledge is more than knowledge of facts and algorithms – it requires knowledge of facts, algorithms and their organizing concepts (the substantive structure) and knowledge of the legitimacy principles for the rules (the syntactic structure) of the subject domain.[5] We may know *how to* add fractions but knowledge of *why* the routines are legitimate is what finally gives power to the teaching act and separates education from mere training.[6] The various ways of justifying mathematics actually make up an essential part of designing instruction so that it is persuasive: an essential of effective pedagogy. Sharing the question 'Why is it so?' with children can stimulate their subject matter knowledge growth, while the question 'How can I best introduce and justify this mathematics?' can drive the development of teachers' pedagogical (content) knowledge.

The transformation of subject matter knowledge into pedagogical content knowledge is a significant focus in teacher education and we suggest that teachers and pre-service teachers who investigate their own mathematical errors, misconceptions and strategies, in order to reorganize their own subject matter knowledge, create an opportunity to develop a rich pedagogical content knowledge at the same time. We do not advocate 'corrective' strategies to address weak subject matter knowledge but rather something more scientific – an investigation of one's own knowledge so that the teaching act is informed by reflection.

When teachers plan, we all occasionally experience that insightful moment of connectedness when the subject matter ideas all 'fit', perhaps for the first time. In teaching we make our own understanding explicit in order to make the subject matter comprehensible to others. In finding the 'fit', we most likely investigate our own understanding in terms of *representations* of underlying concepts: selecting examples, contexts and models that best introduce the idea at hand but that will also be worthwhile in making other mathematical ideas 'fit' as well.[7] We discuss below strategies that pre-service teachers use and representations that they may hold for important mathematical concepts uncovered by our research on their errors.

The research base: primary pre-service teachers

The pre-service teacher errors reported here come from a research study of a large cohort in an Australian university.[8] The students in this cohort were enrolled in the first year of a range of primary teacher undergraduate degree courses and postgraduate certificate courses – they were representative of the usual selected intake for teacher training courses in Australia. A smaller cohort in England in the second year of their undergraduate course was found to have similar patterns of response to the test questions.[9]

The multiple-choice questions were written to test a 'primary teacher curriculum' that reflected functional numeracy: number, measurement, space and shape, chance and data, algebra, and reasoning and proof.[10]

Primary teachers' errors in number: decimal place value

A fundamental concept in number is place value, and we expect teachers to have a very secure understanding of this concept. The extension of 'number' from the whole numbers to decimal fractions is a significant step in mathematical development – we see this at the historical level and also mirrored at the personal level by the learner.[11] For decimal fractions the place value headings for whole numbers (hundreds, tens, units) are now extended to include fractional parts of one unit (tenths, hundredths, thousandths, and so on). The *decimal point* becomes an important marker for the anchoring of the place values: to the left are the whole units, to the right are the fractional parts. How is the decimal point actually conceived by learners?

It was found that 24 per cent of the research sample could not correctly write $912 + {}^4/100$ in decimal form (see Figure 8.1).[12] The most common error response, made by 12 per cent of the teachers, was 912.004 but another error made by 6 per cent of them was 912.25. These are interesting responses. What misconceptions lie beneath these errors?

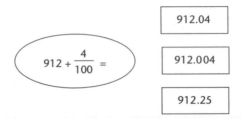

Figure 8.1   Fraction to decimal notation.

The 912.004 response may indicate that some of the future teachers have created a misconceived place value heading of *unit-ths* coming before tenths and hundredths, reflecting the whole number headings about the decimal point. If so, then a conception of 'unit-ths' could fruitfully be investigated in teacher education discussions. Alternatively this error may be a rote procedural response of 'the number of zeros in the denominator is the number of zeros required in the decimal notation'. How was this shortcut constructed? Has it been generalized from multiplication by tens?

The other interesting error is 912.25. Where did it come from? It is possible that four hundredths was (correctly) converted to the unit fraction one-twenty-fifth and the denominator 25 (erroneously) became the decimal part 0.25. Perhaps the *unit fraction* was used as a mediating fraction for the construction of decimal fractions here. The 'unit fraction denominator as decimal part' strategy works for ten hundredths where it is correctly converted to the unit fraction one-tenth and then the decimal part is correctly written as 0.1(0). So why does this strategy not work for four hundredths? Does it work for any other number of hundredths? This could productively be investigated in teacher discussion focusing on argument and justification. Unit fractions were historically significant and they are usually the first experience learners have with quantities smaller than one.[13] A misconception of 'decimal as unit fraction denominator' is also suggested by those 9 per cent of the sample who said that 0.3 was one-third and by those 8 per cent who said that 0.125 was ${}^1/125$.

Figure 8.2 Dividing decimal numbers by 100.

Other conceptions of decimal numbers and the role of the decimal point are suggested by the responses to operations on decimal numbers. It was found that 31 per cent of the sample could not give the correct answer to '300.62 ÷ 100' (see Figure 8.2).

The most common error made by 22 per cent of the sample was 3.62, where the 'whole' and 'decimal' parts may have been treated as separate entities rather than as parts of the one number. One *separation strategy* may be to detach the whole number and decimal number parts and work with the whole number part only (300 ÷ 100) and then reattach the parts (3 and the 0.62). Another separation strategy may be to detach the parts and treat them both as whole numbers: 300 and 62. The processing is then 300 ÷ 100 and 62 ÷ 100. These are sophisticated strategies of decomposition but they are prone to 'bugs' in terms of the conceptions of the nature of the numbers separated. Alternatively these students may believe it is procedurally legitimate to 'cross off' or 'cancel' the same number of zeros in such a dividend and divisor. Discussion relating to when such cancelling is legitimate could be fruitful. Similarly, discussion of how to in fact correctly use a separation strategy would be useful for pre-service teachers examining their own knowledge.

It was found that 24 per cent of the sample could not give the correct answer to '2304.3 × 10'. The most common error made by 11 per cent was 23040.3, where a separation strategy may have been used or a rote procedure of 'add a zero' to one or both parts invoked.

The separation strategy, as can be seen above, is error-prone but it is diagnostically significant. Incorrect use of a separation strategy in these instances indicates that the student has not extended the place value conception to fractional numbers and does not make effective use of the fundamental relationship between neighbouring digit places. The conception of numbers like 2304.3 or 300.62 as *one* number where multiplication or division by 10s, 100s and 1000s has the effect of 'moving' the position of all digits up or down the *places* is fundamental to understanding base 10 notation (or similarly any other base).

When multiplying two decimal numbers the difficulties relating to place value become even more evident. That 64 per cent of the research sample could not give the correct answer to '0.3 × 0.24' indicates widespread problems (see Figure 8.3). The most common error of 0.72 was given by 41 per cent. This

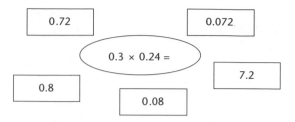

Figure 8.3 Multiplying decimal numbers.

response may involve a procedural bug in attach-and-reattach decimal points or it may involve a consistent use of the 'decimal as unit fraction denominator' misconception where 0.3 is $^1/_3$ and 0.24 is $^1/_{24}$ with the answer $^1/_{72}$ written as 0.72 (it may even be 'backed' by a 'multiplication makes bigger' conception).

Another 15 per cent answered $0.3 \times 0.24 = 7.2$, suggesting a procedural bug with placement of the decimal point perhaps after treating the decimal parts as whole numbers or seeing 0.3×0.24 as equivalent to 3×2.4 (or 30×24), where the digits or the decimal points are simply moved but the answer is not altered to compensate for such moves. Another 6 per cent appear to have treated 0.3 as one-third and then taken one-third of 0.24 to give either 0.08 or 0.8 as their response.

Misconceptions about the decimal point and place value are at the root of the well-known 'decimal point ignored' (DPI) and 'longest is smallest' (LiS) errors that children make when ordering decimals.[14] Children making these errors would argue that 0.3 is smaller than 0.15 because 3 is smaller than 15 (DPI) while other children would argue that 0.625 is smaller than 0.5 because 0.625 is a 'longer' decimal (LiS). The separation strategies have not taken account of the fractional nature of the place value of these numbers. The separation strategies that the pre-service teachers used above are similarly misconceived.

What are the *images* that these pre-service teachers have of decimal numbers? From the errors detailed above it appears that some pre-service teachers use the decimal point as a marker of reflection of the whole number place value headings. Interestingly, 8 per cent of the pre-service teacher sample physically located 0.4 to the left of zero on a number line, which suggests a reflection conception, this time about zero.

What do these errors tell us about how some pre-service teachers have constructed their understanding of decimal numbers? What representations do pre-service teachers have for decimals? Are they simply operating procedurally and without conceptual understanding, or have whole number concepts been overgeneralized for decimal numbers? How is the decimal point conceived? We do not yet know enough about this, but it appears that some pre-service teachers overgeneralize and use prototypes in constructing their mathematical understanding of decimal place value, much as their pupils do.

Teachers' errors in number: fractions

One of the most difficult topics for children in primary school and early secondary school is fractions.[15] It is a significant growth point for mathematical development and several important conceptions are involved. The part–whole conception for fraction rests on recognition that the parts must be equal, yet 16 per cent of the pre-service teacher sample selected a square shape divided into unequal parts as representing quarters (see Figure 8.4).

Figure 8.4   Which pictures show ¼ shaded?

'Fraction as number' is also an important conception, but 25 per cent of the sample could not correctly identify $^4/_7$ on a number line (see Figure 8.5). The most common error was made by 15 per cent, who named it as $^4/_6$ by apparently counting inner scale-tick marks on the number line rather than checking for equal parts of the line segment.

0   ?   1

Figure 8.5   Locating fractions on a number line.

Contexts of course are imperative for mathematization.[16] A sharing context is thought to support the dual conception of 'fraction as process' and 'fraction as number'.[17] 'There are 3 chocolate bars to share equally between 4 people. How much will each person receive?' This problem requires sharing/dividing a smaller by a larger number (see Figure 8.6).

There are 3 chocolate bars to share equally between 4 people.
How much will each person receive?

Figure 8.6   Sharing.

For this question 26 per cent of the sample could not give the correct answer. The most common error of $^1/_4$ was given by 15 per cent of the sample. A 'realistic' solution drawing on the part–whole conception is to divide each of the 3 unit bars into 4 equal parts, creating 12 smaller quarter bars (or 'wholes') to distribute between 4 people (who each get 3 of the quarter bars). That is, the problem is converted to a 'larger by smaller' division/share. Here quarters are constructed first and this unit fraction is the answer given by 15 per cent of the sample.

Operating with fractions uncovers interesting errors and provides insight into fraction conceptions. For a subtraction like $^4/_7 - ^1/_3$ an incorrect answer was given by 21 per cent of the sample (see Figure 8.7). The most common errors were $^3/_4$, given by 9 per cent, and $^3/_{21}$, given by 8 per cent. In the first case we assume a 'separation strategy' was used where the numerators and denominators were subtracted independently; in the second case the numerators were subtracted and the denominators multiplied.

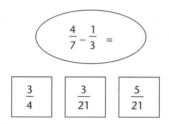

Figure 8.7   Subtracting fractions.

Teachers' errors in number: computation

An examination of computational skills can indicate problems with place value. It was found that 23 per cent of the pre-service teachers could not give the correct answer to the subtraction '6701 – 1592'. The most common error made by 10 per cent of the sample was 5209. If these pre-service teachers are using an algorithm based on place value the problem lies with subtracting *from* a zero place holder. Another 10 per cent answered 5201 or 5291, which both suggest a 'smaller from larger digit' strategy being used with compounding problems when subtracting from zero.

Subtraction of decimals also uncovered place value misconceptions. It was found that 30 per cent of the sample could not give the correct answer to '6.8 – 1.972'. The most common error made by 11 per cent was 4.972, where the problem lies again in subtracting from zero. Another 9 per cent answered 5.172 using a 'smaller from larger digit' strategy. Surprisingly, a further 8 per cent omitted this question.

Division also uncovers place value misconceptions. It was found that 36 per cent of the sample could not give the correct answer to '4949 ÷ 7'. The most common error of 77 was made by 30 per cent. Again, it appears that *zero as a place holder* is problematic for many pre-service teachers.

Teachers' errors in chance and measurement

A 'chance and data' question on the numerical likelihood of an event showed that pre-service teachers were making the same error as children. This item uncovered the *equiprobability intuition* that if there are two outcomes (in this case, red or green) they are assumed to be equally likely to occur.[18] Thirty-one per cent of the sample did not select the correct answer and 17 per cent made the equiprobability error for this question (Figure 8.8).

Here is a spinner for a game. What is the probability of it landing on green?

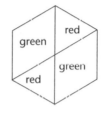

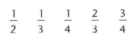

Figure 8.8 Probability intuitions.

A 'measurement' item uncovered fundamental misconceptions related to the *measure of line segments* (see Figure 8.9). Nearly two-thirds of the pre-service teachers gave incorrect responses to the question, which was similar to one given to 12-, 13- and 14-year-olds decades ago with similar results.[19]

A 6-sided figure is drawn on a centimetre square grid as shown. The distance around the edge of the figure is:
   (a) 12 cm
   (b) More than 12 cm
   (c) Less than 12 cm
   (d) You cannot tell

☐ Grid unit 1cm²

Figure 8.9 Length of a diagonal line segment item.

The responses here from the sample suggest important misconceptions about the length of a line drawn between grid lines. Only 34 per cent of the sample was correct; a further 36 per cent did not distinguish between the horizontal and sloping side measures of the hexagon.

Other errors

We have outlined several errors that pre-service teachers made and discussed the misconceptions that may be at the root of the errors. In summary the research sample had place value misconceptions, bugs in whole number, integer and decimal computation (for example, subtract smaller-from-larger digit, have problems with zero), did not recognize that fraction parts must be equal, had bugs in fraction computation (for example, add or subtract numerators and denominators), misinterpreted calculator displays (for example, the 'remainder'), found reverse computation problems difficult (for example, when finding a missing percentage), and used an additive strategy for ratio.

They had scale misconceptions (for example, counted the 'tick marks' rather than the 'gaps'), used scale prototypes (for example, treated all scales as unitary), and used incorrect conversions (for example, 100 minutes in an hour, 100 grams in a kilogram).

They misinterpreted data tables, had statistical misconceptions (for example, the mean average must appear in the data set), reversed Cartesian coordinates, used graph prototypes (for example, all straight line graphs are of the form $y = mx$) and generalized a rule on a single x-y data point in a graph or table. There were also errors in spatial and measurement vocabulary (for example, perpendicular/diagonal/hypotenuse confusion and area/perimeter confusion).

Making use of your own errors: a personalized mathsmap

At the start of the chapter we suggested that errors are constructed for good reasons and that productive investigation of their own errors may support teacher development as they actively reconstruct their conceptual base. A pre-service teacher first needs to know in which areas of the mathematics curriculum they are strong and in which they are weak. Second, they need to know what sort of errors they are making.

There is more to know than whether you got a question right or wrong on a particular test: for example, how hard were the questions, what would you have been expected to get right, what particular errors were you making, which areas of the curriculum do you need to work on?

Jennifer sat a 45-multiple-choice-question test. She answered 29 questions correctly and 16 incorrectly, which gave her a total score of 64 per cent. However, such a score gives little detail about her achievement. A *mathsmap* details her responses according to how difficult the questions were overall.[20] She can then investigate her areas of strength and weakness, and what her particular errors were.

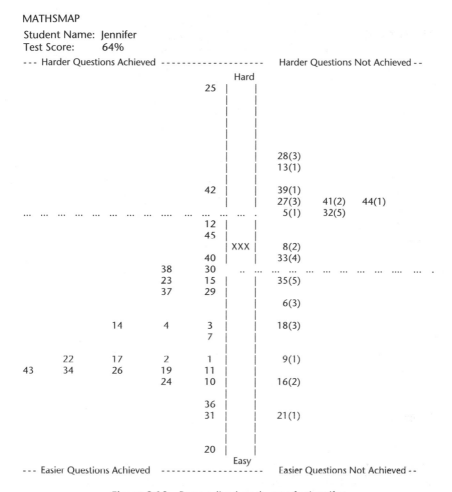

Figure 8.10 Personalized mathsmap for Jennifer.

Jennifer's mathsmap (see Figure 8.10) has all the test questions arranged vertically from bottom to top in terms of how hard the questions were overall: question 20 at the bottom was the easiest and question 25 at the top was the hardest. Then Jennifer's own responses are sorted horizontally left or right: her correct responses go to the left and incorrect ones to the right. Jennifer answered the hardest question, number 25, correctly but the next hardest question, number 28, incorrectly. She answered the easiest question, number 20, correctly but the next easiest question, number 21, incorrectly.

Not everyone who scored 64 per cent answered the same 29 questions correctly. Given her overall score Jennifer would have been expected to have answered the easiest 29 (or so) questions correctly, but she actually answered a

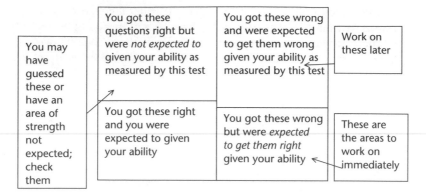

Figure 8.11   How to read your mathsmap.

different set of 29 questions correctly. The three Xs marked in the middle of the mathsmap show where Jennifer would have been expected to have been in terms of her ability (the dotted lines show the margin of error for this expectation). However, she was achieving harder questions than expected (top left corner) and not achieving easier questions (bottom right corner). These two corners of the mathsmap are therefore immediately useful to her diagnostically (see Figure 8.11).

The questions Jennifer answered incorrectly (shown on the whole right side of the mathsmap) also indicate which *particular* errors she made. Table 8.1 details Jennifer's particular areas of weakness and the misconception she may have in each curriculum area.

Jennifer has a range of errors indicated in the bottom right-hand corner of her mathsmap (and also in the top right-hand corner). She does not have each

Table 8.1   Analysis of Jennifer's 'easier not achieved' items

Question (error)	Question description	Inferred misconception
8(2)	Algebra: general statements	Variable as specific number
33(4)	Number: identifying ratio within several ratios	Additive tendency
35(5)	Number: calculating surface area	Area/volume confusion
6(3)	Space: Cartesian coordinates	Coordinate reversal
9(1)	Reasoning: logic	Triangle prototype (equilateral)
18(3)	Measurement: grams to kilograms	100 g is 1 kg
16(2)	Number: fraction representation	Unequal parts of whole treated as equal
21(1)	Algebra: words to symbols	'More than' implies multiply

particular test question but only a description of what it covered and the misconceptions that may lie beneath her response. As a professional development exercise she now needs to make sense of both of these. We believe this is more empowering professionally than drill and practice of particular test questions.[21]

Researching teacher knowledge and teacher education

The previous section offered one method for encouraging teacher reflection by having pre-service teachers personally confront their errors and misconceptions with a mathsmap. Another fruitful research-based strategy involves assessing teachers on their pedagogical knowledge of their pupils in various ways. For instance, the teacher can be asked to complete a diagnostic assessment or test given to their class of children, but rather than simply work out their answers, have them predict the difficulty of the question for their pupils and the likely errors that their pupils would make on the same items.[22]

One study of teachers' probability knowledge (in fact of the representativeness heuristic discussed in Chapter 7) showed, perhaps unsurprisingly, that teachers were generally better able to predict what their pupils would do in answer to the question if they knew the mathematics themselves. But, in addition, experienced teachers were better predictors of their pupils than novice student teachers. These rather obvious results give some confidence that the methodology is working in a valid way, and that teacher educators and researchers might usefully adopt this approach.[23]

In another experiment, teachers were asked to predict the difficulty of certain graphicacy items on a 1–5 Likert scale: by plotting the actual difficulty of the item with that predicted by the teachers, the general trend line was produced and outliers identified.[24] These outlier questions, where the teachers predict quite wrongly as a collective, seem interesting for research. Two reasons for this collective breakdown in pedagogy seemed to be (i) faulty subject matter knowledge (the teachers answered the items incorrectly according to the mark scheme and therefore thought the items 'easier' than the analysis showed them to be (see Chapter 7 for an example where teachers answered a graphicacy item with a linear prototype that was considered unacceptable); and (ii) faulty pedagogical content knowledge, in that the teachers thought the task would be done in a more sophisticated way than the pupils actually performed on the task.

This also seems a promising line of work for researchers and teacher educators; surprisingly little is known and very little research is going on currently in pedagogical content knowledge, at least from a survey, quantitative, point of view. We believe this is a promising area of teacher education research.

Conclusion

Like others we think that teachers need a blend of mathematical and pedagogical knowledge – this includes knowledge of mathematics and of children's conceptions, complemented by expertise in making connections between the mathematics, models and tasks used in teaching.[25] Such teacher knowledge may be uniquely enhanced by investigating one's own misconceptions. We have shown how a personalized mathsmap can provide information about subject matter knowledge so that particular misconceptions can be identified and then investigated productively by pre-service teachers themselves.

A teacher educator could also use whole-cohort patterns of response as the basis for conflict peer group discussion of different conceptions to support pre-service teacher learning and simultaneously model good practice.[26] Within such group discussion, students can be asked to listen to others via discussion, justification, persuasion and finally even change of mind, so that it is the student who reorganizes their own understanding. Toulmin's model of argument is helpful here and a range of errors is valuable in such conflict discussion.[27] In Chapter 3 we outlined ways to set up purposeful mathematical discussions for children, strategies for sustaining their dialogue and models of argument based on reasoning and persuasion. For the beginning teacher such opportunities for the articulation of reasoning and shifts in understanding challenge the transmission model of pedagogy that has failed so many.

Notes

1   Shulman's (1986) three categories of teacher content knowledge – subject matter knowledge, pedagogical content knowledge and curricular knowledge – are intertwined in practice. Pedagogical content knowledge includes 'an understanding of what makes the learning of specific topics easy or difficult: the conceptions and preconceptions that students of different ages and backgrounds bring with them . . . If those preconceptions are misconceptions, which they often are, teachers need knowledge of the strategies most likely to be fruitful in reorganizing the understanding of learners' (pp. 9–10). Pedagogical content knowledge is characterized as including 'the most useful forms of representation of . . . ideas, the most powerful analogies, illustrations, examples, explanations, and demonstrations – in a word, the ways of representing and formulating the subject that make it comprehensible to others' (p. 9).

2   Skemp (1976) contrasts instrumental understanding of mathematics (knowing what to do) and relational understanding (knowing both what to do and

why) in terms of efficiency and adaptability. Instrumental understanding is limited to particular situations and thus may make heavy demands on memory, while relational understanding depends on the building of a conceptual structure (schema) useful for making connections across unlimited situations.

3   Askew *et al.* (1997).

4   The Subject Knowledge in Mathematics (SKIMA) group is a collaboration of researchers from the universities of Cambridge, Durham and York and the Institute of Education at the University of London, which has researched the connections between teacher subject matter knowledge (SMK), planning and competence in the primary classroom. The importance of 'secure' SMK is discussed in Goulding *et al.* (2002).

5   Substantive and syntactic knowledge are components of subject matter knowledge proposed by Schwab (1978).

6   There are different terms to describe this contrast: Skemp's terms are instrumental and relational, and Hiebert's terms are procedural and conceptual. Skemp (1976); Hiebert and Lefevre (1986).

7   This is the idea of a multivalent model – one that can be used across different situations. For instance, the circle is useful for demonstrating the part–whole conception of fraction but the rectangle can show both the part–whole conception and fraction of a fraction.

8   This study of 426 students is reported in Ryan and McCrae (2005).

9   This study of 86 students is reported in Ryan and McCrae (2006).

10 Functional numeracy is defined as the ability to use mathematics at a level necessary to function at work and in society in general. It was interpreted here as reflecting a grade C at GCSE in England and level 6 in Australia. The primary teacher curriculum was constructed from a consideration of England's initial teacher training curriculum (DfEE, 1998; TTA, 2003), the Australian (Victoria) curriculum framework (Board of Studies, 1995, 2000) and the Australian curriculum (Curriculum Corporation, 1994).

11 Freudenthal (1983); Kieren (1993).

12 Results from a study of 426 Australian pre-service teachers were replicated by a study of 86 pre-service teachers in England (Ryan and McCrae, 2006).

13 The Ancient Egyptian fractions were expressed as the sum of unit fraction (with the exceptional case of two-thirds).

14 Assessment of Performance Unit (1982).

15 Streefland (1991).

16 Freudenthal (1968).

17 Sfard (1991); Gray and Tall (1994).

18 Green (1982); Lecoutre (1992).

19 Hart (1981).

20 The mathsmap is produced by Quest software: Adams and Khoo (1996).

21 Ryan and McCrae (2006).

22 Hadjidemetriou and Williams (2002b, 2003, 2004); Williams *et al.* (2004).
23 Afantiti-Lamprianou *et al.* (2005).
24 Hadjidemetriou and Williams (2002b, 2003, 2004).
25 Shulman (1986).
26 Ryan and Williams (2003).
27 Toulmin (1958).

9 Learning and teaching mathematics: towards a theory of pedagogy

Introduction

In this chapter we will draw together the threads from previous chapters to outline a conceptual framework (or theory) of teaching practice – that is, of pedagogy as an activity. We have adopted Freudenthal's perspective on mathematics-for-all, as a 'human activity', but we inscribed it in a sociocultural theory of learning-and-pedagogy as 'joint activity', drawing on Vygotsky and Cultural-Historical Activity Theory (CHAT) after Leont'ev, Cole and Engestrom, and others.[1] We saw that classroom discourse, and especially what we called mathematical 'dialogue', was the ideal essential medium of this joint activity. We have pointed out the significance of the work of Bakhtin, Bernstein, Halliday and Hasan, Mercer, Sfard and others on 'voice' and discourse. We hope that our view of mathematics as a particular genre of communication has been given sufficient emphasis; we argue that mathematics provides powerful models for communication and thought, offering learners deep understandings of, and hence power over, their world. Learners who adopt this point of view themselves not only become competent mathematically, but acquire a mathematical identity of some kind.

We identified a contradiction between mathematics as a scientific activity and mathematics embedded within everyday knowledge and activity. An important part of the pedagogy we promoted involved engaging in conflict between the two. Indeed the joint activity of learner-teacher was thought of as a manifestation of the back-and-forth engagement of the 'everyday' and the 'scientific/academic' mathematics that we have called modelling. Errors and misconceptions are the inevitable, even vital, product of the learner's engagement in such joint activity. We argued in Chapter 2 that they are the result of intelligent engagement and should be prized. They arise from an essential contradiction between the everyday-intuitive conceptions and more advanced mathematical conceptions. As such they are the essential source of the dynamic of pedagogic and learning activity. As we argued in Chapter 3, a problematic or conflict is an essential prerequisite for productive pedagogic dialogue.

Curriculum and assessment practices often frustrate such a pedagogy. In Chapters 4 to 7 we examined errors and misconceptions across the curriculum and everyday contexts, situations and models that provided resources for teachers to engage with them. Contexts can be a vital resource for situated intuition – that is, everyday intuition harnessed in the service of mathematics, as we discussed in Chapters 4, 5 and 6. Modelling provides the vital pedagogic link between the everyday and academic mathematics. Additionally, we argued in Chapters 6 and 7, many models can offer spatial and embodied channels of communication: for many learners this is a critical and often missing side of mathematics. In this chapter, then, we will assemble all these threads in an outline sketch of a sociocultural theory of pedagogy (paraphrasing Fermat, we do not have space for the full theoretical exposition here).

Sociocultural versus behaviourist and information processing approaches

Let us make a few comments on what we think Freudenthal meant when he asserted that mathematics was, or should be, a human activity. First, he meant to include all the activities that people in their everyday lives do that involve mathematics, from checking the change on the bus and interpreting the graphs in the newspaper, to building a spreadsheet, or proving the four-colour theorem – mathematics as a human activity is truly 'for all'. Second, he emphasized mathematics as 'process' first and foremost: finding and solving problems, organizing and analysing the world mathematically, generalizing, symbolizing, communicating, and so on. Third, he implied that mathematics is a social, cultural and historical practice. When humans learn or use mathematics, they are the agent of action, which implies the activity has to have meaning and purpose for them. In CHAT, individual action is always *goal* driven, albeit that it is part of a jointly accomplished, and socioculturally mediated, activity that has some 'larger' object and aim; the point is that the meaning of the action for the 'acting' subject is in this goal.

So, for us, learning mathematics is part of learning to act purposefully with mathematics, and so is a process of becoming active with mathematics. We find behaviourism and even cognitive information processing perspectives on learning deficient in this regard.

Traditionally, theories of learning begin with a definition of learning as some kind of change. A behaviourist typically defines learning as a change in a person's 'behaviour'; a cognitive theorist of learning looks to a change in cognitive structure; and a social theorist looks to a change in social position and status, or social identity. Instead of 'change' here we might say 'relatively stable change'; in addition, we might try to assert that 'growth' or 'progress' in some sense is implicated.[2]

The teacher can see or hear behaviour, but has to infer what the learner knows. As we have seen in previous chapters this involves a cognitive interpretation of behaviour, an explanation perhaps based on the child's own rationalizations. We argue that these inferences should be informed by a pedagogic theory, and one that can stand the test of empirical grounding by a research community. By and large, common sense will not do.

Behaviourist theory was empirically grounded in many experiments initially with animal learning in laboratory situations, and then later with adults and children learning in labs and classrooms. These provided evidence, for instance, that behavioural reinforcement can 'work' to support discrimination and accelerate learning, that positive reinforcement is more effective than negative, and that sporadic reinforcement can be sufficient once the behaviour has become established, after which it can gradually be allowed to diminish. This approach seems most credible when the targeted learning outcome is mastery of a physical behaviour – for instance, when a child is learning to eat or ride a bicycle, a sportsman to perform expertly or a pupil to stand up with the class when the teacher enters the classroom. The rules recommended for managing classroom behaviour make substantial use of behaviourist theory: teachers are exhorted to establish good behaviour by 'reward and praise' rather than 'punishment', and so on.

However, early behaviourism failed to engage with the cognitive mediation of learners' behaviour; thus, extrinsic rewards used to reinforce behaviours can undermine the intrinsic reward from enjoyment or pleasure that engagement in learning might bring. This is a clear hint that 'agency' is at stake. if the teacher controls the learning then they may need to implement rewards and punishments and a behavioural regime. Foucault's account of regimes of truth, discipline and punishment, and technologies of surveillance spring to mind (inspection, league tables, accountability).

But to the extent that the learner is in control then rewards will need to be intrinsic to the activity itself. This location of agency is what is really at the heart of the problem with behaviourism, and much of the information processing cognitive psychology that followed it. Our view of mathematics as a human activity implies that we must reject the assumption that the teacher rather than the learner has the agency in mathematical activity; rather pedagogy needs to develop activities that have intrinsic worth and so provide the 'reward' that behaviourists insist is essential to reinforce learning.

The influence of behaviourism on education in general and mathematics education in particular has been deep and is evident everywhere. Its legacy is clearly visible in traditional approaches to syllabuses, objectives and their assessment, and to planning practices in which periods of teaching time are focused on mastery of bite-sized objectives. Thus even cognitionists, like

Gagné, who saw learning as change in states of knowledge 'in the head', built their frameworks on the same assumptions as the behaviourists in regard to learning outcomes and agency.[3] As a result, we suggest, school systems everywhere alienate learners from mathematics.

Furthermore, the psychological evidence for structured approaches to mastery of learning, based on a 'mind-as-computer' metaphor, is in our view not ultimately convincing, despite our appreciation of some work on 'cognitive load' (see Chapters 2 and 7).[4] We recall that in practice children often learn things other than that which is explicitly planned.[5] While we struggle to memorize a nine-digit telephone number by rote, we can recall a tune, a story or a face with ease (in theory, each implicating millions of bits of 'data'). The explanation lies in the fact that a tune is more than the sum of its notes, a face is more than the sum of eyes, nose, and so on. Indeed the best way to recall a nine-digit number might rather turn out to be to develop a complex story from which the digit-string derives 'sense'. Meaning generally comes from the whole activity, from the top down. We conclude that humans tend to think and talk in complete (if complicated) stories, structured by a narrative sense of purpose, and that perhaps mathematics should be learnt this way too.[6]

We saw in several chapters that, in mathematics, rote learning without understanding typically (and perhaps predictably) leads to the manufacture of bugs in procedures.[7] We claimed that rote learning or 'training' without meaning is a major source of failure in motivation *and* performance. On the contrary we emphasized that any particular mathematical action makes sense or derives meaning only as part of a child's 'larger' social activity, usually in joint work with others (see Chapters 4 and 6). In these cases we have argued that mathematics draws sense from models and representations used in solving practical problems; this provides the larger activity in which the mathematics is embedded.

Constructivist and developmental theories

Piaget is usually cited as the authority and influence behind a constructivist view of learning, in which the learner is regarded as the central agent in a knowledge construction process. A biological model of growth inspired this view: the learner is viewed as constructing their knowledge through processes of assimilation of experience to cognitive schemes or models (such as the 'cardinality of number' or the 'ratio schema/model') but where necessary accommodating these schemes when they are inadequate to the task. As an active and adaptive 'organism', the learner explores the physical and social environment, and reshapes or reconstructs cognitive schemes or models where necessary. Thus we saw in Chapter 3 how an inadequate understanding of decimals may be contradicted, leading the learners to rethink their knowledge, to 'accommodate' their cognitive structures to achieve a new state of 'equilibrium'. These contradictions or 'cognitive conflicts' are regarded as the key moments in learning from this point of view.

The early, so-called 'concrete' stage of development of number conceptions, for instance, involves the 'conservation of number' – that is, the recognition that the number/numerosity of a set of objects is conserved even when transforming the set (moving the objects in the set, spreading them out, and so on). The ability to identify the concept that is invariant under a set of transformations is characteristic of this whole stage of intellectual development, and includes the conservation of length (invariant under translation), mass (invariant under deformation), and volume (for example, invariant when liquid is poured into different-shaped vessels).[8] However, the fact is that the acquisition of conservation comes much earlier for number than for mass and capacity; this leads one to question in what sense it is helpful to say they are 'the same' across contexts, or 'in the same stage'. It is not realistic to believe, for instance, that the learner can benefit from attempts to connect these different cases. However, the teacher/theoretician can make use of the general idea of conservation, arguing that awareness of and reflection on the relevant transformations and their reversibility via inversions is *in general* a vital generative element and hence relevant to a theory of pedagogy. We made use of this notion in Chapter 5 when we argued that attention must always be paid to the salient properties (and non-properties) of any conception if prototyping is to be avoided.

On the other hand, the acquisition of the formal stage of reasoning is quintessentially completed when the logic of hypothesis testing or 'proof by contradiction' is formally mastered. One can see that the properties of this stage do enter the awareness of the learner; they must enter the learner's as well as the pedagogue's or theoretician's mind's eye, precisely because reflection on one's argumentation (that is, metacognition) is the hallmark of this stage of intellectual development.[9]

The Piagetian, constructivist perspective has had a strong influence on research in child development, and particularly mathematics education. However, Piaget's work has also been criticized as having underestimated what young children know and can do, mainly because his work was insufficiently sensitive to the problems adult researchers might have in communicating effectively with children in 'clinical interviews'. It seems that children are able to reason in more advanced ways in certain contexts, when the context is made meaningful to them, while not achieving the same level 'in general'.[10] For Wood, this is a misreading of Piaget: he argues that a stage is complete only (and precisely) when the schema that paradigmatically typify that stage have been mastered across contexts – that is, in general.[11] Our view, a sociocultural view, is that the weakness in Piaget's perspective rests in the interpretation of it or the expectation that stages are in any sense mechanistic. Dynamics can and usually do arise precisely because there are inconsistencies across contexts in what children are able to do; for instance, these can provide for cognitive conflict in the most productive of ways, as we have shown in earlier chapters. The task, then, is for pedagogy to devise meaningful activity in which these contradictions can arise.

Piaget's work has been criticized because many researchers found that most populations of children were not as developed as the children he studied. In particular, it is believed that Piaget's children were socially privileged, and the fact is that many children do not reach the formal stages of intellectual development by age 11 or even 16 years. In relation to the formal understanding of hypothesis testing and proof by contradiction, psychologists have shown that it is not uncommon for students at university to have difficulty with these. In general, sociologists will argue that these intellectual developments are the acme of middle-class labour: intellectual labourers operate with symbols just as the traditional manual working class operate with their hands, with 'hammer and sickle'.[12] Alongside the question of class, there are also arguments about mathematics from the point of view of gender, sexuality, race and colonialism. All these concerns are refracted in our notion of agency and identity. 'Mathematics for all' has sociopolitical implications never addressed by Piaget and early theorists' views of mathematics learning.

Nevertheless, despite the critics, the work of all who follow has been profoundly influenced by Piaget's thinking and theory. In particular, we have emphasized throughout the earlier chapters the importance of children reflecting (usually in and through discussion) on their work; for Piagetians, reflective abstraction is a key process for activating accommodation, or restructuring one's knowledge schema/models. This is big talk for the proposition that children learn from talking about and reflecting on their mathematical ideas and solutions/strategies with others. The discussion in Chapter 6 on van Hiele particularly exemplifies how this reflection is essential to the vertical progress of mathematics, where the processes at one level become the objects at the next.

Piaget's influence in the 1960s and 1970s on professional practice was substantial but perhaps in ways he might not have intended. In the primary years, child-centred approaches involving practical work with mathematics were encouraged. Later, learner-centred classroom activities involving problem solving and investigation developed in secondary school. Some of these trends were criticized as leading to 'rote' practical work: it was argued that 'child-centred learning' should involve active, meaningful learning, but that this could be achieved in many different ways, and is largely verbally and socially mediated. For instance, Ausubel argued that meaningful learning results from the child assimilating new learning using already existing cognitive structures: 'The most important single factor influencing learning is what the learner already knows. Ascertain this and teach accordingly.'[13] If the expertise (and we would argue crucially the motivation) were available to do this through meaningful 'reception' learning, he argued, then a rote discovery pedagogy would be detrimental.

The child-centred trend was also criticized for promoting ideas of 'readiness' to learn, or waiting for children to naturally develop intellectually before they can learn certain things. While Piaget perhaps should not be blamed for the use others made of his work, the concept of 'readiness to learn' seems to arise logically from his approach to 'stages of development'. Arguably this suggests, for example, that without having reached a formal stage the child could not be expected to be able to assimilate formal topics. In fact, Vygotskyan theorists have argued and some researchers have shown the reverse – that is, that teaching for the next stage must be the means of helping children to develop.

An important example of this is the CASE project, which showed that intervening in development with teaching of intellectual skills of the kind Piaget identified with the onset of formal thinking at age 11 to 12 years could lead to much greater success years later.[14] Originally the project targeted science learning, and many of the requisite skills and teaching were related to mathematics, including the ratio schema, the systematic organization of data, and so on. An important element of these intervention lessons is also the way in which inquiry, discussion and reflection are encouraged, motivated by Piagetian notions of the need for reflective abstraction. The fact that the improved examination results were recorded across a diverse range of subjects could be explained by a Piagetian cognitive perspective, that there is a set of intellectual schema that children need to master to be successful in learning the secondary curriculum. On the other hand, it could be that the children learnt *social* skills related to inquiry, discussion and metacognition that we have argued are germane to effective learning. For Vygotsky, these are not incompatible suggestions – the one is the internalization of the other. The social activity is the precursor for its internalization as metacognitive awareness and knowledge.

Social, social constructivist and sociocultural theories of learning

Vygotsky argued that the child's construction of knowledge is led right from the beginning by social interactions with adults.[15] Almost the first cry and the first pointing gestures become social by virtue of the activation of a parental response (the cry leads to a feed, the pointing to a fetching, and so on). Indeed, while Vygotsky still sees the child as the agent of learning activity, he emphasizes the social context mediating all learning and development, and thereby the evolution of successive generations of culture.[16] For Vygotsky, learning in the 'zone of proximal development' should always be in advance of the child's stage of development. That is, in effective learning, the learner is performing in joint activity with others in more advanced mathematics than they can on their own without support. Thus typically the child learns the use of a word in a social, active context with others before internalizing it in verbal thought, through inner speech. Later these ideas were represented by some educationists as 'scaffolding': the social support in joint activity of the parent, guide, teacher, peer group, and so on, provides scaffolding for the child's own construction of new knowledge and expertise. As the child becomes increasingly well practised in the new activity, the scaffolding becomes less and less necessary, less and less often.

The social primacy of mediated learning is usually summed up in Vygotsky's notion of internalization. Vygotsky's formulation of the general law of cultural development is that 'Any function . . . appears twice . . . First it appears on the social plane, then on the psychological plane. First it appears between people as an interpsychological (intermental) category, and then within the child as an intrapsychological (intramental) category.'[17] (Note that the bracketed '-mental' replaces psychological in some Russian translations.) For Vygotsky, the school is instrumental in providing the resources for the essential interactions 'between people' that can allow them to access and internalize the best, scientific (as opposed to the 'everyday') concepts from our culture. The overlap between the scientific and the everyday was expressed in the idea of the 'pseudo-concept' that learners would first grasp: a necessary stage when joint attention and discussion of the concept could be negotiated from the advanced as well as the everyday point of view. In general, CHAT theorists argue that concepts begin their development somewhat abstractly, as relatively 'empty words', but become filled with meaning as they are progressively used in repeated, diverse mathematical practices. The highest stage of such mathematics is in our view the pedagogical one: only when the mathematics is organized conceptually in explaining to another person is the understanding completed. This explains why teachers often say they only 'really' understood a topic for the first time when they taught it. It is also why we value dialogue as the principal medium of pedagogy, for those that explain at least as much as those who listen.

We argued in Chapter 3 that dialogue can sometimes provide a zone of proximal development – or, less ambitiously, a learning zone – for learners. This requires a significant problematic that can be resolved only through more advanced conceptions. This can be realized through tasks in a context that, as Freudenthal suggested, 'begs to be organized' mathematically. The quality of the task may consequently engage pupil agency. Social norms of joint activity must further require a dialogue to arise, so that the children engage with the arguments voiced, and take part in evaluating all the points of view, from the most primitive to the most sophisticated in the group. In this way mathematical activity can draw on a rich social, discursive resource. Mathematics is a genre of communication, and mathematical activity is activity that is interwoven with this and other discourses.[18] Further, we argue that the need for mathematical progress in the dialogue, in the sense of the dialogue providing for more advanced learning for all, in general requires the introduction of new cultural tools: new concepts, instruments and models that need to be introduced into the activity. The introduction of the number line into the dialogue about decimals described in Chapter 3 is of this kind. Thus the activity draws on a cultural resource, the new mathematics, in its proper cultural context.

The notion that a theory of knowledge and learning, and hence pedagogy, requires a cultural perspective is encouraged by anthropology, whose focus is the study of human culture in context. Culture – a difficult concept to define simply – is the totality of artefacts, rites, stories and customs shared in a given human social group (traditionally geographically located, that may be quite widely distributed but 'made close' by technologies of communication – surfers, trekkies, academics, and so on). Here cultural artefacts are viewed as (i) primary – tools for working on nature (axes, gardens, houses, computers, and so on); (ii) secondary – rules, recipes, stories, narratives and customs for operating with primary tools; and (iii) languages (including mathematics), which provide the means for communicating, including the reading and writing of the narratives in (ii).[19] In this view, then, mathematics is properly situated in activities that allow a powerful scripting of mathematically mediated recipes and rules, which manifest themselves these days in all kinds of algorithms, programs, spreadsheets, and so on, that derive sense from their operations on real, material objects. Failure to connect mathematics in this way may lead to a disembedded, disembodied, self-referential discourse that will not make sense to learners, at least in the early stages.[20]

Anthropology insists that everything that can be known about a culture must be understood in context, that knowledge is itself always 'situated' and that this situated-ness is essential to the knowledge. Those who have examined mathematical activity in context have helped us to better understand why 'transfer' across contexts is often so problematic. To take a simple example, communal activities using ratios in the three contexts of nursing (distributing drugs), cooking (recipes) and schooling are profoundly different, because the three cultural contexts offer such different resources for mediating the work.[21] They occur in distinct social situations, solve different practical needs, involving different materials, tools and artefacts. Indeed the people who do these activities know them in distinct ways, and they tell different stories about them. But also, modern anthropology recognizes the significance of the two worlds involved: the Culture under study in its context and the academic culture of the anthropologist.[22] In our context, then, mathematics pedagogy must recognize the two, differently structured worlds: the 'everyday world' of phenomena that may beg to be organized scientifically, and the 'schooling world' that might provide the mathematical tools, discourses and dispositions needed to so 'organize' the world.

CHAT's theory of activity helps to understand this structuration: a communal activity shared by a group typically has a communal 'object', in schooling we might say the object is the 'task' to be carried out by the children and teacher. It has as its aim, or 'intended outcome', that the children should learn something, usually explicitly determined by the teacher, perhaps negotiated with the children. The actual context of activity is then structured by the system of activity: the instruments used for the action (calculators or not, models or not, common sense or not, mathematical and other concepts, and so on); and also the social division of labour and rules for sharing the work and outcomes (who does what with whom, and how, when, where, and so on).

Reviewing the mathematics of 'the street', of supermarket shopping or of the kitchen from this point of view, one can account for the fact that mathematics in these practices is intimately connected with 'other stuff', executed on the hoof, shaped by the resources to hand, and in the service of objectives that make very particular requirements of the mathematics.[23] Typically, the context shapes the requirement for accuracy (quantities in cooking need not be exact but prices, costs and change must be) and fallibility (dosages in nursing must be error free, but supermarket shopping is not critical). The mathematics may be informative rather than decisive (the large bottle is 'better value' but will not fit in the fridge) and practised within constraints and affordances shaped by the infrastructure and the instruments to hand (drug doses are usually made almost foolproof by modern dispensing tools; supermarkets sometimes provide calculators with the trolleys and purchases are scanned for price; microwave cookers allow one to enter the type of food and the weight, and so on).

The very distinct nature of the knowledge involved in schooling then becomes apparent: only in 'schooling' is the intended outcome 'certificated learning', wherein 'learning' as such is explicit, but also certificated as a rite of passage into your social class. The rules about the use of instruments or the rules about 'who does what' then follow: there will be an assessment regime, a division of labour between teacher and child about who decides what, and the technology will be controlled. Indeed 'schooling ratios' do look very different from 'nursing ratios', and while nurses' dosages need to be foolproof, it may be that schooling requires a degree of failure to be socially functional in a class society. Similar arguments may be brought to bear on gender divisions in school mathematics, as social constructions of mathematical identity and femininity may contradict one another. Hence the central contradictions in schooling arise from the constitution of knowledge as a commodity and as gendered.

An important development of CHAT is the method of analysis of change as a result of contradictions between interacting activity systems that share some object: the paradigmatic example is the research and design system that works on a production system's tools to produce new, more advanced systems. The production tools are boundary objects that link the two systems. In this view 'everyday mathematics' becomes a boundary object that operates within everyday activity (and so engages people's intuition and understandings from the everyday practice) as well as within schooling activity. The purpose of pedagogy is to help connect the 'scientific' essence – that is, the mathematics – with the everyday. For the learner, then, whose intuitive models and schemes were made and remain situated in the everyday phenomena, pedagogy seeks to engage and to contradict these models with more advanced, more mathematical ones. Our cognitions are 'made' in situations, but we cross the boundaries between distinct situations and take our knowledge with us in ways that induce conflicts of meaning for us and for others.[24] Thus the knowledge that develops intuitively in one situation can be a source of significant learning when activated in another situation, such as in school mathematics. We argue that this can be a powerful resource for intuitive learning of mathematics, as well as, even because of, the obstacles and misconceptions that this kind of transfer across situations and activities always engenders.[25]

Social identity and situated cognition

The idea that cognition is socially situated is not new, but has recently become fashionable, especially among those who are interested in informal learning, tacit knowledge, identity, and especially learning or apprenticeship in the workplace. Learning can always be seen as social – that is, a matter of changing one's social position, status and identity in relation to social communities. So an apprentice – a student teacher perhaps – acquires a new identity by virtue of completing their apprenticeship. It is suggested that this is a crucial context for understanding the motivation, agency, and hence the structure of all learning activity.[26]

Further, a social theory of learning implicates the changing relevance of mathematics to a learner's identity as they grow up. If we accept for the moment that the leading, predominant activity of the infant is found in 'play', and of the adult is found in 'work', then schooling must provide for transitional activities and identities between those of 'play' and 'work'. Many teachers and curriculum designers are intuitively aware of this and structure mathematical activities around play, playful-work and work in various ways. A theory of pedagogy should address this directly: what is the meaning of school-going as transitional between these two?

The recognition that people learn without schooling or any explicit teaching, often very successfully, is more than a curiosity for pedagogy. The fact that apprentices often reach mastery without any official curriculum or teaching suggests that there can be, maybe *must* be, significant, tacit elements to all learning, including schooling. The hidden curriculum of many mathematics classrooms includes social and sociomathematical norms, perhaps: that mathematics need not make sense, that problems and tasks come in packages of between two and ten minutes, that the teacher always knows and arbitrates the answer, that maths gets 'hard' and is better left to 'others' (the boys, those who talk like 'teacher', or whatever).

These 'hidden messages' are believed to be the most important means of transmitting ideology and shaping identity: what is hidden cannot be so easily challenged or controlled, what is explicit can be. In thinking about how certain kinds of pupils are alienated from mathematics, we argued that one should make these hidden rules and values explicit, as they determine much of what it means to become a mathematician, or a non-mathematician. The argument was that mathematics should be a social activity involving sense making and collective argumentation, and in the final analysis this is an argument to make mathematicians with a particular social identity. The traditional view that mathematics is difficult, that everyone is eventually dropped from maths at some level, or that it is a white-middle-class-male subject, is a deeply ideological and elitist view that is transmitted through the pedagogic discourses of schools and classrooms. On the contrary, a view that mathematics pedagogy is a human activity that everyone engages in is also a deeply ideological and inclusive one: the task of pedagogy is to operationalize it in practice.

The requirements of a theory of pedagogy

Before there was any *theory of teaching* there was always craft knowledge, or know-how, of 'teaching'. Parents and adults have always taught children. Indeed research into how this is done has been and continues to be inspirational to theorists. Infant–parent interaction studies and studies of tutoring have inspired the development of notions of scaffolding; and master–apprenticeship contexts have inspired social theorizations of learning and the significance of identity in pedagogy.[27]

Theories of teaching have tended to be predicated on theories of learning. In fact, one is struck by the relative poverty of scientific understanding of teaching in comparison to that of learning. Most twentieth-century educational psychology focused on learning, especially in theoretical work. Often pedagogy is relegated to the 'implications for teaching' section of a text reporting research on learning. Thus, behaviourists typically drew inferences for the classroom from theories of learning that emerged from laboratory studies; the tradition, then, is to draw inferences for the design of teaching and perhaps then to evaluate the teaching from gains in learning.

However, it seems that while theories of learning will be important in their various implications, only Vygotsky's approach provides a theory of learning-and-teaching as a joint activity. This is because, for Vygotsky, learning is for development, and school teaching is central to a certain critical stage of development. Here we will attempt to develop this as a theory of mathematics teaching as such, or at least lay down the essential elements for building a theory of mathematics pedagogy.

First, there are some candidates for 'theory of pedagogy' that deserve to be discussed and dismissed. One school of thought involves constructing a checklist of 'good practices' involved in teaching. Government agencies and inspectorates are keen on checklists, and even enforce them via classroom observations and inspections.[28] This might establish or shape a pedagogy in practice, but cannot provide a theory of pedagogy because such a theory must by its nature be a general conceptual framework that teachers and researchers can, at least in principle, communally share as a tool for understanding and exploring pedagogic practices in diverse situations. In other words, to be a theory it must be general, flexible and communally negotiable. At the very least these checklists are too particular to constitute a theory.

A second, similar candidate for a theory of pedagogy involves cherry-picking various practices that seem to work in 'effective' schools – for example, those perceived to be 'more effective' school systems internationally or, for example, textbook use in Singapore or Holland, whole-class teaching from Hungary or use of homework from Japan. This might be a sensible thing to do but it is not possible to construct a theory from such an empirical soup.

Finally, there is an argument that every teacher must themselves, through their reflective work, possibly through action research, construct their own personal theory of teaching. Action research or professional development through teachers' inquiry groups are surely good things to do to improve practice, and especially if collectively and systematically pursued they are likely to lead to important gains and insights, but this approach in itself is not likely to lead to a significant pedagogic theory. This is because it is too insular: such theory emerges from within the confines of and bounded by local practice, and is therefore too locally determined. The problems education faces may be too great to be completely solved locally. A theory worthy of the name must surely listen and speak to a wider research community, preferably globally.

An example of a pedagogic theory might be that espoused in the Plowden report; some have criticized it as an 'ideology'.[29] It was strongly influenced by Piaget's theory of cognition, learning and development, and underpinned an era of child-centred teacher education in primary school pedagogy. Better, some neo-Piagetian theorists developed a diagnostic and 'conflict' theory of pedagogy that systematically attempted to provide the individual learner with relevant experiences of cognitive conflict. As described in previous chapters, the learners' inadequate schema are thereby confronted with an experience they cannot merely assimilate. At this point, when the learner has been dis-equilibrated, the more advanced schema or modified schema can be presented and lead the learner to cognitive change, or even 'development'. A good deal of empirical research has been done in this tradition, and this provided pedagogy with the theory of assessment for learning that this book has largely built on.[30]

We have argued in previous chapters that the key principles are (i) the choice of powerful tasks from 'rich', meaningful cultural mathematical practices; (ii) the introduction of powerful organizers, models, metaphors and representations; and (iii) management of a progressive dialogue involving the articulation of different arguments that provide opportunities for weaker formulations or conceptions to be contradicted by stronger ones. The Realistic Mathematics Education (RME) literature adds two key ideas to this: the use of a model can provide 'horizontal modelling', whereby contexts are modelled with mathematics; and 'vertical modelling', where new mathematics is itself introduced to organize and schematize. This provides leverage for new mathematics to be constructed. The articulation of the two types of modelling together allows for the growth of new mathematical concepts that organizes cultural knowledge from outside mathematics. We drew on this work in Chapters 4 to 7, and showed how the use of an appropriate model and the shift from 'modelling of' a context to 'modelling for' mathematics can provide for progressive mathematizing, from the horizontal to the vertical.

While these latter theorizations make significant contributions to a theory of mathematics pedagogy, we argue that they are not general or complete enough to be called a 'theory' without CHAT, which situates mathematics pedagogy within a cultural, historical and political analysis of human activity and development.

CHAT, pedagogy and inquiry

According to Vygotsky, 'good learning' is always in advance of individual development. That is, an individual learner, working in joint activity with others 'in the zone of proximal development', is helped to perform tasks at the next level of development; with practice, such a learner comes to achieve this competence on their own. A few examples of efforts to provide for mathematical development have been researched in the Activity Theory (AT) tradition in Russia, with reported success. These are theoretically articulated as being cultural-historical in a very direct sense that is quite close to Freudenthal: the mathematics is designed as the solution to a practical problem in much the same way that the theorist believes mankind historically might have solved the problem. In one experiment, early number conceptions were built from problems induced by measurement tasks.[31]

A possible misconception of this theory is that tasks need to be individualized, in the sense that a task set to a whole class of individuals at different levels is likely to be in the 'zone' for some but not all. In this view, the more diverse the class, the more problematic it is for pedagogy. However, this inference involves a misunderstanding of 'joint activity'. In the CHAT tradition, joint or 'communal' activity involves the sharing of a joint enterprise directed to a common object, but mediated by a set of tools, and, crucially, a division of labour and associated norms and expectations regarding collaboration. In a classroom where learners simply replicate a teacher's performance, doing the same thing individually, there is a 'poor' division of labour, and not much collective activity. In such a case we can predict that the quality of community, talk, language, and so on, is poor, with very little social engagement. On the other hand, a complex task engaging the whole community in inquiry might be expected to raise many demanding questions that offer a challenge for all, including the teacher. This involves the creative activity of learners, possibly at different levels of development, all in their own way perhaps contributing to the communal effort.

Various authors and researchers have characterized such a classroom in various ways as a 'community of inquiry', a 'knowledge-building' community or a 'community of practice'.[32] Many have indicated that the classroom discourse or dialogue in the community can provide each learner with a zone of proximal development, or at any rate a learning zone, a resource that potentially can lead to internalization. The curriculum in many places has even been rewritten to include this aspect – the idea in science education, for instance, being that to 'become a scientist' is to learn to 'talk science'.[33] In this view, the pedagogy must provide for learners' verbalization of mathematics in joint activity with others, of 'talking maths' in a dialogue before they are expected to internalize and perform independently.[34]

As well as talk, one should expect to see mathematics being predominantly written for an audience, addressed to others to some purpose – perhaps making a case, persuading, arguing, and so on, and so revealing an authentic communicative competence. We have rarely seen this in practice, though coursework and group problem solving followed by class reporting has some of these characteristics. Most of the richest examples we have seen have involved cross-curricular projects often engaging tasks with meaning outside the classroom and even school (for example, improving the school environment, making a case for traffic calming in a neighbourhood, and so on).

Thus, a rich pedagogy is one that allows for the activation of the community's resources, and hence the development of a rich division of labour, with norms that include the properties of good dialogue previously mentioned. Our preference is for Wells' conception of a 'community of inquiry', which is most often associated with the notion that a community works together through its communal dialogue in the sense explored in Chapter 3.[35] Those in the children's philosophy movement have characterized such communities in ideal, even idyllic, terms: the community in search of 'truth', where everyone 'listens' and contributes to the dialogue, and respect for all contributions and persons is expected, but at the same time all are expected to help the community in the advancement of the inquiry.[36] Cobb and his colleagues refer to these 'rules' as being social norms, and point especially to 'socio-mathematical' norms, such as 'what counts' as a good mathematical argument. Thus, 'Guessing is good, but to have a reason is better' might be an early sociomathematical norm for a Year 1 classroom.[37] Our pedagogy needs to define itself, then, in terms of community activity, and this must specify norms and values.

This account is an essentially social theory of pedagogy, but does not yet quite deserve to be called cultural (or sociocultural). While the interactions of chimpanzees should certainly be called 'social', the term 'cultural' is properly reserved for human societies, in which the social is almost always mediated or 'translated' in time and space by artefacts, especially through language. Just as Dickens famously talked incessantly with his characters, a lone human on a desert island engages socially (at a lapse in time) with Dickens and those same characters, and with the human species as a whole, by reading his book.

So a critical element of the zone of proximal development in the practice and the dialogue of the classroom is provided by culture – that is, the advanced mathematics is introduced into the activity as a requirement for solving the task. The learners – and the whole classroom community – appropriate this mathematics as they become more practised with these tools. A culturally rich pedagogy therefore reaches out to wider resources and communities through its tools, mathematics texts, models and manipulatives, but also through computers and e-networks, to users of mathematics in society, societies of mathematicians, engineers, analysts, and so on. This then puts the culture (especially the mathematics) at the heart of the pedagogical theory: the curriculum should situate powerful 'kernels' of mathematics within meaningful cultural tasks that, on reflection, open the door to new worlds.[38]

Pedagogical models mediating mathematics

A reminder: Freudenthal and his followers emphasized two points about mathematics pedagogy. First, entirely consistent with the Vygotskyan theoretical tradition, Freudenthal looked to culture and history to humanize mathematics. The growth points for mathematics are to be found in cultural contexts and problems that 'beg to be organized' mathematically. 'A bus stops. Three people get off the bus, while five people get on. What has happened to the number of people on the bus?' Or, 'Jan sets off to walk from the

15-kilometre mark and gets to the 23-kilometre mark. How far has he walked?' Second, the dual use of mathematical and pedagogical models (*model of* the situation and *model for* the mathematics) allows strategies that are intuitive in a familiar cultural context to translate into mathematical strategies and, on reflection in dialogue, translate into new, intuitively grounded mathematical knowledge. For example, the case of integers and the double abacus described in Chapter 4 illustrated how vertical mathematization can link new mathematics to situated intuitions.

A central place in our pedagogy has been found for mathematical 'communication' and this follows from all that has been argued from a Vygotskyan perspective. In a sense, all classroom discourse and even all mathematics text *is* communication. This point of view allows for our pedagogy to benefit from linguistics and semiotic theory. One can then analyse mathematical models as metaphors in the cognitive linguistic and 'embodied cognition' tradition.[39] In this view mathematics is situated in the body, in space and time, as well as socioculturally and historically. This can allow one to 'place' mathematics spatially in relation to one's body, and hence in relation to non-verbal, gestural and deictic, embodied elements of communication. Thus the number line has been shown to 'embody' the various models of number that we need, such as number as 'point on a line of ordered points', number as 'stick of a certain length'; but it has also been shown that the number line thereby offers pedagogical communication about number that is 'embodied' in gestures and deictic modes of communication. This informality of communication is vital in the critical, exploratory stages of problem solving and of significant learning, as Barnes and others suggested.[40]

It has become a cliché that 80 per cent of communication in face-to-face situations is non-verbal, but there is good evidence to suggest that non-verbal and informal verbal communication is critical at certain significant moments, and grows in importance especially when there are mathematical models present to give them explicit meaning. This is the case with the number line, the graph, the use of any sort of table or diagram that mathematically organizes space. In the context of mathematics and science the gestural content of new learning can be, at the crucial moment, in contradiction to, and often *in advance* of the verbal.[41] This fits well with the research that also suggests that when a new thought is to be verbalized, the gesticulation that serves to summon the word to consciousness occurs in advance of the verbalization. It seems that we have mental actions that are constructed from or with bodily actions that have been mentally internalized with a spatial structure – facial gestures reveal the internal spatial organization of memory when one is asked to recall some incident – typically the eyeball looks upwards in its socket as the accompaniment to this recall activity.

To take the simple example of the work on integers, we argued in Chapter 5 that the physical-spatial structure of the double abacus affords gestures and deictics, and that these precede the crucial 'semiotic contraction' of the term 'score', which is the pre-algebraic equivalent of the integer. Understanding the culturally mediated semiotics of communication is therefore essential to our pedagogy.[42] In addition to the use of gestures, the use of deictics in such informal communication has been emphasized in our research. For instance, it was shown that the provision of a simple picture into a group discussion can lead to the increase in use of deictics in the ensuing discussion (see Chapter 4, on ratio).

In conclusion, models that help to mediate mathematics spatially have crucial affordances that correlate with bodily as well as verbal communication between people, and thus also between speech-and-gesture and internalization. The RME notion of 'model of' that is found to be so practical in pedagogic design now seems theoretically well grounded in theoretical principles of communication. We associated the shift to 'model for' mathematics with the shift in activity that comes in schooling when it is recognized that the teacher has the right to introduce new mathematical signs to an activity. Thus the Freudenthal shift is associated with the CHAT notion of activity that is at the boundary of two systems: on the one side is the 'everyday world' that is 'begging to be organized' and on the other is the 'schooling' world that provides scientific tools – in this case mathematical signs and concepts with which to do the organizing. The schooling activity that the pedagogy crucially mediates proves its value to the extent that mathematics truly does reveal scientific value – that is, essential insights into the everyday world that remain hidden if discourse is restricted to 'common sense'.

Conclusion

We have argued for a theory of pedagogy that includes:

- Vygotsky's theory of learning and teaching as joint mathematically mediated activity in the CHAT sense, with 'everyday mathematics' serving as the *object* of 'schooling' activity mediated by richly distributed pedagogic discourses
- Freudenthal's didactical phenomenology of mathematics as a 'human activity' invoking reinvention, through modelling and problem solving
- 'dialogue' between conflicting argumentations based in the contradiction between the 'everyday' situated, intuitive discourse and the 'scientifically' more advanced mathematical pedagogic discourse[43]
- purposeful mathematical activity in classrooms as dialogically and collectively mediated communication and inquiry
- modelling (of and for) and models and metaphors that afford

spatial, embodied and informal deictic forms of mathematical communication

- a critical mathematical 'literacy' mediated by explicit pedagogic discourses in the sense of mathematics mediating learners' leading activity, and hence
- multiple models of ways of becoming some kind of mathematician – a user, a learner or a professional mathematician.

In this description we are aware that our original contribution has been small, perhaps in some of the studies in small-group argumentation and small-group teaching experiments, in our development of the theory of modelling and models, and in surveys of performance that reveal the scale of the need to address misconceptions and errors. We hope, though, that we have here helped a new generation of mathematics educators to begin to see the relevance of theory, the need for much more research, and to envision how current work might begin to help make sense of mathematics education.

Notes

1 Engestrom (1987); Cole and Engestrom (1993); Engestrom and Cole (1997).
2 Telos, after Lave (1996). This can be harder than it sounds: when a mathematician learns arithmetic they typically forget the early stages through which they progressed. We would argue this 'forgetting' is an essential part of mathematical growth and development.
3 Gagné's 'conditions of learning' was a key influence in the field and in mathematics in particular. The debate continues with psychologists in that tradition, such as Anderson *et al.* (see next note).
4 Anderson *et al.* (1996, 1997). The isolation of particular skills that demand practice and perfection is contrasted with the embedding of the practice within a cultural context – for example, of problem solving.
5 Denvir and Brown (1986) showed this.
6 Bruner's work over several decades has evolved in this direction: Bruner (1966, 1986, 1990, 1996).
7 For example, see Ashlock (2005).
8 Piaget and Inhelder (1974).
9 Piaget (1970).
10 Donaldson (1978); Hughes (1986).
11 Wood (1998).
12 Bernstein (1996).
13 Ausubel (1968).
14 Adey and Shayer (1994).
15 Vygotskii (1987).

16 Vygotsky (1978)

17 Vygotsky (1981, p. 163). Empirically Vygotsky was able to demonstrate the validity of this in regard to the egocentric and inner speech of the child; in contrast to Piaget's view that this speech dies away as the child becomes less egocentric, he found that egocentric speech was the transitional means by which the child comes to control their own play activity, and hence the means by which language becomes internalized at the higher-level mental functions.

18 Sfard (1998, 2001).

19 Wartofsky (1979) notes the reflexivity in (iii) – that is, languages can speak of themselves.

20 Williams and Wake (2007a) have offered a number of these from workplace activity.

21 Noss *et al.* (2002); Lave (1988); Chaiklin and Lave (1993).

22 Strathern (2000, 2006).

23 Nunes *et al.* (1993).

24 Tuomi-Grohn *et al.* (2003) on the importance of boundaries to introducing contradictions.

25 Williams, Corbin and McNamara (under review).

26 Lave and Wenger (1991); Wenger (1998).

27 Lave (1988).

28 Corbin *et al.* (2003); Williams, Corbin and McNamara (under review).

29 Mercer (1995).

30 Bell *et al.* (1985).

31 See accounts of work by Galperin and Davydov in Cobb *et al.* (1996); Renshaw (1996); Stetsenko and Arievitch (2002); and Chaiklin (2002). In fact Freudenthal (1991) criticized Galperin's approach, and Cobb *et al.* developed this critique to Davydov's pre- and post-glasnost formulations of AT in mathematics education, both regarding it as not mathematically humane or child centred: the Russian literature was then and is still not easily available in the West, leading to probable misunderstandings, but the critique is that 'mathematics' is conceived of as in modern mathematics as structural, modern, professional mathematics. What the essence of 'mathematics' *is* remains a critical question.

32 Wells (1999); Bereiter (1997).

33 Lemke (1990).

34 Mercer (2000).

35 Wells (1999).

36 Lipman *et al.* (1980). See also many others, such as Splitter and Sharp (1995).

37 Cobb and Bauersfeld (1995); Cobb *et al.* (2000).

38 Stetsenko and Arievitch (2002); Chaiklin (2002).

39 Williams and Wake (2007b); Lakoff and Nunez (2000); also the work on gestures – for example, Radford (2003).

40 Barnes (1976); Barnes and Todd (1995).

41   Roth (2001). See also Williams (2005) for older references to McNiel, Kendon, Goldin-Meadow, Radford and many others.
42   Koukkoufis and Williams (2006, in press).
43   A crucial assumption in this pedagogy is that the curriculum is right – that is, that it really does offer more mathematically advanced scientific concepts for apprehending important aspects of the learner's concerns in leading activities.

Appendix 1: Common errors and misconceptions

This appendix provides a selection of data from the Mathematics Assessment for Learning and Teaching (MaLT) project database, which comprises a set of written paper-and-pencil tests standardized on large national samples for each age group from 5 to 14 years. These tests are complemented by computer adaptive versions for primary and secondary ages. The whole package is published by Hodder & Stoughton.

For each 'interesting' item selected here we give:

- the descriptor for the question and the percentage of the relevant year group who correctly answered the question (the facility)
- the significant error made on that test item and its frequency as a percentage of the year group
- the explanation or 'diagnosis' we suggest for each error, based where possible on previous research – this should be regarded as provisional, even hypothetical
- a description of the item and its reference in the MaLT tests so that it can be located for further study and research (see MaLT, 2005); we also give the scale score (SS) for the item, which is a measure of difficulty of the item independent of the year group.

So, looking at the first row of the table, the question designed to assess 5-year-olds' ability to 'Count reliably up to ten everyday objects in a row' was successfully completed by 77 per cent of the sample of 5-year-olds (actually the population was a representative sample of approximately 1000 English reception classes in March 2005); 6 per cent of the 5-year-olds 'miscount by one', which we interpret as a 'faulty numeral sequence' OR 'faulty one-to-one principle'. In fact the question asks the children (orally by the teacher) to, 'Circle 5 (of 8) candles', the brackets round the 8 serve to suggest that the picture in the children's response booklet offered 8 candles. The question M5.1 can be found in MaLT5, question 1 of the test for 5-year-olds. In fact we discuss this item in Chapter 4 and a rough approximation to its figure can be seen there. (Incidentally the computerized version targeted at those aged 8 years and above does not offer oral items and operates only on the items from the written tests.) Finally, the scale score is 27, so this is clearly a very easy item.

Technical note

The scale score (SS) is obtained from a vertical equation of all the items and children in the database, as in Figure 1.1, where 1 logit = 5 scale score points; indeed the equation is SS = 61 + 5*(logit). This is best interpreted with the following average scale scores in mind:

Table of average (median) scale scores for ages 5 to 14 years

Age (years)	5.0	6.0	7.0	8.0	9.0	10.0	11.0	12.0	13.0	14.0
Average scale score	35	44	50.5	56	60	64	68	70	71	73

Add to this that the interquartile range is about 2 logits = 10 scale score points and this provides for approximate conversions for facility in a given year group to scale score, and vice versa. It also allows the teacher-researcher to build a subscale of items from different years; an example is given in Chapter 4 (see page 64).

5-year-olds: oral items

NUMBER AND MEASUREMENT Descriptor (Facility)	Error Description (Making error)	Diagnosis of error	Item MaLT reference Scale score
Count reliably up to ten everyday objects in a row 77%	Miscounts by one 6%	Faulty numeral sequence OR Faulty one-to-one principle	Circle 5 (of 8) candles M5.1 SS 27
Work out *how many more* to make a larger number of objects 15%	'Counts all' rather than 'counts on' when comparing sets of objects in alignment 42%	Two-step task complexity OR 'How many more' heard as 'how many'	How many more girls (9) than boys (6) M5.6 SS 47
Use language such as 'more' to compare two quantities of objects 83%	Identifies the longer set of objects in alignment 14%	'Longer is more' misconception for a set of objects	Circle who has more bears (5 spread out) M5.16 SS 25
Work out by counting *how many more* to make a larger number in a practical problem context 45%	Counts only one set of objects 26%	Two-step task complexity	7 children and only 4 brushes – how many have not got a brush? M5.23 SS 36
Multiplicative problem in real context: (3×2) 19%	Attends to only one number in the problem 44%	Two-step task complexity	Each bun 2 cherries, how many on 3? (one bun shown) M5.18 SS 43
Count reliably up to ten everyday objects in a complex array 69%	Counts one more or one less 18%	Loses track of starting object	Count beads on a necklace (9) M5.19 SS 30
Write *one more than* a number from 1 to 10 75%	Correct number but reverses numerals: 01 for 10 6%	Writing reversal	(Book shown) . . . the page just after 9 M5.20 SS 27

Write *one less than* a number from 2 to 10 54%	Writes next digit for 'one less than 7' 19%	Confuses 'just before' with 'just after'	(Book shown) Write page just before 7 M5.28 SS 34
Begin to relate addition to combining two groups of objects by counting all the objects 65%	Counts only one set of objects 11%	Misunderstanding of 'altogether'	5 hats and 2 hats (visible) M5.22 SS 31
Begin to relate the addition of *doubles* to counting on 20%	Counts visible objects only 37%	Lack of imagery	Two cars have _ wheels altogether? (cars show 2 each) M5.25 SS 44
Begin to relate subtraction to 'taking away' and counting how many are left from a set of objects 72%	Writes the number taken away 7% $5 - 2 = 4$: counts 5, 4 5%	Two-step task complexity Counting numerals	. . . 5 cakes, she eats 2 (5 shown) . . . how many left? M5.26 SS 29
Begin to relate addition to combining two groups of objects 60%	Writes number in one set only 13% 6 objects and 3 objects is 8 objects: counts 6, 7, 8 6%	Two-step task complexity Counting numerals	6 apples and 3 more (all visible) M5.27 SS 32
Perform simple addition to a total of 10: number bonds 21%	Selects $5 + 5$ only 17% Selects $2 + 8$ only 9%	Two-step task complexity	Cards that add up to 10? ($2 + 8$, $5 + 5$) M5.29 SS 43
Find a total by counting on when one group of objects in hidden 48%	Counts only the visible objects 24%	Two-step task complexity OR Misunderstanding of 'altogether'	Pack of three (not visible) and 5 more M5.30 SS 36

SHAPE AND SPACE Descriptor (Facility)	Error Description (Making error)	Diagnosis of error	Item MaLT reference Scale score
Use language to describe flat shapes: square 80%	'Vertical' rectangle identified as square 12%	Square is common window shape (shape prototype)	Tick the square (rectangles also given) M5.2 SS 26
Use language to describe flat shapes: triangle 46%	Does not include non-prototypical triangles 33%	Equilateral prototype OR Orientation prototype	Circle all triangles (various incl. curved sides shown) M5.9 SS 37
Recognize and recreate simple sequence of shapes 32%	Interprets shape pattern as a single alternating: A B B A B B A B A 41%	Two-step task complexity OR pattern means alternating	Shape that comes next? A B B A B B A B _ M5.15 SS 40

6-year-olds: oral items

NUMBER Descriptor (Facility)	Error Description (Making error)	Diagnosis of error	Item MaLT reference Scale score
Count back in ones from any small number on number line 25%	Counts forwards from left 'end-point' of number line: 1, 2, . . . rather than back from 4: 4, 3, 2 71%	Ordinal prototype OR No zero in number sequence	Put tick at '2' on line marked _, _, _, _, 4, _, 6, 7, 8, _ M6.2 SS 51
Read numerals from 0 to at least 20 88%	Reads two numerals back to front (e.g. selects 12 for '21') 9%	Place value misconception OR Reading reversal	Identify the number 'twenty-one' as '21' M6.3 SS 30
Write numerals from 0 to at least 20 75%	Writes 61 for 'sixteen' 9%	Place value misconception OR Writing reversal	Write the number 'sixteen' M6.7 SS 36
	Writes 16 for 'sixteen' and reflects or rotates the 6 8%	Writing reversal	
Extend number sequences from 0 to 20 or more 73%	7, 8 Does not identify counting by 2s 11%	'Sequences go up in 1s' prototype	Write the next two numbers: 2, 4, 6, _, _ M6.8 SS 36
Extend number sequences for 0 to 20 or more 40%	Identifies counting by 5s as by 1s 18%	'Sequences go up in 1s' prototype	Write the next number 5, 10, 15, 20, 25, _ M6.4 SS 45
	Identifies counting by 5s as by 10s 5%	'Sequences go up in 10s' prototype	
Extend number sequences for 0 to 20 or more 55%	Does not identify counting down by 10s 36%		Write down the number that comes next: 60, 50, 40, 30, _ M6.24 SS 42
	Counts up rather than counts down by 10 4%	Two-step task complexity	

Begin to use the signs for addition and equals in a number sentence 38%	Counts on inaccurately: 15 + 5 = 19 9%	Counts numerals	Write the missing number 15 + _ = 19 M6.6 SS 47
Begin to use the signs for subtraction and equals in a number sentence 55%	9 – 3 = 7 Counts back 9, 8, 7 8%	Counts numerals	Write in the missing numbers: 9 – 3 = _ M6.25a SS 42
	Counts on in a subtraction problem 8%	Addition number sentence prototype	
Begin to use the signs for subtraction and equals in a number sentence 37%	Counts back inaccurately: 9 – 7 = 3 11%	Counts numerals	Write in the missing numbers: 9 – _ = 3 M6.25b SS 47
Count pairs reliably up to 10 everyday objects 79%	Counts pairs of socks rather than number of socks 7%	Two-part complexity Comprehension problem	How many socks are there altogether? (7 pairs shown) M6.15 SS 35
Count reliably up to 10 everyday objects in pairs 42%	Counts number of mittens rather than pairs of mittens 43%	Does not see a pair as a unit	How many pairs of mittens are there altogether? (7 pairs shown) M6.19 SS 45
Know doubles of numbers to at least 5 65%	Writes 33 for the number that is 'double 3' 11%	Literal conception of 'double'	What number is double three? M6.16 SS 40
	Writes the next number: 4 3%	No conception of 'double'	
Know doubles of numbers more than 5 43%	Writes 77 for 'double 7' 12%	Literal conception of 'double'	What is double 7? M6.17 SS 46
	Writes next number: 8 9%	No conception of 'double'	

Find a total by counting when one group of objects is hidden (and circle answer on a number line) 51%	Writes visible number of objects only 5%	Comprehension problem	3 eggs in a box (shown) and 8 eggs in the other (hidden) . . . altogether? M6.21 SS 43
	Writes *hidden* number of objects only 13%	Comprehension problem	
Add pairs of numbers with a total up to at least 20 (and circle answer on a number line) 45%	Recognizes that counting is required but doubles one short $9 + 9 = 19$ 13%	Counting the numerals in a problem-solving context	9 eggs in each box. How many altogether? M6.22 SS 45
Write one more than a number from 1 to 30 75%	Writes number one before 5%	Confuses 'just after' with 'just before'	What number comes just after nineteen? M6.23a SS 36
	Correct but reflects number: 02 for 20 6%	Writing reversal	
Write one less than a number from 1 to 30 54%	Writes incorrect number one less than 30 39%	Counting through a ten problem	What number comes just before thirty? M6.23b SS 42
Begin to know what each digit in a 2-digit number represents and solve problems 11%	3 bundles of ten sticks and 2 single sticks less 3 sticks is 2 sticks 23%	Confuses 'tens' and 'units' suggesting a place value misconception	How many sticks are left? (3 bundles of ten and 2, take away 3) M6.28 SS 58

MEASUREMENT **Descriptor** **(Facility)**	**Error** **Description** **(Making error)**	**Diagnosis of error**	**Item** **MaLT reference** **Scale score**
Measure using non-standard units with end-points aligned 74%	Counts units correctly but reflects the answer digit 7 17%	Writing reversal	The toothbrush is _ paperclips long? M6.10 SS 37
Measure using non-standard units with end-points of 'object' not aligned to 'ruler' 50%	Counts all the units shown in the 'ruler' 36%	End-points of paperclips not matched to end of comb	The comb is _ paperclips long? M6.11 SS 44

Measure and compare lengths in non-standard units: *how much longer* 18%	Counts only the longer measure 50%	Two-step task complexity AND/OR Misunderstands 'How much longer?' instruction	The toothbrush is _ paperclips longer than the comb? M6.12 SS 54
Suggest suitable measuring equipment to measure length or capacity 19%	Does not agree that a ruler can measure a door 55%	Ruler must be longer than item measured	. . . measure with a ruler: weight of parcel, height of door, width of book?' M6.13 SS 53
Understand the vocabulary related to time and read clocks 25%	Selects clock for last mentioned hour: 2 hours later than 11 o'clock is 2 o'clock 37%	Two-step task complexity	Clock faces: . . . 11 o'clock . . . 2 hours later . . . what time? M6.18 SS 51

7-year-olds: oral items

NUMBER Descriptor (Facility)	Error Description (Making errror)	Diagnosis of error	Item MaLT reference Scale score
Count back in steps of 5 from any given 2-digit number (sequence . . . 25, 30, 35 . . .) 68%	Does not continue sequence: 35, 30, 25, *15* 7%	Two-step task complexity	Write 15 in number line: _ _ _ 25 30 35 _ _ M7.2 SS 47
Count back in 10s from any given 2-digit number (sequence . . . 53, 63, 73, . . .) 38%	Counts forwards from left 'end-point' of number line: 3, 13 rather than back from 53 20%	Prototype sequence OR Skips a ten	Tick the box where 13 goes M7.8a SS 53
Count forward in 10s from any 2-digit number (sequence 53, 63, 73, . . .) 30%	One number off target 17% End-point of number line 38%	Skipping through 100 'Largest number to end' prototype	Put a cross where 113 goes M7.8b SS 57
Complete a number sentence 'ten less than *what* is 40' 47%	Subtracts rather than adds 22%	Number sentence syntax complexity: working backwards	Ten less than forty is what? M7.10 SS 52
Find 'ten more than' any given 2-digit number 73%	Correct but reverses the 9 digit in 90 6%	Writing reversal	Ten more than eighty is what? M7.9 SS 44
Count on in ones from a 2-digit number (sequence . . . 47, 48, 49, . . .) 66%	One number short of target *bridging through* a ten 12%	Skipping through a ten	Write 53 in the correct box M7.5 SS 46
Recognize multiples of 5 39%	Includes 51 as a multiple of 5 40%	Multiples have a 5 digit anywhere OR No knowledge of term	Circle all the . . . multiples of five M7.7 SS 54
	Selects only one multiple 10%	Multiples of 5 end in 5 OR No knowledge of term	

MEASURE Descriptor (Facility)	Error Description (Making error)	Diagnosis of error	Item MaLT reference Scale score
Recognize one half of a small number of objects (4 oranges on plate and 4 off) 14%	Selects ¼ as fraction for 4 out of 8 objects 38%	Identifies wrong unit suggesting a ratio–fraction misconception	What fraction of these oranges are on the plate? M7.11 SS 63
	Selects ¼ as fraction for 4 out of 8 objects 7%	Unit fraction prototype	
Understand the = sign and add 3 single-digit numbers 71%	$8 + 3 + 5 = 15$ 7%	Counting numerals OR Faulty number bonds	Fill in the missing . . . $8 + 3 + 5 = \_$ M7.14a SS 45
Understand the = sign and add 3 single-digit numbers 53%	$8 + 7 + 1 = 14$ OR $22 + 7 + 1 = 14$ Adding visible numbers 8%	Number sentence syntax complexity: working backwards	$\_ + 7 + 1 = 14$ M7.14b SS 50
Use mental recall of the 3 and 4 times multiplication table, or count all in 4 boxes of 3 61%	Counts visible units 7%	Lack of multiplicative reasoning	A box contains 3 balls. In 4 boxes there are _ balls M7.15a SS 48
Subtract numbers with 2 digits 19%	Subtracts smaller from larger digit in a horizontal number sentence 7%	'Smaller from larger' digit subtraction prototype	$42 - 27 = ?$ M7.19 SS 60
Choose appropriate operation to solve problems 30%	Selects addition $(12 + 6)$ for multiplication problem 33%	Lack of multiplicative reasoning OR Additive prototype	. . . 12 rows, 6 bottles in each . . . select . . . M7.25 SS 57
MEASURE Descriptor (Facility)	**Error Description (Making error)**	**Diagnosis of error**	**Item MaLT reference Scale score**
Recognize right angle (as a turn) 53%	Selects answer on right-hand side of page 26%	Lack of knowledge of the term 'right angle'	Circle the right angle M7.17 SS 50

SHAPE AND SPACE Descriptor (Facility)	Error Description (Making error)	Diagnosis of error	Item MaLT reference Scale score
Use language to describe 3D shapes 61%	Names a cube as a 'square' 30%	2D prototype	'Circle . . . name' for cubes M7.1 SS 48

HANDLING DATA Descriptor (Facility)	Error Description (Making error)	Diagnosis of error	Item MaLT reference Scale score
Extract and interpret data in a bar chart (times to travel home) 68%	Selects person with tallest box 26%	Two-step task complexity OR prototype	Who arrives home first? M7.6 SS 46

8-year-olds

NUMBER Descriptor (Facility)	Error Description (Making error)	Diagnosis of error	Item MaLT reference Scale score
Extend number sequences by counting on in 10s (62, 72, ?, 92, ?) 89%	Counts correctly by 10s up to 100 only 8%	Counting through 100 problem	Fill in the missing numbers M8.1b SS 41
Know number bond pairs to 100 for numbers of tens 84%			60 + _ = 100 M8.3a SS 44
Know number bond pairs to 100 for numbers of tens and units 46%	79 + 31 = 100 12% Answers 20 or 30 11%	Counting on to 100 problem Ignoring units	79 + _ = 100 M8.3b SS 56
Recognize unit fractions such as one-quarter 81%	Shades all 4 sectors of the shape for 'one-quarter (¼)' 3%	No part–whole conception of fraction OR Shade denominator value	Shade ¼ of cake (4 sections visible) M8.4a SS 45
Recognize unit fractions such as one-quarter and use to find fractions of shapes 39%	Shades 1 sector of the shape divided into 8 equal sectors 43%	Unit-fraction prototype	Shade ¼ of cake (8 sections visible) M8.4b SS 58
	Shades 4 sectors of the shape 9%	Shade denominator value	
Recognize unit fractions such as one-quarter 26%	Selects only one correct shape or includes an incorrect one 22%	Multi-step task complexity?	Tick the shape/shapes with ¼ shaded M8.10 SS 62

Identifies ⅓ as 'one-quarter (¼)'
9%
Ratio-fraction misconception

Recognize simple fractions that are several parts of a whole and simple equivalent fractions 7%	Selects ¼ for shaded ⅛ 33% Recognizes ½ but not equivalences ¾ and ⅛ 26%	Ratio-fraction 'unit' misconception Equivalence misconception	Tick statements that are true for circle (4 out of 8 parts shaded): ½, ¼, ¾, ¼, ⅛ shaded M8.19 SS 71
Demonstrate subtraction facts for each number to 20 78%	20 – 7 = 17 7%	Avoidance of counting down strategy	20 – 7 = _ M8.7b SS 48
Understand and use notation for money (£ and p) to solve a word problem 65%	Selects £1.08 or 18p for £1.80 22% Selects £180 for £1.80 7%	Place value problem with decimal currency Ignoring monetary unit	A choc bar costs 60p. . . . three choc bars cost . . . 18p, £1.08, £1.80, £180 M8.8 SS 51
Understand and use notation for money (£ and p), and make sensible decisions about rounding in a division problem context 33%	Writes 'I can buy 3 pencils (at 35p each) with £1' 22%	Rounding in context problem	. . . costs 35p. How many for £1.00? M8.14 SS 60
Write a number halfway between two 1-digit numbers 72%	5 is halfway between 3 and 9 10%	Estimation	Number line: . . . halfway between 3 and 9 is _ M8.9a SS 49
Write a number halfway between two 2-digit numbers on a number line 71%	Counting intervals on scaled number line 9%	'Unit scale' prototype	Number line: halfway between 50 and 70 is _ M8.9b SS 49
Recognize multiples of 5 61%	Identifies only some of the multiples 13% Includes 51 as a multiple of 5 11%	Multi-step complexity Multiples have a 5 digit anywhere OR No knowledge of term	Circle the . . . multiples of 5 M8.12 SS 52

Find the double of a number without bridging through a ten 69%			Double 24 M8.13a SS 50
Find the double of a number without bridging through a ten 50%	Double 38 is 68 8%	Ignoring the units digit when doubling	Double 38 M8.13b SS 55
Count back and forwards in 30s from a given 3-digit number 23%	Makes mistake bridging through a hundred 20%	'Sequences go by 10s' prototype OR Miscounting through a hundred	Fill in . . . _, 900, 870, 840, 810, _ M8.18 SS 63
Recognize that addition is commutative but subtraction is not 23%	States $a - b = b - a$ 25%	Subtraction is commutative misconception	Tick/cross: $125 + 285 = 285 + 125$ $546 - 124 = 124 - 546$ M8.21a SS 63
Recognize that multiplication is commutative but division is not 24%	States $a \div b = b \div a$ 27%	Division is commutative misconception	Tick/cross: $25 \times 2 = 12 \times 25$ $400 \div 80 = 80 \div 400$ M8.21b SS 63
Subtract 2-digit numbers 44%	Subtracts smaller from larger digit in horizontal number sentence 6%	'Smaller from larger' digit subtraction prototype	$37 - 18 = \_$ M8.22 SS 57
Know what each digit represents in a 4-digit number 22%	Selects 8012 for 8 hundred and 12 units 23%	Place value misconception	. . . 8 hundreds, 0 tens, 12 units = _ M8.28 SS 64
	Selects 80012 for 8 hundred and 12 units 16%	Place value misconception	
Write whole numbers in figures and words 51%	Writes 214 or 20014 for 'two thousand and fourteen' 13%	Place value misconception	Two thousand and fourteen M8.33b SS 55

Choose appropriate operation to solve problems 17%	Selects multiplication sign for division problem 26%	Partial recognition of a multiplicative situation	12 eggs in a box . . . Jack has 60 eggs. Which calculation . . . for how many boxes? M8.29 SS 65
	Selects division sign but incorrect order 13%	Division is commutative misconception	
Demonstrate basic division facts 28%	Interprets division sign as addition 15%	Division sign not known	Fill in: ÷ = 5 M8.34 SS 61

MEASUREMENT Descriptor (Facility)	**Error Description (Making error)**	**Diagnosis of error**	**Item MaLT reference Scale score**
Estimate the weight of an object when rounded to the nearest 10 grams 19%	Interpreting 'to the nearest 10' as 'to within 10 of' 30%	Syntax problem: working backwards	. . . 170 g to the nearest ten . . . could be _ grams M8.11 SS 64
Use units of time and know the relationships between them 25%	Treats hours and minutes separately 16%	100 minutes in an hour misconception	. . . at 9:20, . . . 50 minutes later = _ M8.16 SS 62
Read scales accurately in whole numbers 32%	Counts each interval on a scale as one unit 17%	'Unit scale' prototype	Write down the measurement on the ruler, in cms M8.23 SS 60
	Ignores scale 27%	Estimating	
Read analogue clock to the quarter hour 25%	Misreads hands of clock 31%	Hour and minute hand confusion	What time does this clock show? (2:45) M8.30 SS 62
	Next hour for 'quarter to' the hour 11%	Reading closest hour numeral for hour	

SHAPE AND SPACE Descriptor (Facility)	Error Description (Making error)	Diagnosis of error	Item MaLT reference Scale score
Recognize half-turns of a shape 28%	Selects the quarter-turn 27%	Confusing half- and quarter-turns	This card . . . by its corner . . . turns . . . a half turn M8.15 SS 62

HANDLING DATA Descriptor (Facility)	Error Description (Making error)	Diagnosis of error	Item MaLT reference Scale score
Interpret numerical data in a pictogram 33%	Does not use key (book = 5) in pictogram 56%	'Picture as single unit' prototype	How many books (in pictogram) M8.17a SS 60

9-year-olds

NUMBER Descriptor (Facility)	Error Description (Making error)	Diagnosis of error	Item MaLT reference Scale score
Subtract 2-digit numbers 75%	Writes 40 – 21 = 29 5%	Making a 'carry' error	Fill in . . . 40 – 21 = _ M9.3 SS 52
	Subtracts smaller from larger digit in *horizontal* number sentence 4%	'Smaller from larger' digit subtraction prototype	
Subtract 3-digit numbers using written methods 30%	Subtracts smaller from larger digit in *vertical* layout 17%	'Smaller from larger' digit subtraction prototype	Vertical format: 458 – 162 = _ M9.26 SS 65
Round positive integer to the nearest 10 48%	Rounds some but not all numbers 31%	Multi-step task complexity	Circle the numbers that . . . make 50 when rounded to the nearest ten M9.6 SS 59
	Rounds 59 to 50 as the nearest ten 10%	Rounding understood as truncating	
Understand and use notation for money (£ and p) 39%	Writes £3.5(0) for £3.05 50%	Place value misconception	How much . . . altogether: £1+£1+£1+5p = _ M9.8 SS 63
Find 100 less than a 4-digit number on a scaled number line 45%	Counts back by 10 rather than 100 15%	Scale 'unit of 10' prototype OR Place value problem	What number does arrow point to? (one step of 100 short of 6000) M9.9 SS 61

Complete a number sentence involving division 21%	$1 \div 9 = 9$ 26%	Syntax error: reads ÷ as 'into' OR Division is commutative misconception OR Number sentence syntax complexity: working backwards	Write in missing number: _ $\div 9 = 9$ M9.14b SS 69
	Interprets division sign as addition 8%	Division sign not known	
Recognize and order negative numbers in a temperature context 52%	Orders integers by digit only: 0, –1, 5, –10, 20 23%	'Negative sign ignored' error	Write in order: 5, –10, 0, 20, –1 (°C) M9.16 SS 59
	Orders negative numbers by digit: –1, –10, 0, 5, 20 6%	Integers conceived as two separate objects: 'sign' and 'the number'	
Choose appropriate operation to solve a problem 39%	Selects multiplication sign for a division problem 24%	Incomplete multiplicative conception	24 go sailing, 4 in each boat . . . circle the (calculation) M9.23 SS 62
	Selects $4 \div 24$ for $24 \div 4$ 17%	Syntax error: reads ÷ as 'into' OR Division is commutative misconception	
Recognize unit fractions: one-quarter (¼) 3%	Includes shape divided into unequal parts as one-quarter 75%	Incomplete part–whole fraction conception OR Visual distraction of equal width of strips	Circle all the shapes . . . one-quarter (¼) shaded M9.27 SS 79
Count back in 10s from any whole number up to 10,000 32%	$4000 - 10 = 3090$ 18% $4000 - 10 = 3900$ 9% $4000 - 10 = 3000$ 8%	Place value misconception OR 'Carrying' error	What . . . is ten less than 4000? M9.30 SS 65

Recognize fraction equivalence between thirds and sixths 15%	Selects ⅔ = 3/2 56%	Numerator-denominator comparison misconception	. . . the same as ⅔: ¾, ½, 3/2, 4/6, ⅓? M9.34 SS 71
	Selects ⅔ = ¾ OR ⅔ = ½ 13%	Additive misconception	
Know that division is the inverse of multiplication 10%	? ÷ 5 – 45 Answers ? = 9 38%	Number sentence syntax problem OR Use visible numbers and operations conception	Fill in: _ : 5 = 45 M9.35 SS 74

MEASUREMENT **Descriptor** **(Facility)**	**Error** **Description** **(Making error)**	**Diagnosis of error**	**Item** **MaLT reference** **Scale score**
Find perimeter of a simple shape by counting 20%	Counts the grid squares surrounding the shape rather than edges 26%	Counting objects rather than lengths	'. . . distance round the outside' of compound shape M9.10 SS 69
Interpret non-unit scales accurately using decimals 10%	Counts each interval on a scale as one decimal unit 49%	'Unit scale' prototype	Read non-unit scale and convert to unit scale M9.21 SS 73
Find the area of a simple shape using counting 44%	Counts half squares as whole squares 15%	Consistency of unit ignored	'Find area of shape' with half-grid units shaded M9.22 SS 62
	Counts whole squares only 14%	Fractions ignored	
Convert kilograms to grams 51%	Writes 2 kilograms is 200 grams 18%	100 g in a kg (derived from 100 p in a £)	Two kilograms is same as 2, 20, 200, 2000 grams M9.32 SS 59

SHAPE and SPACE Descriptor (Facility)	Error Description (Making error)	Diagnosis of error	Item MaLT reference Scale score
Identify a hexagon from a mixed set of shapes 60%	Includes six-pointed star as hexagon 10%	Vertex misconception	Tick all the shapes that are hexagons M9.13 SS 57
	Identifies the regular but not irregular hexagon 7%	Regularity prototype	
Identify shapes with no lines of symmetry 48%	Parallelogram has a line of symmetry 21%	Visual distraction of sloping parallel sides	Two of the shapes have no line of symmetry. Tick them. M9.31 SS 60
Identify the reflection of a simple shape in a mirror line parallel to one side of shape (vertical to page) 62%	Identifies the shape shifted as a reflection 15%	Reflection confused with translation	Which of the following shows a reflection? M9.37 SS 55

HANDLING DATA Descriptor (Facility)	Error Description (Making error)	Diagnosis of error	Item MaLT reference Scale score
Read and use the calendar 17%	Misses one condition of a three-part problem 9%	Multi-step task complexity	'. . . magazine . . . every two weeks on Mondays . . . First publication' next month is ? M9.11 SS 71
	Misses two conditions 15%	Multi-step task complexity	
Interpret numerical data in a pictogram 73%	Does not use key in pictogram 19%	'Picture as single unit' prototype	30 ice creams sold on Monday. How many on Wednesday? M9.15 SS 53

Interpret data in a table involving time in seconds (to 2 decimal places) 68%	The winning time in a race is the biggest number 12%	Two-step task complexity	. . . Table shows time taken to run 400-metre race. What is the winner's time? M9.19 SS 54
	62.50 < 62.32 5%	'Largest decimal is smallest' error	
Organize data on a Venn diagram (two criteria) 50%	Manages one criterion only 42%	Does not know that intersection represents 'both' criteria satisfied on Venn diagram	Write 40 in correct place: sets 'numbers with 4 in tens column' and 'even numbers' M9.7b SS 60
Read coordinates of points (first quadrant) not on axes 50%	Reverses coordinates: writes (2, 3) for (3, 2) 16%	Lack of knowledge of convention	Write coordinates for A M9.38a SS 60
Read coordinates of points (first quadrant) on an axis 32%	Reverses coordinates 11%	Lack of knowledge of convention	Write coordinates of B M9.38b SS 65
	Writes (1, 4) or (4, 1) for (0, 4) 21%	Rejects a zero coordinate	

10-year-olds

NUMBER Descriptor (Facility)	Error Description (Making error)	Diagnosis of error	Item MaLT reference Scale score
Write a number halfway between two 2-digit numbers on a number line 83%	Writes number one after or one before end-points 10%	Ignoring scale	Number line marked 17, 21, 25, 29 with arrow halfway between 17 and 21. 'Write the correct number' M10.2 SS 53
Divide a 3-digit number by a 2-digit number to solve a problem 15%	$280 \div 80 = 3$ 15%	Rounding down avoiding fractional time in hours	Car travels at 80 km per hour . . . How long to travel 280km? _ hours M10.19 SS 74
	$280 \div 80 = 4$ 10%	Rounding up avoiding fractional time in hours	
Reduce a fraction to simplest terms 59%	$\frac{4}{6} = \frac{1}{3}$ 6%	Unit fraction prototype OR Additive error (numerator and denominator difference)	Fill in the missing number: $\frac{4}{6} = \_/3$ M10.3a SS 60
	Doubles rather than halves: $\frac{4}{6} = \frac{8}{3}$ 8%	Multiplicative direction error	
Find simple percentages of numbers 40%	Writes 50% of $8 = 16$ 17%	Number sentence complexity: reversal	Fill in missing number: 50% of _ = 16 M10.5a SS 66
Find one-quarter of a number 31%	Writes A quarter of $4 = 16$ 25%	Number sentence complexity: reversal	Fill in missing number: a quarter of _ = 16 M10.5b SS 68

Find simple fraction of a shape 36%	Shades 2 parts of 6 parts for ⅔ 35%	Shade numerator value: fraction as 2 objects misconception	Rectangle divided into 6 equal parts: 'Shade in ⅔ of the shape'
	Shades 3 parts of 6 parts for ⅔ 15%	Shade denominator value: fraction as two separate objects – 'numerator' and 'denominator'	M10.9 SS 67
Solve simple problems using ideas of ratio and proportion using *doubling* 62%	Multiplies wrong numbers in recipe proportion (20 × 4): 10:4 = 20:*80* 7%	No proportional reasoning	Soup recipe for 10 using 4 potatoes. 'How many potatoes needed for soup for 20 people?' M10.10a SS 60
Solve simple problems involving ratio and proportion using *times-and-a-half* 25%	10:4 = *12*:6 16%	Additive error	Soup recipe for 10 showing 4 potatoes. 'She used 6 potatoes . . . how many people can she serve?' M10.10b SS 70
Choose and use appropriate operations to solve a problem 50%	Rounds incorrectly in a division task 23%	Failure to consider context (of packs)	Pack of 4 batteries: 'Each pack . . . costs £3.40. How many . . . with £10?' M10.14 SS 63
Recognize negative numbers in temperature context 64%	Locates −15 at +15 position on number line 19%	'Negative sign ignored' error	Thermometer (−30 to 20°C): 'Draw arrow to show −15°C' M10.15 SS 60
	Locates −15 at −5 position on number line 8%	Counting in wrong direction from −10	
Order positive and negative integers 42%	Orders negative numbers by digit: −5 > −1 28%	Integers conceived as two separate objects: 'sign' and 'the number'	True or false: −5 > −1 M10.29 SS 65
Order a set of whole numbers and one decimal number 62%	Orders 47, 143, 62.5 19%	'Whole number' prototype: decimals are 'other'	Write numbers in order . . . smallest to largest: 143, 62.5, 47 M10.17a SS 59

Order a set of whole numbers and decimal numbers 18%	Orders the decimals according to decimal digit(s): 62.5, 62.36, 62.72 34%	'Decimal point ignored' error	Write numbers in order from smallest to largest: 143, 62.5, 62.36, 47, 62.72 M10.17b SS 73
	Orders whole numbers first 20%	'Whole number' prototype: decimals are 'other' AND 'Decimal point ignored' error	
Count on in steps of 0.2 52%	0.2, 0.4, 0.6, 0.8, 0.10 34%	Bridging through a unit problem/decimal point ignored	Fill in missing number in sequence: 0.2, 0.4, 0.6, 0.8, _ M10.23 SS 63
Add 3-digit numbers using written methods (missing addend digit) 25%	Makes a carry error in vertical layout 20%	Structural complexity	Vertical layout: Write in missing digit: 3 _ 9 + 135 = 524 M10.24a SS 70
	Attempts to subtract 19%	Distraction	
Add decimals to 2 places 16%	Writes $0.7 + 0.51 = 0.58$ in horizontal layout 55%	Place value misconception: decimal part as whole number	Calculate: $0.7 + 0.51 = $ _ M10.30a SS 74
Use multiplication facts up to 10-times-10 in problem solving 24%	$61 \times 7 = 441$ 10%	Structural complexity AND $1 \times 7 = 1$	Vertical layout: Write the missing number: $6\_ \times 7 = 441$ M10.24b SS 71
Find a missing number in a division number sentence 41%	$1 \div 5 = 5$ 22%	Syntax error: reads $\div$ as 'into' OR Division is commutative misconception OR Number sentence syntax complexity: working backwards	Complete the number sentence: _ $\div 5 = 5$ M10.28b SS 65

MEASUREMENT Descriptor (Facility)	Error Description (Making error)	Diagnosis of error	Item MaLT reference Scale score
Read analogue clock and calculate time duration in minutes 28%	Writes 1 hour 30 minutes as 130, 1.3, 150 or 1.5 minutes 19%	Decimal time prototype OR 100 minutes in an hour misconception	Two clocks showing 11:15 and 12:45: Clocks show time film started and finished. How long did film last, in minutes? M10.4 SS 69
Convert grams to kilograms 7%	Writes 65 grams is 6.5 kilograms 41% Divides by 100 28%	Patterning from example: 1500 g given as 1.5 kg 100 g in 1 kg OR Patterning by estimation	Table shows weights of some fruits. A bag of pears 1500 grams is 1.5 kilograms. A bag of grapes 65 grams is _ kilograms M10.6b SS 77
Read non-unit scales accurately using decimals 20%	Counts each (0.2) interval on a scale as one decimal unit (0.1) 35%	'Unit scale' prototype	Scales show apples weighing between 2 and 3 kg. Scale marked in 0.2 intervals M10.18 SS 72
	Reads scale to nearest half or quarter fraction 16%	Avoiding decimal notation	

SHAPE and SPACE Descriptor (Facility)	Error Description (Making error)	Diagnosis of error	Item MaLT Reference Scale score
Recognize a 90° clockwise turn 54%	Selects anti-clockwise 90° degree turn 17%	Clockwise and anti-clockwise confusion	The number card (for 9) is turned clockwise through 90°. Circle correct card. M10.21 SS 62
	Selects half-turn 13%	'Half-turn' prototype	

Find the reflection of a simple shape in a mirror line parallel to one side of shape (sloping to page) 70%	Selects correct shape orientation but incorrect location 11%	Task complexity	Shape on grid with diagonal mirror line: Which picture shows the correct reflection of the triangle? M10.31 SS 57

HANDLING DATA **Descriptor** **(Facility)**	**Error** **Description** **(Making error)**	**Diagnosis of error**	**Item** **MaLT reference** **Scale score**
Interpret and compare numerical data in a pictogram 64%	Does not use key in pictogram 12%	'Picture as single unit' prototype	Children voted for favourite colour. How many more children voted red than blue? M10.11 SS 58
Extract and interpret information in tables (grouped data) 57%	Reads single interval '31 to 40' for '31 or older' 23%	Two-step task complexity	Table with 6 age bands: This table gives the ages of swimmers . . . How many are 31 or older? M10.13 SS 61
Extract and use information in tables (discrete intervals) 34%	Uses 'up to 3 hours' interval for '3 hours 25 minutes' 22%	Misinterprets interval description	Table with car park fees: Anne stayed for 3 hours and 25 minutes. How much did she pay? M10.16b SS 67
	Estimates proportional value 20%	Inappropriate interpolation in a discrete interval context	
Organize data on a Venn diagram (two criteria) 74%	Manages one criterion 18%	Does not know Venn diagram: intersection represents 'both'	'Multiples of 5' and 'multiples of 7': Write 45 and 56 in correct places M10.20 SS 56
Read and interpret a distance–time graph 19%	Rounds to nearest hour 28%	Rounding up or down avoiding fractional time in hours	Graph of journey. Hourly axis marked in quarter-hour scale: How many hours was she away from home? M10.32a SS 71

11-year-olds

NUMBER Descriptor (Facility)	Error Description (Making error)	Diagnosis of error	Item MaLT reference Scale score
Complete a number sentence involving division (using a calculator) 63%	$7 \div 5 = 35$ 27%	Syntax error: reads ÷ as 'into' OR Division is commutative misconception OR Number sentence syntax complexity: working backwards	Write in the missing number: _ ÷ 5 = 35 CALC M11.1 SS 64
Identify and use appropriate operation (*multiplication*) to solve 'real-life' word problems (using a calculator) 63%	Incorrectly inserts a decimal point for money when reading from a calculator display: 7044 becomes £70.44 14%	Patterning on experience of money	587 people went to the zoo. Each paid £12. Calculate total amount of money paid. CALC M11.6 SS 64
Identify and use appropriate operation (*division*) to solve 'real-life' word problems (using a calculator) 45%	Incorrectly rounds down rather than up OR Truncates decimal 19%	Does not check with real-life context	560 pupils went to a zoo by bus. Each bus carries 42 pupils. How many buses did they use? CALC M11.9 SS 69
Subtract 3-digit numbers using written methods (non-calculator) 68%	Subtracts smaller from larger digit in *vertical* layout 13%	'Smaller from larger' digit subtraction prototype	Vertical layout: Subtract: 567–185 M11.14 SS 62
Multiply a 3-digit number by a 1-digit number 43%	Makes a carry error in a vertical layout 5%	Two-step task complexity AND/OR Multiplication facts	Complete the long multiplication: 238 × 5 = _ _ _ 0 M11.34 SS 70

Add integers (positive and a negative) 66%	Add +4 and −5: (+)1 5%	Attach first sign strategy OR Difference conception Integer conceived as two separate objects: 'sign' and 'the number'	Add +4 and −5 M11.16 SS 63
	Add +4 and −5: Answers +9 or −9 4%		
	Add +4 and −5: Answers 3 4%	Reversed image of negative numbers: −5, 0, 1, 2, 3	
Recognize negative decimal numbers on a number line 45%	Locates numbers smaller than −4 to its right 25%	Ignoring sign OR Number line direction misconception	Number line marked with −6, −4, −2 and arrow at −3.5 position: What number does the arrow point to? M11.20 SS 69
Solve simple problems involving ratio and proportion *using times-and-a-half* 52%	Multiplies wrong numbers: 8:4 = 12:*48 or 96* 17%	No proportional reasoning	8 bottles of water cost £4.00 . . . How much do 12 bottles cost? M11.17 SS 67
	8:4 = 12:*8* 5%	Additive error	
Round any integer up to 10,000 to the nearest 100 73%	Rounds down instead of up 11%	Truncating for rounding	Round 951 to nearest 100 M11.22b SS 61
Multiply decimals by 10 to complete a sequence 54%	Writes $0.25 \times 10 = 25$ 11%	Place value error	. . . sequence made by multiplying for ten each time . . . continue: 0.025, 0.25, _, _ M11.19 SS 67
Multiply 2 numbers both with 1 decimal place 9%	Writes $0.2 \times 0.4 = 0.8$ 68%	Decimals conceived as two separate objects: 'point' and 'the number'	$0.2 \times 0.4 = \_$ M11.28 SS 82
Recognize square numbers to at least 12×12 36%	Calculates $4^2 + 5^2 = 9^2 = 81$ 27%	Order of operations misconception	$4^2 + 5^2 = \_$ M11.23 SS 72
	Calculates 'square' as 'double' 7%	Index notation error	

Order a set of whole numbers (W) and decimal numbers (D) 36%	W DDD W: orders decimals according to decimal digit(s) 18%	'Decimal point ignored' error only	Order . . . smallest to largest: 73.2, 73.65, 25, 120, 73.5 M11.26 SS 71
	WWDDD: orders whole numbers first 11%	'Whole number' prototype: decimals are 'other' AND 'Decimal point ignored' error	
	DDDWW: orders decimal numbers first and then according to decimal digit(s) 7%	'Decimal numbers are less than whole' misconception AND 'Decimal point ignored' error	
	DDDWW: orders decimal numbers first and according to 'largest is smallest' 6%	'Decimal numbers are less than whole' misconception AND 'Largest is smallest' error	
Find simple percentages of small whole numbers 51%	Interprets shade 10% of 40 as shade 10 29%	'Percentage sign ignored' error	Grid 8 by 5: . . . made of 40 squares; shade 10% . . . M11.24 SS 67
Add fractions with a common denominator 33%	Added numerators and denominators 30%	Fractions conceived as two separate objects: 'numerator' and 'denominator'	$3/8 + 2/8 = \_$ M11.29 SS 72

MEASUREMENT Descriptor (Facility)	**Error Description (Making error)**	**Diagnosis of error**	**Item MaLT reference Scale score**
Find the area of rectangles in a compound shape 18%	Finds perimeter by adding visible measures only 24%	Area–perimeter confusion AND Two-step task complexity	Find area given 4 of the 6 side measures CALC M11.10 SS 77
	Finds the perimeter 11%	Area–perimeter confusion	

Find the perimeter of simple shapes 34%	Finds the area 36% Counts diagonal of a unit square as 1 13%	Area–perimeter confusion 'Diagonal and side of square measure' misconception	Select two shapes with same perimeter (on grid) M11.15 SS 73
Select the smallest angle from a group of angles 83%	Selects angle with smallest arms as the smallest 7%	Arms-turn misconception	Angles drawn on grid with varying orientation and arm lengths. Select smallest angle M11.18a SS 57
Compare angle sizes 66%	Matches angle size by distance between arm end-points 23%	Length-turn misconception	Select two angles the same size M11.18b SS 63
Compare measures in metres and centimetres 53%	Converts 1 metre 20 centimetres to 12 or 1020 metres 23%	10 or 1000 centimetres in a metre misconception	High jump . . . bar starts at 1 metre . . . moved up 20 cm . . . how high now: 1.02 m, 1.2 m, 12.0, 1020 cm, 102 m M11.36 SS 67
SHAPE AND SPACE Descriptor (Facility)	**Error Description (Making error)**	**Diagnosis of error**	**Item MaLT reference Scale score**
Recognize where a shape will be after rotation in a real-life context 19%	Incorrectly models a rotation as a reflection 63%	Two-step task complexity: reality constraints	Shapes printed stamp: Which with same stamp? M11.31 SS 77

HANDLING DATA Descriptor (Facility)	Error Description (Making error)	Diagnosis of error	Item MaLT reference Scale score
Extract and interpret data in a table to solve problems 77%	Uses one condition only: selects day for largest number rather than largest total 12%	Two-step task complexity	Table shows costs for park rides on 3 different days: Which day took most money? CALC M11.8b SS 59
Find the average of a set of data (using a calculator) 24%	Partially correct but rounds to nearest whole number of seconds 11%	Avoiding decimals	Table for times in 100 metre race: Calculate average (mean) time . . . CALC M11.11a SS 76
Extract and interpret data in a table to solve problems involving time in hours and minutes 40%	Uses 1 hour is 100 minutes 13%	Decimal time prototype OR 100 minutes in an hour misconception	Table with 3 trips with time taken and cost per person: They came back from coach trip at 5:15 pm. What time did the coach leave? M11.12c SS 70
Use the language associated with probability 68%	Expects WGWG W 18%	'Gambler's fallacy': likelihood based on pattern of recent events	Spinner results for first 4 spins. WGWG _ What can you say about 5th? M11.30 SS 62
Read and plot coordinates in all 4 quadrants 49%	Incorrectly identifies a negative coordinate as positive 13%	Ignoring negative sign error	P in 3rd quadrant: Select coordinates M11.32 SS 68
	Reverses coordinates 10%	Lack of knowledge of convention	

12-year-olds

NUMBER AND ALGEBRA Descriptor (Facility)	Error Description (Making error)	Diagnosis of error	Item MaLT reference Scale score
Identify and use appropriate operation (*division*) to solve 'real-life' word problem (using a calculator) 46%	Incorrectly rounds down rather than up OR Truncates decimal 15%	Does not check with real-life context	. . . 90 minutes' practice spread equally over 7 days . . . how much each day . . . nearest minute?
	Selects multiplication instead of division 12%	Decimal avoidance	CALC M12.3 SS 70
Divide a 3-digit number by a single-digit number using written methods 59%	621 ÷ 3 = *27* 7%	Place value error	621 ÷ 3 = _ M12.17 SS 67
Understand decimal notation 18%	Writes one ten-thousandth *0.001* or *0.00001* 12%	Place value error	Write one ten-thousandth as a decimal M12.29 SS 80
	Misreads thousandths as thousand 5%	Reading problem	
	Writes *10.000* 7%	Place value misconception	
Add decimals numbers to 2 places 57%	Writes 8.04 + 1.6 = *9.1(0)* in horizontal layout 6%	Place value misconception: decimal part as whole number	8.04 + 1.6 = _ M12.25 SS 67
Find a number *100 times greater than* a number with 1 decimal place 53%	'100 times greater than 8.2' is *82* or *8200* 12%	Place value misconception	What number is 100 times greater than 8.2? M12.26 SS 68

Extend mental methods of calculation to include decimals 60%	Writes $6 \times 0.5 = 30$ or $0.3(0)$ 9%	Place value misconception: decimal part as whole number	$6 \times 0.5 = \_$ M12.28 SS 66
Solve a problem using addition or subtraction of decimals 64%	Selects subtraction instead of addition 11%	Distracted by the opposing directions of the signposts in the diagram	Signpost: Town A is 2.4 km to the left and B is 13.3 km to the right. How far from A to B . . .? M12.16 SS 65
Extend written methods of multiplication to decimals with 2 places 26%	Calculates 'double' for 'square' 27% Selects 4.25 or 4.10 as 'the square of 2.5' 21% Selects 0.5 as 'the square of 2.5' 14%	Square–double misconception Decimal number conceived as two whole numbers separated by a point Place value misconception	The square of 3 is 9 because $3 \times 3 = 9$: select the square of 2.5: 5, 0.5, 4.235, 6.25, 4.10 M12.31 SS 76
Find a fraction of a number (calculator available) 17%	Writes $\frac{3}{10}$ of $6 = 2$ 14%	Divides by numerator error OR $\frac{3}{10} = \frac{1}{3}$ misconception	Table: Nutritional value of 30 g serving of cereal always $\frac{3}{10}$ of that of 100 g serving. For 100 g value is 6, so for 30 g is _ CALC M12.10a SS 79
Subtract two fractions by writing them with a common denominator 22%	Subtracts numerators and denominators 34%	Fractions conceived as two whole numbers separated by a fraction sign	$\frac{3}{8} - \frac{1}{4} = \_$ M12.36 SS 77
Find simple percentages of a number of *people* in a word problem (using a calculator) 21%	28% of 45: Divides larger number by the percentage number 14%	% sign prompts division error	. . . survey of 425 . . . 28% chose blue. How many chose blue? CALC M12.5 SS 77

Find simple percentages of *money* in a word problem (using a calculator) 15%	4% of £50: divides larger by smaller number 20%	% sign prompts division error	. . . earned interest for one year on £50 at 4% per year. Interest earned is £_ CALC M12.11 SS 80
Use the equivalence of decimals and percentages 17%	Writes *2* for 20% 6%	Decimal–percentage misconception OR % sign prompts division of whole number	. . . T-shirt costs £8, price reduced by 20%. Write decimal number to calculate the saving: £8 × _ M12.32 SS 79
Understand the operations of multiplication and division, and their relationship to each other (*doubling and halving*) 34%	Extends a doubling sequence forwards correctly but incorrectly backwards by taking differences rather than halving 29%	Arithmetic sequence prototype OR Whole number sequence prototype OR Fraction avoidance	. . . sequence, next number is twice previous number . . . fill in: _, _, 1, 2, 4, 8, _ M12.21 SS 73
Understand the operations of multiplication and division, and their relationship to each other in the context of inequalities 9%	Selects $0.6 \times 0.3 > 0.6 \div 0.3$ as true 46%	'Multiplication makes bigger' misconception	Mark each true/false: $60 \times 3 > 60 \div 3$ $60 \times 0.3 < 60 \div 0.3$ $0.6 \times 0.3 > 0.6 \div 0.3$ M12.33 SS 83
Understand the relationship between ratio and proportion to calculate a percentage 41%	Uses ratio part-to-part instead of part-to-whole 13%	Ratio misconception	. . . mixes paint 4 parts red and 1 part yellow to make orange. What percentage of mixture . . . was yellow? CALC M12.9 SS 71
Solve simple problems using ideas of ratio and proportion using *times-and-a-half* 24%	$3{:}10 = 4{:}15$ OR $3{:}10 = 5{:}15$ Rounds up or down to nearest integer 24%	Whole number preference OR Estimation	3 loaves to make 10 sandwiches . . . how many loaves to make 15 sandwiches? CALC M12.12b SS 76

	$3:10 = 50:15$ Reverses the terms of the problem 5%	Working in whole numbers preference	
Recognize approximate proportions of a whole as a percentage 46%	Confuses percentage with degrees for a shaded circle sector 5%	Pie chart degrees prototype	Circle marked in eighths (about 28% shaded): Approximately what percentage shaded? M12.18 SS 70
Simplify linear algebraic expressions by collecting like terms 38%	Simplifies 'add 5 to $3n$' as a number (e.g. 8 or 9) 13%	'Letter as specific unknown' error OR Ignoring the letter	Write in simplest form: Add 5 to $3n$ M12.22b SS 72
	Simplifies as $8n$ 17%	'Letter not used' error: seeking closure of algebraic object	
Simplify linear algebraic expressions by collecting like terms 19%	Simplifies 'add 5 to $n + 3$' as a number (e.g. 8 or 9) 15% Simplifies as $8n$ 8%	'Letter as specific unknown' error OR Ignoring the letter 'Letter not used' error: seeking closure of algebraic object	Write in simplest form: Add 5 to $n + 3$ M12.22a SS 77
Interpret an algebraic function machine (flow diagram) 41%	For the inverse function of a temperature scale conversion, reverses the operations but not the order 9%	'Order of operations' error	An approximate conversion method for Celsius to Fahrenheit is . . . What is method for converting . . . back to Celsius: F _ _ C M12.37 SS 71
Generate terms of a pattern number sequence 35%	Generates next number (4th) rather than the number requested (6th) 9%	One-step patterning	Counters pattern for sequence of 3 Z-shapes shown. Complete table: pattern number 1, 2, 3, . . ., 6 and counters used: 7, 10, 13, . . ., _ M12.39a SS 73

Describe the general term of a pattern number sequence 3%	Writes a number rather than an expression for the nth term 21%	Generality misconception	Write an expression for number of counters for the nth shape in sequence M12.39b SS 91
	Writes an algebraic expression for iterative patterning 11%	Additive error based on one-step patterning OR Iterative patterning error	

MEASUREMENT Descriptor (Facility)	Error Description (Making error)	Diagnosis of error	Item MaLT reference Scale score
Read and interpret scales on a measuring instrument where the interval represents 5 units 72%	Counts each interval on scale as one unit (81 for 85) 4%	'Unit scale' prototype	Speedometer dial with major intervals: 20, 40, 60, . . . 200. What is reading . . .? M12.35 SS 63

SHAPE AND SPACE Descriptor (Facility)	Error Description (Making error)	Diagnosis of error	Item MaLT reference Scale score
Visualize and describe 3D shapes from 2D representations 24%	Confuses 'triangular-based' with square-based pyramid 31%	Two-step task complexity	Tetrahedron shown: . . . triangular-based pyramid with 4 faces and 4 corners . . . How many edges . . .? M12.14 SS 76
	Counts only visible edges of tetrahedron 20%	Lack of imagery	
Recognize parallel lines 54%	Selects as parallel only those with lines of same length 21%	Parallel lines prototype	Five sets of lines given M12.20 SS 68

Understand and use the language of rotations 16%	Rotates triangular shape about a vertex clockwise rather than anti-clockwise 6%	'Direction of turn' error	Triangle on Cartesian grid with point of rotation at (1, 1) on a vertex M12.38 SS 79

HANDLING DATA Descriptor (Facility)	**Error Description (Making error)**	**Diagnosis of error**	**Item MaLT reference Scale score**
Extract and use information in a table to solve a problem 33%	Interprets 'under 6' to include 6 31%	Boundary condition error and task complexity	Table of ticket prices for adults and children: A is 6 years and B is 12 years old. How much saving for family ticket . . .? CALC M12.4 SS 73
Interpret data in a frequency diagram 29%	Calculates Σf for all $x > 0$ instead of Σxf 30%	Multi-step task complexity	Frequency chart for pupils with different number of pets: How many pets do the pupils . . . have altogether? CALC M12.7b SS 75
	Calculates Σf for all x instead of Σfx 30%	Multi-step task complexity	
Calculate the *mean* of a discrete set of data 39%	Calculates the total of the data 16%	Two-step task complexity	. . . rolls a die 7 times . . . gets 3, 3, 4, 2, 5, 6, 5. Calculate the mean score . . . M12.27a SS 72
Find the *range* of a discrete set of data 25%	Writes an expression for the range (e.g. '3 to 6') rather than a numeric value 13%	Lack of knowledge of convention	. . . 3, 3, 4, 2, 5, 6, 5. What is the range of the scores? M12.27b SS 76
	Does not order the set of data first 5%	Two-step task complexity OR Incomplete concept	

13-year-olds

NUMBER AND ALGEBRA Descriptor (Facility)	Error Description (Making error)	Diagnosis of error	Item MaLT reference Scale score
Solve whole number problems involving division with a remainder (using calculator) 55%	Selects division correctly but does not round the answer for the context 17%	Two-step task complexity	. . . bag of rice weighs 4000 g. Each serving weighs 75 g. How many whole servings . . .? CALC M13.2 SS 68
Extend mental methods of calculation to include decimals 70%	$0.5 \times 8 = 40$ or $0.4(0)$ 9%	Place value misconception: decimal part as whole number	$0.5 \times 8 = \_$ M13.19 SS 63
Add decimals to 2 places 57%	Calculates: $2.02 + 1.8 + 2.13 = 5.23$ in horizontal layout 13%	Place value misconception: decimal part as whole number in context	Ribbon pieces 2.02 m, 1.8 m and 2.13 m. What is total length? M13.23 SS 67
Subtract decimals to 2 places 51%	$12.09 - 1.5 = 11.(0)4$ 17%	Place value misconception: decimal part as a whole number	$12.09 - 1.5 = \_$ M13.30 SS 69
Extract information from a table and subtract decimals to 2 places 40%	Calculates $9.05 - 7.2$ as $2.(0)3$ 18%	Place value misconception: decimal part as whole number in context	Table with monthly rainfalls (cm): What is difference between November and October? M13.24 SS 73
Extend written methods of division to include decimals to 2 places 30%	Calculates a quarter of 0.16 as 0.4 16%	Place value misconception: decimal part as whole number	Next number in sequence is a quarter of previous number. 10.24, 2.56, 0.64, _, _ M13.27 SS 75

Use division with decimals to 2 places 42%	Writes $0.64 \div 8 = 0.8$ 11%	Place value misconception: decimal part as whole number	$0.64 \div 8 = \_$ M13.34 SS 72
Understand the operations of multiplication and division, and their relationship to each other in the context of inequalities 12%	Selects 0.8×0.4 as larger than $0.8 \div 0.4$ 35%	'Multiplication makes bigger' misconception	Which gives largest answer each time: 8×4 or $08 \div 4$ 8×0.4 or $8 \div 0.4$ 0.8×0.4 or $0.8 \div 0.4$ M13.38 SS 82
Reduce a fraction to its simplest form 57%	Selects $^{12}/_{20} = ^{29}/_{12}$ 14%	Division is commutative misconception	Which fraction is equivalent to $^{12}/_{20}$? M13.33 SS 67
	Selects $^{12}/_{20} = ^{19}/_{18}$ 10%	Additive error	
Solve word problems involving percentage parts of quantities (using calculator) 21%	Finds percentage buts does not round in context 8%	Two-step task complexity	In 70 journeys train was delayed 69% of the time. How many journeys . . .? CALC M13.4 SS 79
	Ignores the % sign 4%	Percentage misconception: sign ignored	
Determine which number to consider as the 'whole' when finding percentages (using calculator) 18%	Uses original value as 'whole' rather than an increased value 11%	Two-step task complexity	A bottle . . . used to contain 500 ml now contains 10% extra. David drinks 20% of the bottle . . . how much juice? _ ml CALC M13.8 SS 79
Solve simple problems using ideas of ratio and proportion using *one-and-a-half-times* 27%	$4:6 = 6:8$ 37%	Additive error	4 loaves used to feed 6 animals . . . how many animals can you feed with 6 loaves? M13.39a SS 77
Solve simple problems using ideas of ratio and proportion using *two-and-a-half-times* 24%	$4:6 = 13:15$ 19%	Additive error	4 loaves used to feed 6 animals. How many loaves . . . for 15 animals? M13.39b SS 78

Simplify linear algebraic expressions by collecting like terms 49%	Simplifies 'add 3 to 7y' as a number 6%	'Letter as specific unknown' error OR Ignoring the letter	Write in simplest form: Add 6 to $7y$ M13.15b SS 71
	Simplifies as $10y$ 25%	'Letter not used' error: seeking closure of algebraic object	
Simplify linear algebraic expressions by collecting like terms 36%	Simplifies 'add 6 to $x + 3$' as a number 9%	'Letter as specific unknown' error OR Ignoring the letter	Write in simplest form: Add 6 to $x + 3$ M13.15a SS 73
	Simplifies as $9x$ 9%	'Letter not used' error: seeking closure of algebraic object	
	Simplifies as $6x + 3$ 11%	'Letter not used' error	
Substitute numbers into an algebraic formula (using calculator) 12%	Calculates 'square' as 'double' and then multiplies by 5 4%	'Index notation' error	Formula $d = 5t^2$ gives . . . Find d when $t = 3$ CALC M13.6 SS 82
	Calculates $(5t)^2$ 17%	'Order of operations' error	
Interpret and use an algebraic function machine (flow diagram) 56%	For the inverse of a temperature scale conversion, reverses the operations but not the order 5%	'Order of operations' error	An approximate method for converting Celsius to Fahrenheit is C, ×2,+30, F. Convert 50°F to °C M13.25b SS 68
	Does not use the inverse function (works forward) 7%	Two-step complexity: working backwards	

MEASUREMENT Descriptor (Facility)	Error Description (Making error)	Diagnosis of error	Item MaLT reference Scale score
Recognize and use the sum of angles at a point (using calculator) 26%	Calculates the turn of the minute hand instead of the hour hand on a clock 41%	Two-step task complexity	Clock face shown: Through how many degrees does the hour hand turn in an hour? CALC M13.7 SS 77
Convert from kilometres to metres (using calculator) 28%	Converts 0.34 km to 3.4, 34 or 3400 metres 36%	10, 100 or 10,000 metres in a kilometre misconception	Sound travels at 0.34 km in one second. How many metres does sound travel in one second? CALC M13.5 SS 76
Convert an area measure from square millimetres to square metres (using calculator) 3%	Converts using correct linear ratio 1000:1 12% Makes other decimal place error 31%	Two-step task complexity Two-step task complexity	. . . sheet of paper 210 mm by 297 mm: What is the area . . . in square metres (m²)? CALC M13.10 SS 92
Understand and use the formula for the area of a rectangle 46%	Calculates perimeter rather than area to find a missing dimension 32%	Area–perimeter confusion	Rectangles shown as 12 by 5 and 10 by _: These two rectangles have same area . . . what is the missing dimension? M13.29 SS 70
Calculate the surface area of a compound shape made from cuboids 10%	Calculated volume instead of surface area 19%	Area–volume confusion	Cross shown made from 5 cubes: What is the total surface area of cross? M13.20 SS 84

SHAPE AND SPACE Descriptor (Facility)	Error Description (Making error)	Diagnosis of error	Item MaLT reference Scale score
Recognize line symmetry 37%	Fails to recognize a diagonal line of symmetry 39%	Multi-step task complexity AND Vertical lines of symmetry prototype	Shade in one more section so figure has no lines of symmetry M13.35 SS 74

HANDLING DATA Descriptor (Facility)	Error Description (Making error)	Diagnosis of error	Item MaLT reference Scale score
Understand and use the mean of discrete data: find the total from the mean (using calculator) 58%	Selects division instead of multiplication 9%	Structural complexity: working backwards	In three throws . . ., mean distance is 40.2 m. What is total distance of the three throws? CALC M13.9 SS 68
Understand that different outcomes may result from repeating an experiment 61%	Selects HTHTH as most likely outcome for tossing a fair coin five times 17%	'Representativeness' misconception	Fair coin tossed five times. Which sequence is most likely . . . or all equally likely? M13.26 SS 67
	Selects THHTH as the most likely 12%	'Representativeness' misconception	

14-year-olds

NUMBER Descriptor (Facility)	Error Description (Making error)	Diagnosis of error	Item MaLT reference Scale score
Order decimals to 3 decimal places 81%	Selects largest decimal according to decimal digits rather than decimal place 9%	'Decimal point ignored' error	Circle decimal number with the greatest value: 0.063, 0.80, 0.21, 0.078 CALC M14.4 SS 62
	Selects largest decimal as one with smallest decimal digit(s) 7%	'Smallest is largest' error	
Understand the equivalence between fraction and decimal 53%	Converts $\frac{2}{100}$ to 0.2 or 2 12%	Place value misconception	$\frac{2}{100}$ as a decimal is _ M14.23 SS 71
Add decimals to 2 places 72%	$0.6 + 0.73 = 0.79$ or 0.079 13%	Place value misconception: decimal part as whole number	$0.6 + 0.73 = $ _ M14.22 SS 65
Add fractions by writing them with a common denominator 31%	Adds numerators and denominators 27%	Fractions conceived as two separate objects: 'numerator' and 'denominator'	$\frac{1}{4} + \frac{3}{8} = $ _ M14.35 SS 77
Solve a problem by converting a fraction to a percentage (using a calculator) 38%	Ignores % sign: $\frac{20}{80}$ is 20 31%	Percentage misconception: sign ignored	. . . has 80 books . . . sold 60 books. What percentage of the books . . . unsold? CALC M14.6 SS 75
	Calculates sold percentage correctly ($\frac{60}{80} = 75\%$) but misses one condition in the problem 6%	Two-step task complexity	

Solve word problems involving percentage parts of quantities (using calculator) 49%	Calculates the new total (275) rather than the percentage increase 24%	Expecting two parts in a word problem	. . . carton of orange juice . . . contains 250 ml . . . new carton . . . 10% more. How much *extra* juice . . . new carton . . .? CALC M14.2 SS 72
	Ignores % sign: 10% of 250 is 10 8%	Percentage misconception: sign ignored	
Solve word problems involving percentage parts of quantities (using calculator) 42%	Ignores % sign: calculates new price after 5% reduction as 5 less than original price 19%	Percentage misconception: sign ignored	. . . price of book £25 . . . reduced by 5% . . . What is sale price? CALC M14.10 SS 74
Solve word problems involving percentage parts of quantities (no calculator) 15%	Selects the ratio of the two parts instead of identifying the 'unit' 17%	Identifies wrong unit suggesting a ratio–fraction misconception	. . . 24 pupils travel by bus, the other 6 do not. What percentage of class does *not* travel . . . by bus? M14.31 SS 83
	Identifies correct fraction but fails to convert to percentage 3%	Multi-step task complexity	
Convert a fraction to a percentage (using calculator) 24%	Calculates '24 out of 500' as 500 ÷ 24 11%	'Percent means divide' misconception	. . . 24 out of 500 . . . do not like choc bars. What percentage of people . . .? CALC M14.8 SS 79
Divide positive and negative integers 44%	$(-24) ÷ (+6) = 4$ 12%	Negative sign ignored	$(-24) ÷ (+6) = \_$ M14.18a SS 73
	$(-24) ÷ (+6) = 18$ or -18 7%	Division sign read as subtract	
Subtract positive and negative integers 35%	$(-6) - (+3) = -3$ 27%	Integers conceived as two separate objects: 'sign' and 'the number'	$(-6) - (+3) = \_$ M14.18b SS 76
	$(-6) - (+3) = 3$ 7%		

Write an algebraic expression for a problem situation 85%	Selects $20 - n$ rather than $n - 20$ 9%	Subtraction is commutative misconception	A brother and sister . . . total age 20 . . . brother is n years old. Sister's age . . . M14.21 SS 71
Use letters to represent unknowns in a problem 58%	Writes an equation instead of an expression 9%	Letter evaluated misconception	A packet . . . has N rulers, each costing 20 pence. Write expression for total cost of packet . . . M14.27 SS 69
	Writes $n + 20$ for $20n$ 8%	Additive preference in word problems	
Generate terms of a pattern number sequence 65%	For the 6th term adds 6 to last value (3rd) given 10%	Non-recognition of patterning	Toothpick pattern showing squares. Table:
	Uses double last term for an additive sequence 9%	Generality misconception: patterning on last term only	Squares: 1, 2, 3, . . ., 6 Toothpicks: 4, 7, 10, . . ., — M14.20a SS 67
Describe the general term of a pattern number sequence 43%	Selects algebraic expression for iterative patterning 31%	Additive error based on one-step patterning OR Iterative patterning error	Table given: . . . formula for n squares: $4n$, $3n + 1$, $3 + n$, $n + 7$ M14.20b SS 74
	Selects algebraic expression for the first term 14%	Generality misconception	
Simplify linear algebraic expressions by collecting like terms 60%	$3 + 6y + 1 + 5y =$ $16y$ 7%	'Letter not used' error: seeking closure of algebraic object	$3 + 6y + 1 + 5y$ in simplest form M14.34a SS 69
Identify a linear function from its graph in the form $y = mx + c$ 20%	Selects $V = T + 2$ for $V = T - 2$ 30%	Using x-intercept for c	Graph shown: Circle correct formula. M14.36 SS 81
	Selects $V = 2T + 1$ for $V = T - 2$ 11%	Gradient-intercept confusion	

MEASUREMENT Descriptor (Facility)	Error Description (Making error)	Diagnosis of error	Item MaLT reference Scale score
Calculate the perimeter of a rectangle (using calculator) 68%	Calculated the area 14% Added only the visible lengths 12%	Perimeter–area confusion Word problem confusion?	Rugby pitch . . . length and width shown: Referee ran round the pitch . . . Write total distance CALC M14.1 SS 67
Appreciate the imprecision of measurement and understand 'to the nearest' measure 8%	Ignores 'to the nearest' measure 36%	Two-step task complexity	. . . rectangular strip . . . 100 mm long and 6 mm wide to the nearest mm. What is minimum possible area of strip? CALC M14.13 SS 88

SHAPE AND SPACE Descriptor (Facility)	Error Description (Making error)	Diagnosis of error	Item MaLT reference Scale score
Solve problems using angle properties of intersecting and parallel lines 28%	Writes $180 - x + y$ for $180 - x - y$ 30%	Bracket or order of operations error	Parallel lines with intersecting transversals – 3 angles given as x, y, z: Circle expression that gives z in terms of x and y M14.30 SS 78

HANDLING DATA Descriptor (Facility)	Error Description (Making error)	Diagnosis of error	Item MaLT reference Scale score
Understand and use the mean of discrete data: find the total from the mean (using calculator) 80%	Selects division instead of multiplication 7%	Structural complexity: working backwards	The mean number of goals . . . in 20 matches was 4 goals per match . . . Total number . . . in 20 matches? CALC M14.3 SS 63

Solve a problem using the mean and range of a set of discrete data 14%	Uses only one condition in the problem 40%	Multi-step task complexity	Five cards: _, 6, 7, 8, _. Mean is 7. Range is 8. Write other two numbers M14.26 SS 83
Interpret frequency diagrams (bar chart) 67%	Interprets condition '3 or more' as only '3' OR only 'more than 3' 18%	Boundary condition error OR Two-step task complexity OR Reading problem	Bar chart . . . number of pets each pupil owns: How many own 3 pets or more? M14.14 SS 67
Extract and use information in a table to solve a problem (using calculator) 53%	Ignores one condition in problem 24%	Two-step task complexity	Table of sales – Item; No. sold; Takings per item: How much does the cheapest pizza cost? CALC M14.7 SS 71
Extract and use information in a table to solve a problem in the context of time 40%	Confuses arrival and departure times in a timetable 33%	Multi-step task complexity	Train route and timetable arrival and departure times: Train leaves A . . . how long does it take to travel to C? _ hr _ mins M14.24b SS 74
Find probabilities using methods based on equally likely outcomes 34%	Interprets 'greater than' a number to include that number 12%	Boundary condition error OR Two-step complexity	Two spinners and add their scores. Table of outcomes: . . . probability that the total is greater than _ is $^{10}/16$ M14.29b SS 76
Demonstrate a basic understanding of correlation 37%	Identifies negative correlation as 'no correlation' 13%	Dichotomous intuition: data is correlated or not OR Two-step complexity	Two scatter diagrams. Tick correct statement M14.32b SS 75
Use coordinates in the first quadrant 85%	Reverses coordinates 9%	Lack of knowledge of convention	Graph: Coordinates of P are _ M14.19 SS 60

Appendix 2: Discussion prompt sheets

Discussion prompt sheet 1: Ordering

 Mr Riley

Put these numbers in order from smallest to largest: 185, 73.5, 73.32, 57, 73.64

 Sonia

Just looking at the whole numbers, it's 57, 73 then 185, so I went 57 then 73.5 then 73.32 then 73.64 then 185

Why the point 5 then point 32 then point 64?

Because 5 is less than 32 and 32 is less than 64

 Carol

Yes, because 73.32 has got two digits after the point and 73.5 has got only one

 Diane

I'm not so sure because 73.5 is basically seventy-three and a half. I'm not sure if 73.64 is over a half or under a half…

Try putting some numbers on a number line between 73 and 74; where would you put 73.5?

Who do you agree with?

How could you persuade the others that they are wrong?

Use a number line.

Discussion prompt sheet 2: Thermometer

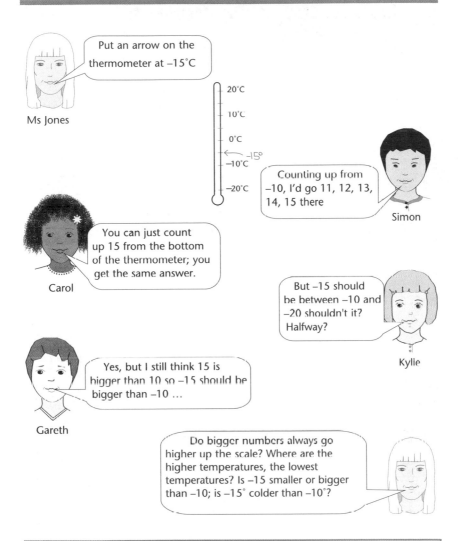

Ms Jones: Put an arrow on the thermometer at −15°C

20°C
10°C
0°C
← −15°
−10°C
−20°C

Simon: Counting up from −10, I'd go 11, 12, 13, 14, 15 there

Carol: You can just count up 15 from the bottom of the thermometer; you get the same answer.

Kylie: But −15 should be between −10 and −20 shouldn't it? Halfway?

Gareth: Yes, but I still think 15 is bigger than 10 so −15 should be bigger than −10 …

Do bigger numbers always go higher up the scale? Where are the higher temperatures, the lowest temperatures? Is −15 smaller or bigger than −10; is −15° colder than −10°?

Who do you think is right?
How would you persuade the others that you are right?

Discussion prompt sheet 3: Houses

Who do you agree with?

Can you help work out the perimeter?

Is the answer in squares or centimetres?

Discussion prompt sheet 4: Scales

Mr Riley: Write down the reading on the weighing scale as accurately as you can

Robin says ...

Is it 2.4 kilograms or 2400 grams? A fifth of a kilogram is 200, so ... and there's two and it goes up to 400. So that's 2400 grams

Where did you get the fifth from?

Robin says ...

There was five lines: there's one, two, three, four, then 3 (kg) is the five

David says ...

I get 1, 2, 3, 4, 5, 6; I get 6 lines

... later, Gareth says ...

I got 2.2 – I know it was wrong, but ...

Kylie says ...

I think I know why you put 0.2 there. You go up in ones, but it goes up in twos: 200, 400, 600, 800, up to 1000

Are there 4, 5 or 6 lines on the scale between 2 kg and 3 kg?

Why is each gap a fifth of 1000 grams?

Why do you think some children say 2.2 or 2200?

Pretend I'm one of your friends and you're going to teach me how to answer this question.

Discussion prompt sheet 5: Missing Numbers

Ms Williams

How do you do this?

 $\boxed{?}$ x 6 = 9 x 4

Sonia

I did 9 x 4 = 36, and wondered 'what' times 6 would equal 36? I thought through my table.

Gareth

Well to be honest I didn't know 9 times 4 quickly, so I just changed it round and took 4 off the 40, because 10 x 4 is 40. Then I thought 5 x 6 is 30, so I added 6 to get 36.

?

I knew 8 times 4 is 32, so I added another four. And that would be 'something' times 6 would be 36. And I looked through my tables and 6 x 6 equals 36.

Robin

?

I have a different way for the nine times table. Say it was 9 x 6: you go one down from the 6, that's 5. Write it down. Then what added to the 5 is 9? Which is 4. Write down the 4. So the answer is 54. My mum taught me that.

How do you work out your nine times tables?

Can you help the teacher understand Gareth, Robin and Sonia's methods?

Can you use Sonia's method for the 9 times table? Does it always work? (Try 9 x 11).

Do you know any other methods for finding out times tables?

Discussion prompt sheet 6: Points

Ms Jones

Add 0.75 to 3.5 in your head... and I want you to remember and tell me how you do it.

75 and 5 makes 80, so I get 3-point-eighty, 3.80

Sonia

Carol

I put 3-point-8, isn't that the same?

I got 4.25, because you add the 5 and the 7 to get 12, another ten to the three to make 4, that's 4.2, then you still have the 5, that's 4.25

David

Kylie

Yes, I did 3.5 is 3-and-a-half, then add three quarters, so a half makes 4, then a quarter is 4.25

So we have 3.80, 3.8 or 4.25. Any other answers?

Who do you agree with? Why?

Can you work out why the mistakes came about?

What would you say to persuade the children you are right?

Glossary

This glossary is designed to help the reader with technical terms used in the text; the pages cited against the entry in the index will offer more help.

In general we have tried to explain how we have used these terms in this text rather than provide formal or comprehensive scientific definitions that the reader can access from the *Oxford English Dictionary* or other sources. Occasionally an implicit statement or a generic example seemed best suited to this purpose.

If an entry does not appear here this is because we think that the text in which the term appears provides the best explanation we can manage or because the usage is not 'technical' to mathematics education per se and a dictionary is the best recourse.

Word	Entry
7-year gap	This phenomenon refers to a seven-year range in performance in a typical UK cohort of children. For example, within a cohort of 10-year-old children there will be significant numbers of children who are performing at the average standard for 7-year-olds and others performing at the average standard for 14-year-olds (see Hart, 1981).
Activity theory	A Marxist, cultural-historical theory of activity attributed to revolutionary Russian psychologists Vygotsky, Luria and Leon'tev, which focuses on the notion of joint, tool-mediated, goal- or 'object'-orientated activity as the basis of mental development or learning. (See also *CHAT*.)
Additive tendency	The tendency to respond with an addition (or subtraction) when a multiplicative response is required.
Affordances	Characteristics of an object or situation that present opportunities or potential for some achievement (as opposed to constraints).
Algorithm	A set of ordered routines or steps for carrying out a mathematical computation or process.
Argumentation	A chain of reasoning that seeks to establish a proposition or decision, or to persuade others.
Artefact	Anything made by humans (including tools, recipes, concepts, and so on).
Assessment for learning	Assessment directed at and that therefore supports or informs learning, usually involving formative or diagnostic feedback.

Word	Entry
Asymmetry	Lack of symmetry.
Backing	A term used by Toulmin (1958) to indicate a part of logical argument where grounds, reasons or evidence are stated for making an assertion. (See *Toulmin's model of argument*.)
Bee-bot	Programmable floor robot for young children.
Black box	Used here when a process becomes hidden from view (or consciousness) as if it were in a black box.
Boundary object	An object at the boundary between two systems.
Cardinality	The number of a set of objects – that is, how many there are in the set (as distinct from ordinality).
Chain of signs	A semiotic term: meaning is understood or represented as a chain of signs, each of which connects the previous sign to a new interpretant.
CHAT	*Cultural-Historical Activity Theory*. (See also *Activity theory*.)
Cognitive conflict	A cognitive conflict arises when there is a conflict between two positions, understandings or arguments – for example, when a learner's mental model conflicts with the reality manifested ('Ah, that does not fit!').
Cognitive load	The mental demand of the learning task for the learner.
Community of inquiry	A community collectively and cooperatively engaged in inquiry.
Commutative principle for multiplication	In multiplication the order of operation does not affect the outcome: $a \times b = b \times a$.
Compensation strategy	An adjustment to attain equality (arithmetic) or fairness (social).
Constraints	See *Affordances* for contrast.
Cuisenaire rods	A set of coloured wooden rods created by Cuisenaire and promoted by Gattegno to teach children arithmetic.
Cultural-Historical Activity Theory (CHAT)	See *Activity theory*. The CHAT perspective has emerged from modern developments of activity theory that developed its concerns for culture, diversity, multiple voices, communities and identity.
Definition move	When teaching a concept, a 'definition' move provides a salient property of the concept. (See also *Exemplification move*.)
Dialogical pedagogy	Pedagogy that recognizes or prioritizes dialogue (also see Bakhtin (1981) on 'dialogism').
Dienes blocks	Set of wooden blocks created by Dienes to support understanding of place value. The sets come in different number bases.
Embodied cognition	Understanding situated in the body, in space and time, as well as socioculturally and historically.
Embodiment	An idea or abstraction expressed or represented physically or concretely.

Empirical research	Research based on primary data – for example, observation.
Enculturate	Establish competence in the customs of the culture.
Euclidean geometry	Euclid's geometry was published as a set of theorems proved logically from a (nearly) minimal set of axioms and modes of deduction.
Exemplification move	When teaching a concept, this is a move that involves providing an example or a counterexample (as contrasted with a *Definition move*, which provides a salient property of the concept).
Function machine	A model of the function concept – usually a diagram showing input numbers 'processed' in a 'machine' with the resulting output numbers.
GCSE	The General Certificate of Secondary Education in England, which assesses children's attainment at the end of compulsory schooling.
General pedagogic strategy	A teaching move that focuses on learning in general rather than mathematical learning in particular.
Genetic approach	An approach that pays due regard to how a concept or idea was conceived, born and grew up/old.
Graphicacy	Understanding of graphical forms and ability to use graphical information.
Heterogeneous grouping	See *Homogeneous and heterogeneous grouping*.
Heuristics	The means to discover solutions to problems.
Homogeneous and heterogeneous grouping	Homogeneous groups are 'of a kind' (for example, all the same ability) whereas heterogeneous implies groups that are 'different' or diverse (for example, mixed ability).
Hoopla set	A traditional game where rings or hoops are thrown to land on a wooden pole (also quoits).
Horizontal mathematization	Mathematizing can be directed 'horizontally' at phenomena outside mathematics (in the 'real' world perhaps) or 'vertically' at the mathematics itself. (See also *Vertical mathematization*.)
Inquiry groups	Groups of people (for example, teachers, children) sharing inquiry together.
Internalization (Vygotsky)	The acquisition of a concept (or knowledge generally) in the mind that was formerly presented in social interaction.
Intersubjectivity	That understanding (emotion and so on) which is shared between people and subjects.
Learning trajectory	A possible or actual learning path, perhaps to some educational goal.
Linear prototype	The presumption that a relationship should prototypically be linear.
Logits	Logarithm of the odds ratio: $\ln(p/1 - p)$.

Word	Entry
LOGO	A programming language also suitable for children as a learning and problem-solving tool.
Mathematization	The process of representing or modelling with mathematics.
Metacognition	Knowing about your own thinking, learning and problem-solving processes.
Metaphorical entailments	Properties of the metaphorical world or model that may (but may not always) hold faithfully to those of the structure it is used to represent.
Modelling	Using or making models to solve problems. We refer in Chapter 2 to the way mathematics is *connected* with a 'real' everyday world.
Multiplicative field	The conceptual field including multiplication, tasks demanding multiplication, fractions, proportion, ratio, and so on.
Neo-Piagetians	Followers of Piaget, who developed notions/theories of teaching for cognitive development.
Number and numeral	The numeral is the symbolic label given to a number, such as '5' is the number of fingers on one hand.
Numeral	The numerical quantity (for example, cardinality).
Numerosity	The numerical quantity (for example, cardinality).
Oracy	Oral competence.
Pedagogical content knowledge	Knowledge about how to represent and formulate a subject so that it is comprehensible to others (see Shulman, 1986).
Peircean analysis	Peirce was a leading thinker in semiotics; a Piercean analysis implies a semiotic analysis involving the 'interpretant'.
Performativity	The requirement that activity should be performed according to some (usually external) standards.
Problematic	A problematic is a problem that is unresolved or not trivially resolved.
Procedural bug	An error in a procedure, usually a bug implies some consistency of use.
Prototype	A culturally typical example of a concept; often associated with narrative ways of knowing.
Quantitative–qualitative dichotomization	The separation of qualitative from quantitative research, philosophically or practically.
Rasch model	Rasch invented a measurement model that helps construct objective, scientific measurement from tests.
Realistic Mathematics Education (RME)	A mathematics education reform movement originated by Freudenthal and his followers in Holland, based on the principle that mathematics is a human activity rather than a mechanistic one.

Referents	Referents are things that refer or represent other things – for example, *Unifix cubes* are referents for number, counting, and so on.
Reification	The making of a process into an object or a 'thing' – for example, subtracting becomes subtraction.
RME	See *Realistic Mathematics Education*.
Roamer	A programmable floor robot designed to represent the *LOGO* turtle.
Scale score	The score (on our scale from about 10 to 100) used to identify pupils' 'attainment' across the whole raft of tests (often called 'ability' by psychometricians).
Schema	A pattern, model or representation that organizes complex reality to assist in explaining experience, mediating perception or guiding response.
Semiotic contraction	Occurs when a chain of signs becomes contracted into one new object or sign.
Semiotic objectification	The making of a new sign by associating and reifying a signifier with some signified.
Semiotics	The science of communication, which studies the interpretation of signs and symbols in different fields.
Situated cognition	The assertion that knowledge and meaning is always essentially tied to the situation or context.
Situated intuition	An intuition (that is, a cognitive belief) that arises spontaneously from engagement with a situation or cultural practice – for example, unfairness in games.
Social norms	The expectations associated with a social practice – for example, the interpersonal behaviours that are expected of children to support the classroom dialogue.
Sociocultural theory	Theory that foregrounds the social and the cultural as inseparable contexts in which any activity can be understood, theorized or analysed.
Sociomathematical norms	The expectations associated with mathematics learning practice – for example, the interpersonal behaviours that are expected of children to support *mathematical* dialogue.
Spatial embodiment	See *Visuo-spatial*.
Standardized assessments	An assessment is standardized if the assessment outcomes are comparable with what is 'normal' for the group against whom the score is being judged or 'standardized' (thus age standardization compares scores with those of the population of the same age).
Toulmin's model of argument	Toulmin analyses argumentation as a structure by which data (for example, I was born in Yorkshire) are used to *Warrant* (you can only play for the Yorkshire cricket team if you are born in

Word	Entry
	Yorkshire) claims (I can play for the team), and *Backing* (I was told this as a boy) is offered when necessary to justify these 'warrants'. Changing the rules of argumentation usually involves a new regime of what constitutes legitimate 'backing' arguments.
Unifix cubes	Interlocking coloured plastic cubes used to develop children's understanding of number.
Vertical equating	When a test score is to be equated with a score on a different test, the two tests need to be 'equated'; this can be done through a statistical analysis of performance by pupils on both tests.
Vertical mathematization	New mathematics is often built 'vertically' from modelling of problems in mathematics, thus fractions can emerge from 'vertical mathematization' of division of whole numbers, with the aid of models such as pizzas/circles. (See also *Horizontal mathematization*.)
Visuo-spatial	Visual (seeing) and spatial (three-dimensional space) perception and knowledge is connected, and so is often described as 'visuo-spatial' – a context that allows abstractions to be visualized through some figure or model in space is described as a visuo-spatial context or visuo-spatial model.
Warrant	The justification for a claim based on data in an argument is called its warrant. (See *Toulmin's model of argument*.)
Zone of proximal development (ZPD)	Vygotsky's term to denote the gap between a learner's current developmental level and their potential level; the difference between the child's competence without support and their competence in joint activity with others.

References

Adams, R. J. and Khoo, S. T. (1996) *Quest: The Interactive Test Analysis System.* Melbourne: ACER.

Adey, P. and Shayer, M. (1994) *Really Raising Standards: Cognitive Intervention and Academic Achievement.* London: Routledge.

Afantiti-Lamprianou, T. (2006) *The Representativeness Heuristic in Children's and Teachers' Probabilistic Thinking.* PhD, University of Manchester.

Afantiti-Lamprianou, T. and Williams, J. (2003) A scale for assessing probabilistic thinking and the representativeness tendency. *Research in Mathematics Education*, 5, pp. 173–96.

Afantiti-Lamprianou, T., Williams, J. S. and Lamprianou, I. (2005) A comparison between teachers' and pupils' tendency to use a representativeness heuristic. In H. L. Chick and J. L. Vincent (eds) *Proceedings of the 29th Conference of the International Group for the Psychology of Mathematics Education*, Vol. 2, pp. 9–16. Melbourne: University of Melbourne.

Amir, G. S. and Williams, J. S. (1994) The influence of children's culture on their probabilistic thinking. In J. P. Da Ponte and J. F. Matos (eds) *Proceedings of the 18th Conference of the International Group for the Psychology of Mathematics Education*, Vol. 2. Portugal: University of Lisbon, pp. 24–31.

Amir, G. S. and Williams, J. S. (1998) Cultural influences on children's probabilistic thinking. *Journal of Mathematical Behavior*, 18 (1), pp. 85–107.

Anderson, J. R., Reder, L. M. and Simon, H. A. (1996) Situated learning and education. *Educational Researcher*, 25 (4), pp. 5–11.

Anderson, J. R., Reder, L. M. and Simon, H. A. (1997) Situative versus cognitive perspectives: form versus substance. *Educational Researcher*, 26 (1), pp. 18–21.

Anghileri, J. (2001) *Principles and Practices in Arithmetic Teaching: Innovative Approaches for the Primary Classroom.* Buckingham: Open University Press.

Ashlock, R. B. (2005) *Error Patterns in Computation: Using Error Patterns to Improve Instruction.* Upper Saddle River, NJ: Merrill Prentice Hall. 9th ed.

Askew, M., Brown, M., Rhodes, V., Johnson, D. and Wiliam, D. (1997) *Effective Teachers of Numeracy: Final Report.* London: King's College.

APU (Assessment of Performance Unit) (1982) *A Review of Monitoring in Mathematics 1978–1982.* London: DES.

Ausubel, D. (1968) *Educational Psychology: A Cognitive View.* New York: Rinehart & Winston.

Bakhtin, M. M. (1981) The dialogic imagination: four essays. In M. Holquist (ed.)

The Dialogic Imagination: Four Essays by M. M. Bakhtin. (transl. C. Emerson and M. Holquist). Austin: University of Texas Press.

Bakhtin, M. (1986) *Speech Genres and Other Late Essays* (transl. C. Emerson and M. Holquist). Austin: University of Texas Press.

Bakker, A. and Gravemeijer, K. (2006) Historical phenomenology of mean and median. *Educational Studies in Mathematics*, 62, pp. 149–68.

Barnes, D. (1976) *From Communication to Curriculum.* Harmondsworth: Penguin Books.

Barnes, D. R. and Todd, F. (1995) *Communication and Learning Revisited: Making Meaning Through Talk.* Portsmouth, NH: Boynton/Cook Publishers.

Beishuizen, M. (1999) The empty number line as a new model. In I. Thompson (ed.) *Issues in Teaching Numeracy in Primary Schools.* Buckingham: Open University Press.

Bell, A. W., Swan, M., Onslow, B., Pratt, K. and Purdy, D. (1983) *Diagnostic Teaching: Report of ESRC Project.* Nottingham: University of Nottingham, Shell Centre for Mathematical Education.

Bell, A. W., Swan, M., Onslow, B., Pratt, K. and Purdy, D. (1985) *Diagnostic Teaching: Teaching for Lifelong Learning.* Nottingham: University of Nottingham, Shell Centre for Mathematical Education.

Bell, A., Crust, R., Shannon, A. M. S. *et al.* (1993) *Awareness of Learning, Reflection and Transfer in School Mathematics.* Nottingham: University of Nottingham, Shell Centre for Mathematical Education.

Bell, A., Rooke, D. and Wigley, A. (1978) *Journey into Maths: The South Nottinghamshire Project.* Nottingham: University of Nottingham, Shell Centre for Mathematical Education.

Bereiter, C. (1997) Situated cognition and how to overcome it. In J. A. Whitson and D. Kirshner (eds) *Situated Cognition: Social, Semiotic, and Psychological Perspectives.* Hillsdale, NJ: Lawrence Erlbaum Associates, pp. 281–300.

Bernstein, B. (1971) *Class, Codes and Control, Volume 1: Theoretical Studies Towards a Sociology of Language.* London: Routledge & Kegan Paul.

Bernstein, B. (1990) *Class, Codes and Control, Volume 4: Structuring of Pedagogic Discourse.* London: Routledge.

Bernstein, B. (1996) *Pedagogy, Symbolic Control and Identity Theory, Research, Critique.* London: Taylor & Francis.

Black, M. (1962) *Models and Metaphors: Studies in Language and Philosophy.* Ithaca, NY: Cornell University Press.

Black, M. (ed.) (1993) *More About Metaphor.* Cambridge: Cambridge University Press.

Black, P., Harrison, C., Lee, C., Marshall, B. and Wiliam, D. (2003) *Assessment for Learning: Putting it into Practice.* Maidenhead: Open University Press.

Black, P., Harrison, C., Lee, C., Marshall, B. and Wiliam, D. (2004) *Working Inside the Black Box: Assessment for Learning in the Classroom.* Windsor: nferNelson.

Board of Studies (1995) *Curriculum and Standards Framework: Mathematics.* Melbourne: Board of Studies.

Board of Studies (2000) *Curriculum and Standards Framework II: Mathematics. Revised edition*. Melbourne: Board of Studies.

Booth, L. R. (1984) *Algebra: Children's Strategies and Errors: A Report of the Strategies and Errors in Secondary Mathematics Project*. Windsor: nferNelson.

Boulter, C. J. and Gilbert, J. K. (1995) Argument and science education. In J. M. Costello and S. Mitchell (eds) *Competing and Consensual Voices: The Theory and Practice of Argument*. Clevedon: Multilingual Matters, pp. 84–98.

Bourdieu, P. (1990) *The Logic of Practice*. Oxford: Polity Press.

Bourdieu, P. (1997) The forms of capital. In A. H. Halsey, H. Lauder, P. Brown and A. S. Wells (eds) *Education: Culture, Economy, Society*. Oxford: Oxford University Press.

Bruner, J. S. (1966) *Toward a Theory of Instruction*. Cambridge, MA: Harvard University Press.

Bruner, J. S. (1986) *Actual Minds, Possible Worlds*. Cambridge, MA/London: Harvard University Press.

Bruner, J. S. (1990) *Acts of Meaning*. Cambridge, MA/London: Harvard University Press.

Bruner, J. S. (1996) *The Culture of Education*. Cambridge, MA/London: Harvard University Press.

Burkhardt, H. (1981) *The Real World and Mathematics*. Glasgow: Blackie.

Burkhardt, H. (1991) Mathematical modelling in the curriculum. In W. Blum, I. Huntley and M. Niss (eds) *Teaching of Mathematical Modelling and Applications*. Chichester: Ellis Horwood, pp. 271–9.

Burton, L. (1984) *Thinking Things Through: Problem Solving in Mathematics*. Oxford: Basil Blackwell.

Butterworth, B. (1999) *The Mathematical Brain*. London: Macmillan.

Chaiklin, S. (2002) A developmental teaching approach to schooling. In G. Wells and G. Claxton (eds) *Learning for Life in the 21st Century: Sociocultural Perspectives on the Future of Education*. Oxford: Blackwell, pp. 167–80.

Chaiklin, S. and Lave, J. (1993) *Understanding Practice: Perspectives on Activity and Context*. Cambridge: Cambridge University Press.

Cherouvim, N., Kitchen, A., Robbins, P. and Williams, J. S. (1991) *Practical Projects with Mathematics*. Cambridge: Cambridge University Press.

Cipra, B. (1983) *Misteaks . . . and How to Find Them Before the Teacher Does*. Boston, MA: Birkhauser.

Clement, J. (1985) Misconceptions in graphing. In *Proceedings of the 9th Conference of the International Group for the Psychology of Mathematics Education*, Vol. 1, pp. 369–75.

Clements, M. A. and Ellerton, N. (1996) *Mathematics Education Research: Past, Present and Future*. Bangkok: UNESCO.

Cobb, P. and Bauersfeld, H. (1995) *The Emergence of Mathematical Meaning: Interaction in Classroom Cultures*. Hillsdale, NJ: Lawrence Erlbaum Associates.

Cobb, P., Perlwitz, M. and Underwood, D. (1996) Constructivism and activity theory: a consideration of their similarities and differences as they relate to mathematics. In H. Mansfield, N. Pateman and N. Bednarz (eds) *Mathematics for Tomorrow's Young Children*. Dordrecht: Kluwer, pp. 10–58.

Cobb, P., Yackel, E. and McClain, K. (eds) (2000) *Symbolizing and Communicating in Mathematics Classrooms: Perspectives on Discourse, Tools, and Instructional Design*. Mahwah, NJ: Lawrence Erlbaum Associates.

Cole, M. and Engstrom, Y. (1993) A cultural-historical approach to distributed cognition. In G. Solomon (ed.) *Distributed Cognitions: Psychological and Educational Considerations*. Cambridge: Cambridge University Press, pp. 1–46.

Cooper, B. and Dunne, M. (2000) *Assessing Children's Mathematical Knowledge: Social Class, Sex and Problem Solving*. Buckingham: Open University Press.

Corbin, B., McNamara, O. and Williams, J. S. (2003) Numeracy coordinators: 'brokering' change within and between and communities of practice? *British Journal of Educational Studies*, 51 (4), pp. 344–68.

Cross, A., Harrison, M., Kitchen, A. and Williams, J. S. (1991) *Explorations: A Primary Maths Resource*. Blackburn: Unilab.

Curriculum Corporation (1994) *Mathematics – A Curriculum Profile for Australian Schools*. Victoria: Victoria Curriculum Corporation.

Davis, P., Williams, J., Pampaka, M. and Wo, L. (2006) Developmental assessment of data handling performance age 7–14. *Proceedings of the 30th Conference of the International Group for the Psychology of Mathematics Education*, Vol. 2. Prague: Charles University, pp. 401–8.

Davydov, V. V. (1982) The psychological characteristics of the formation of elementary mathematical operations in children. In T. P. Carpenter, J. M. Moser and T. A. Romberg (eds) *Addition and Subtraction: A Cognitive Perspective*. Hillsdale, NJ: Lawrence Erlbaum, pp. 224–38.

de Bock, D., Van Dooren, W., Janssens, D. and Vershaffel, L. (2002) Improper use of linear reasoning. *Educational Studies in Mathematics*, 50, pp. 311–34.

DeCorte, E., Greer, B. and Vershaffel, L. (1996) Mathematics learning and teaching. In D. C. Berliner and R. C. Calfee (eds) *Handbook of Educational Psychology*. New York: Macmillan.

Denvir, B. and Brown, M. (1986) Understanding of number concepts in low attaining 7–9 year olds: Part II – the teaching studies. *Educational Studies in Mathematics*, 17 (2), pp. 143–64.

DfEE (Department for Education and Employment) (1998) *Teaching, High Status, High Standards: Circular 4/98*. London: Her Majesty's Stationery Office.

Diamond, J. (1997) *Guns, Germs and Steel: A Short History about Everybody for the Last 13,000 Years*. London: Vintage.

Dickson, L., Brown, M. and Gibson, O. (1984) *Children Learning Mathematics: A Teacher's Guide to Recent Research*. London: Cassell Educational.

Doig, B., Williams, J., Wo, L. and Pampaka, M. (2006) Integrating errors into developmental assessment: 'time' for ages 8–13. *Proceedings of the 30th Conference of the International Group for the Psychology of Mathematics Education*, Vol. 2. Prague: Charles University, pp. 441–8.

Donaldson, M. (1978) *Children's Minds*. Fontana.

Dunne, E. and Bennett, N. (1994) *Talking and Learning in Groups*. Helsinki: Orienta-Konsultit.

Easley, J. and Easley, E. (1992) *Changing Mathematics Teaching in the Elementary School*. Melbourne: Deakin University Press.

Edwards, D. and Mercer, N. (1987) *Common Knowledge: The Development of Understanding in the Classroom*. London: Methuen.

Engestrom, Y. (1987) *Learning by Expanding: An Activity-Theoretical Approach to Developmental Research*. Helsinki: Orienta-Konsultit.

Engestrom, Y. and Cole, M. (1997) Situated cognition in search of an agenda. In J. A. Whitson and D. Kirshner (eds) *Situated Cognition: Social, Semiotic, and Psychological Perspectives*. Hillsdale, NJ: Lawrence Erlbaum Associates, pp. 301–9.

Fischbein, E. (1987) *Intuition in Science and Mathematics: An Educational Approach*. Dordrecht: Reidel.

Freudenthal, H. (1968) Why teach mathematics so as to be useful? *Educational Studies in Mathematics*, 1, pp. 3–8.

Freudenthal, H. (1973) *Mathematics as an Educational Task*. Dordrecht: Reidel.

Freudenthal, H. (1983) *Didactical Phenomenology of Mathematical Structures*. Dordrecht: Reidel.

Freudenthal, H. (1991) *Revisiting Mathematics Education: The China Lectures*. Dordrecht: Academic Publishers.

Fuys, D., Geddes, D. and Tischler, R. (1988) *The van Hiele Model of Thinking in Geometry Among Adolescents*. Reston, VA: National Council of Teachers of Mathematics.

Gardner, H. (1983) *Frames of Mind: The Theory of Multiple Intelligences*. New York: Basic Books.

Gelman, R. and Gallistel, C. R. (1986) *The Child's Understanding of Number*. Cambridge, MA: Harvard University Press.

Ginsburg, H. P. (2002) Little children, big mathematics: learning and teaching in the pre-school. In A. D. Cockburn and E. Nardi (eds), *Proceedings of the 26th Annual Meeting of the International Group for the Psychology of Mathematics Education*, Vol. 1. Norwich: University of East Anglia, pp. 3–14.

Goldin, G. (2001) Counting on the metaphorical. *Nature*, 413 (6851), pp. 18–19.

Gorard, S. (1999) Keeping a sense of proportion: the 'politician's error' in analysing school outcomes. *British Journal of Educational Studies*, 47 (3), pp. 235–46.

Goulding, M., Rowland, T. and Barber, P. (2002) Does it matter? Primary teacher trainees' subject knowledge in mathematics. *British Educational Research Journal*, 28 (5), pp. 689–704.

Gray, E. M. and Tall, D. O. (1994) Duality, ambiguity, and flexibility: a 'proceptual' view of simple arithmetic. *Journal for Research in Mathematics Education*, 26 (2), pp. 114–41.

Gray, E. M., Pitta, D., Pinto, M. and Tall, D. O. (1999) Knowledge construction and diverging thinking in elementary and advanced mathematics. *Educational Studies in Mathematics*, 38 (1–3), pp. 111–33.

Green, D. R. (1982) *Probability Concepts in 11–16 Year Old Pupils*. Loughborough: Centre for the Advancement of Mathematical Education in Technology, University of Technology.

Greeno, J. G. (1991) Number sense as situated knowing in a conceptual domain. *Journal for Research in Mathematics Education*, 22, pp. 170–218.

Greeno, J. G. (1998) *Thinking Practices in Mathematical and Science Learning*. Hillsdale, NJ: Lawrence Erlbaum Associates.

Groves, S. and Doig, B. (2002) Developing conceptual understanding: the role of the task in communities of mathematical inquiry. In A. D. Cockburn and E. Nardi (eds) *Proceedings of the 26th Conference of the International Group for the Psychology of Mathematics Education*, Vol. 3. Norwich: University of East Anglia, pp. 25–32.

Hadjidemetriou, C. and Williams, J. S. (2002a) Children's graphical conceptions. In J. Winter and S. Pope (eds) *Research in Mathematics Education*, 4, pp. 69–87.

Hadjidemetriou, C. and Williams, J. S. (2002b) Teachers' pedagogical content knowledge: graphs, from a cognitivist to a situated perspective. In A. D. Cockburn and E. Nardi (eds) *Proceedings of the 26th Conference of the International Group for the Psychology of Mathematics Education*, Vol. 3. Norwich: University of East Anglia, pp. 57 64.

Hadjidemetriou, C. and Williams, J. S. (2003) Teachers' theories and strategies in practice of classroom argumentation. In *Proceedings of the British Society for Research into Learning Mathematics*, 23 (1), pp. 25–30.

Hadjidemetriou, C. and Williams, J. S. (2004) Using Rasch models to reveal contours of teachers' knowledge. *Journal of Applied Measurement*, 5 (3), pp. 243–57.

Halliday, M. A. K. and Hasan, R. (1985) *Language, Concept and Text: Aspects of Language in a Social-Semiotic Perspective*. Victoria, Australia: Deakin University Press.

Hart, K. M. (ed.) (1981) *Children's Understanding of Mathematics: 11–16*. London: John Murray.

Hart, K. M. (1984) *Ratio: Children's Strategies and Errors: A Report of the Strategies and Errors in Secondary Mathematics Project*. Windsor: nferNelson.

Hasan, R. (1996) Semantic networks: a tool for the analysis of meaning. In C. Cloran, D. Bull and G. Williams (eds) *Ways of Saying, Ways of Meaning: Selected Papers of R. Hasan*. London: Cassell.

Hasan, R. (2002) Ways of meaning, ways of learning: code as an explanatory concept. *British Journal of Sociology of Education*, 23 (4), pp. 537–48.

Hatano, G. (1982) Learning to add and subtract: a Japanese perspective. In T. P. Carpenter, J. M. Moser and T. A. Romberg (eds) *Addition and Subtraction: A Cognitive Perspective*. Hillsdale, NJ: Lawrence Erlbaum Associates, pp. 211–23.

Haworth, A. (1999) Bakhtin in the classroom: what constitutes a dialogic test? Some lessons from small group interaction. *Language and Education*, 13 (2), pp. 99–117.

Hiebert, J. and Lefevre, P. (1986) *Conceptual and Procedural Knowledge: The Case for Mathematics*. Hillsdale, NJ: Lawrence Erlbaum Associates.

Hughes, M. (1986) *Children and Number: Difficulties in Learning Mathematics*. Oxford: Basil Blackwell.

Janvier, C. (1981) Use of situations in mathematics education. *Educational Studies in Mathematics*, 12, pp. 113–22.

Jones, G., Williams, J., Shimizu, Y., Neubrand, M. and Kieran, C. (2005) What do studies like PISA mean to the mathematics education community? (Plenary Panel.) In H. L. Chick and J. L. Vincent (eds) *Proceedings of the 29th Conference of the International Group for the Psychology of Mathematics Education*, Vol. 1. Melbourne: University of Melbourne, pp. 71–90.

Joseph, G. G. (1991) *The Crest of the Peacock: Non-European Roots of Mathematics*. Harmondsworth: Penguin.

Kahneman, D., Slovic, P. and Tversky, A. (eds) (1982) *Judgement Under Uncertainty: Heuristics and Biases*. Cambridge: Cambridge University Press.

Kaput, J. (1998) Representations, inscriptions, descriptions and learning: a kaleidoscope of windows. *Journal of Mathematical Behavior*, 17 (2), pp. 265–81.

Kieren, T. (1993) Rational and fractional numbers: from quotient fields to recursive understanding. In T. Carpenter, E. Fennema and T. Romberg (eds) *Rational Numbers: An Integration of Research*. Hillsdale, NJ: Erlbaum, pp. 49–84.

Koukkoufis, A. and Williams, J. S. (2006) Integer instruction: an experimental comparison. Paper presented at the British Society for Research in Learning Mathematics, Day Conference, June 2006. Bristol: University of Bristol.

Koukkoufis, A. and Williams, J. S. (2006) Semiotic objectifications of the compensation strategy: en route to the reification of integers. *Revista Latinoamericana de Matemática Educativa*. Special Issue, pp. 157–75.

Kutscher, B., Linchevski, L. and Eisenman, T. (2002) From the lotto game to subtracting two-digit numbers in first-graders. In A. D. Cockburn and E. Nardi (eds) *Proceedings of the 26th Annual Conference of the International Group for the Psychology of Mathematics Education*, Vol. 3. Norwich: University of East Anglia, pp. 249–56.

Lakoff, G. (1987) *Women, Fire, and Dangerous Things: What Categories Reveal About the Mind*. Chicago: University of Chicago Press.

Lakoff, G. and Johnson, M. (1980) *Metaphors We Live By*. Chicago: University of Chicago Press.

Lakoff, G. and Johnson, M. (1999) *Philosophy in the Flesh*. New York, NY: Basic Books.

Lakoff, G. and Johnson, M. (2003) *Metaphors We Live By*. London: University of Chicago Press.

Lakoff, G. and Nunez, R. E. (2000) *Where Mathematics Comes From: How the Embodied Mind Brings Mathematics into Being*. New York, NY: Basic Books.

Latour, B. (1987) *Science in Action: How to Follow Scientists and Engineers Through Society*. Milton Keynes: Open University Press.

Lave, J. (1988) *Cognition in Practice: Mind, Mathematics and Culture in Everyday Life*. Cambridge: Cambridge University Press.

Lave, J. (1996) Teaching, as learning, in practice. *Mind, Culture and Activity*, 3 (3), pp. 149–64.

Lave, J. and Wenger, E. (1991) *Situated Learning: Legitimate Peripheral Participation*. Cambridge: Cambridge University Press.

Lean, G. A., Clements, M. A. and Del Campo, G. (1990) Linguistic and pedagogical factors affecting children's understanding of arithmetic word problems: a comparative study. *Educational Studies in Mathematics*, 21, pp. 165–91.

Lecoutre, M. P. (1992) Cognitive models and problem spaces in 'purely random' situations. *Educational Studies in Mathematics*, 23, pp. 557–68.

Lemke, J. L. (1990) *Talking Science: Language, Learning and Values*. Westport, CT: Ablex Publishing Corp.

Linchevski, L. and Williams, J. S. (1996) Situated intuitions, concrete manipulations and the construction of mathematical concepts: the case of integers. In L. Puig and A. Gutierrez (eds) *Proceedings of the 20th Conference of the International Study Group for the Psychology of Mathematics Education*, Vol. 3. Valencia: University of Valencia, pp. 265–72.

Linchevski, L. and Williams, J. S. (1998) Situating the activity of teaching and learning integers. In A. Watson (ed.) *Situated Cognition and the Learning of Mathematics*. Oxford: Oxford University Department of Educational Studies, pp. 143–57.

Linchevski, L. and Williams, J. S. (1999) Using intuition from everyday life in 'filling' the gap in children's extension of their number concept to include the negative numbers. *Educational Studies in Mathematics (special issue: Teaching and Learning Mathematics in Context)*, 39 (1–3), pp. 131–47.

Lipman, M., Sharp, A. M. and Oscanyan, F. S. (1980) *Philosophy in the Classroom*. Philadelphia: Temple University Press.

MaLT (2005) *Mathematics Assessment for Learning and Teaching*. London: Hodder & Stoughton.

McNeill, D. (1992) *Hand and Mind: What Gestures Reveal about Thought*. Chicago: University of Chicago Press.

McNeill, D. (ed.) (2000) *Language and Gesture*. Cambridge: Cambridge University Press.

McNeill, D. (2005) *Gesture and Thought*. Chicago: University of Chicago Press.

Mercer, N. (1995) *The Guided Construction of Knowledge: Talk Amongst Teachers and Learners*. Cleveland, UK: Multilingual Matters.

Mercer, N. (1996) The quality of talk in children's collaborative activity in the classroom. *Learning and Instruction*, 6 (4), pp. 359–77.

Mercer, N. (2000) *Words and Minds: How We Use Language to Think Together*. London: Routledge.

Mercer, N., Wegerif, T. and Dawes, L. (1999) Children's talk and the development of reasoning in the classroom. *British Educational Research Journal*, 25 (1), pp. 95–111.

Misailidou, C. and Williams, J. S. (2002) Investigating children's thinking on the topic of 'ratio'. In J. Winter and S. Pope (eds) *Proceedings of the British Society for Research into Learning Mathematics*, Vol. 22. University of Durham (February) and University of Bristol (May), pp. 47–52.

Misailidou, C. and Williams, J. S. (2003) Diagnostic assessment of children's proportional reasoning. *Journal of Mathematical Behavior*, 22 (3), pp. 335–68.

Nelson, R. D., Joseph, G. G. and Williams, J. S. (1993) *Multicultural Mathematics*. Oxford: Oxford University Press.

Noss, R., Hoyles, C. and Pozzi, S. (2002) Abstraction in expertise: a study of nurses' conceptions of concentration. *Journal for Research in Mathematics*, 33 (3), pp. 204–29.

Nunes, T. (1996) What is the difference between one, un and yi? In H. Mansfield, N. A. Pateman and N. Bednarz (eds) *Mathematics for Tomorrow's Young Children*. Dordrecht: Kluwer Academic Publishers, pp. 177–85.

Nunes, T., Schliemann, A. D. and Carraher, D. W. (1993) *Street Mathematics and School Mathematics*. Cambridge: Cambridge University Press.

Nunez, R. E., Edwards, L. and Matos, J. F. (1999) Embodied cognition as grounding for situatedness and context in mathematics education. *Educational Studies in Mathematics*, 39, pp. 45–65.

Opie, I. and Opie, P. (1959) *The Lore and Language of Schoolchildren*. Oxford: Oxford University Press.

Paulos, J. A. (2001) *Innumeracy: Mathematical Illiteracy and its Consequences*. New York: Hill & Wang Publishing.

Petridou, A. and Williams, J. (accepted) Accounting for real person misfit using multilevel models. *Journal of Educational Measurement*.

Piaget, J. (1970) *Genetic Epistemology*. New York: Columbia University Press.

Piaget, J. and Inhelder, B. (1974) *The Child's Construction of Quantities: Conservation and Atomisation*. London: Routledge & Kegan Paul.

Pinker, S. (1998) *How the Mind Works*. London: Penguin.

Pirie, S. and Kieren, T. (1994) Growth in mathematical understanding: how can we characterise it and how can we represent it? *Educational Studies in Mathematics*, 26 (2–3), pp. 165–90.

PISA (2003) *The PISA 2003 Assessment Framework*. Paris: OECD.

PISA (2004) *Learning for Tomorrow's World*. Paris: OECD.

PISA (2005) *School Factors Related to Quality and Equity*. Paris: OECD.

Polya, G. (1945) *How to Solve it: A New Aspect of Mathematical Method*. Princeton, NJ: Princeton University Press.

Radford, L. (2002) The seen, the spoken and the written. A semiotic approach to the problem of objectification of mathematical knowledge. *For the Learning of Mathematics*, 22 (2), pp. 14–23.

Radford, L. (2003) Gestures, speech, and the sprouting of signs: a semiotic-cultural approach to students' types of generalizations. *Mathematical Thinking and Learning*, 5 (1), pp. 37–70.

Renshaw, P. (1996) A sociocultural view of the mathematics education of young children. In H. Mansfield, N. Pateman and N. Bednarz (eds) *Mathematics for Tomorrow's Young Children*. Dordrecht: Kluwer, pp. 59–78.

Resnick, L. B. and Ford, W. B. (1981) *The Psychology of Mathematics for Instruction*. Hillsdale, NJ: Lawrence Erlbaum.

Roberts, G. (2002) *SET for Success: The Report of Sir Gareth Roberts' Review – The Supply of People with Science, Technology, Engineering and Mathematical Skills*. London: HM Treasury Report.

Roth, W.-M. (2001) Gestures: their role in teaching and learning. *Review of Educational Research*, 71 (3), pp. 365–92.

Roth, W.-M. and Bowen, G. M. (2001) Professionals read graphs: a semiotic analysis. *Journal for Research in Mathematics Education*, 32, pp. 150–94.

Ruddock, J. (1979) *Learning to Teach through Discussion*. Norwich: University of East Anglia, Centre for Applied Research in Education.

Ryan, J. and McCrae, B. (2005) Subject matter knowledge: errors and misconceptions of beginning pre-service teachers. In P. Clarkson, A. Downtown, D. Gronn, M. Horne, A. McDonough, R. Pierce and A. Roche (eds) *Building Connections: Research, Theory and Practice: Proceedings of the 28th Annual Conference of the Mathematics Education Research Group of Australasia*, Vol. 2. Melbourne: Deakin University, pp. 641–8.

Ryan, J. and McCrae, B. (2006) Assessing pre-service teachers' mathematics subject knowledge. *Mathematics Teacher Education and Development*, Vol. 7.

Ryan, J. and Williams, J. (1998) The search for pattern: student understanding of the table of values representation for function. In C. Kanes, M. Goos and E. Warren (eds) *Teaching Mathematics in New Times: Conference Proceedings of the Mathematics Education Research Group of Australasia*, Vol. 2. Gold Coast, Australia: Mathematics Education Research Group of Australasia, pp. 492–9.

Ryan, J. and Williams, J. (2000) *Mathematical Discussions with Children: Exploring Methods and Misconceptions as a Teaching Strategy*. Manchester: University of Manchester.

Ryan, J. and Williams, J. (2002a) Conflict discussion as a teaching (and learning) strategy. In Teacher Training Agency (ed.) *Learning from Mistakes, Misunderstandings and Misconceptions in Mathematics*. London: Crown.

Ryan, J. and Williams, J. (2002b) Learning from mistakes, misunderstandings and misconceptions in mathematics at Key Stage 2. In Teacher Training Agency (ed.) *Learning from Mistakes, Misunderstandings and Misconceptions in Mathematics*. London: Crown.

Ryan, J. and Williams, J. S. (2003) Charting argumentation space in conceptual locales: tools at the boundary between research and practice. *Research in Mathematics Education*, 4, pp. 89–111.

Ryan, J. T., Williams, J. S. and Doig, B. A. (1998) National tests: educating teachers about their children's mathematical thinking. In A. Olivier and K. Newstead (eds) *Proceedings of the 22nd Conference of the International Group for the Psychology of Mathematics Education*. South Africa: University of Stellenbosch, pp. 81–8.

Schoenfeld, A. H. (1985) *Mathematical Problem Solving*. London: Academic Press.

Schoenfeld, A. H. (1994) *Mathematical Thinking and Problem Solving*. Hillsdale, NJ: Lawrence Erlbaum Associates.

Schwab, J. (1978) Education and the structure of the disciplines. In I. Westbury and N. Wilkof (eds) *Science, Curriculum, and Liberal Education*. Chicago: University of Chicago Press, pp. 229–72.

Seitz, J. A. (2000) The bodily basis for thought. *New Ideas in Psychology*, 18, pp. 23–40.

Sfard, A. (1991) On the dual nature of mathematical conceptions: reflections on process and objects as different sides of the same coin. *Educational Studies in Mathematics*, 22, pp. 1–36.

Sfard, A. (1995) The development of algebra: confronting historical and psychological perspectives. *Journal of Mathematical Behavior*, 14, pp. 15–39.

Sfard, A. (1998) On two metaphors for learning and the dangers of choosing just one. *Educational Researcher*, 27 (2), pp. 4–13.

Sfard, A. (2001) There is more to discourse than meets the ears: looking at thinking as communicating to learn more about mathematical learning. *Educational Studies in Mathematics (special issue)*, 46 (1–3), pp. 13–57.

Sfard, A. and Linchevski, L. (1994) The gains and pitfalls of reification: the case of algebra. *Educational Studies in Mathematics*, 26, pp. 87–124.

Shulman, L. (1986) Those who understand: knowledge growth in teachers. *Educational Researcher*, 15 (2), pp. 4–14.

Skemp, R. R. (1971) *The Psychology of Learning Mathematics*. Harmondsworth, Penguin.

Skemp, R. R. (1976) Relational understanding and instrumental understanding. *Mathematics Teaching*, 77, pp. 20–26.

Smith, A. (2004) *Making Mathematics Count: The Report of Professor Adrian Smith's Inquiry*. London: The Stationery Office.

Smith, J. P., DiSessa, A. A. and Roschelle, J. (1993–94) Misconceptions reconceived: a constructivist analysis of knowledge in transition. *Journal of the Learning Sciences*, 3 (2), pp. 115–63.

Splitter, L. J. and Sharp, A. M. (1995) *Teaching for Better Thinking: The Classroom Community of Inquiry*. Melbourne, Australia: Australian Council for Educational Research.

Steffe, L. (1991) Operations that generate quantities. *Journal of Learning and Individual Differences*, 3 (1), pp. 61–82.

Stetsenko, A. and Arievitch, I. (2002) Teaching, learning and development: a post-Vygotskian perspective. In G. Wells and G. Claxton (eds) *Learning for Life in the*

21st Century: Sociocultural Perspectives on the Future of Education. Oxford: Blackwell, pp. 84–96.

Stigler, J. W. and Hiebert, J. (1999) *The Teaching Gap: Best Ideas from the World's Teachers for Improving Education in the Classroom.* New York: Free Press.

Strathern, M. (ed.) (2000) *Audit Cultures: Anthropological Studies in Accountability, Ethics and the Academy.* London: Routledge.

Strathern, M. (2006) Useful knowledge. *Proceedings of the British Academy*, 139, pp. 73–109.

Streefland, L. (1991) *Fractions in Realistic Mathematics Education: A Paradigm of Developmental Research.* Dordrecht: Kluwer Academic Publishers.

Sweller, J. (1994) Cognitive load theory, learning difficulty, and instructional design. *Learning and Cognition*, 4 (4), pp. 295–312.

Sweller, J. (1998) Cognitive architecture and instructional design. *Educational Psychology Review*, 10, pp. 251–96.

Sweller, J. (2004) Instructional design consequences of an analogy between evolution by natural selection and human cognitive architecture. *Instructional Science: An International Journal of Learning and Cognition*, 32 (1–2), pp. 9–31.

Tanner, H. and Jones, S. (1999) Dynamic scaffolding and reflective discourse: the impact of teaching style on the development of mathematical thinking. In O. Zaslavsky (ed.) *Proceedings of the 23rd Conference of the International Group for the Psychology of Mathematics Education.* Vol. 4. Haifa: PME, pp. 257–64.

TTA (Teacher Training Agency) (2003) *Qualifying to Teach: Professional Standards for Qualified Teacher Status.* London: Teacher Training Agency.

Toulmin, S. E. (1958) *The Uses of Argument.* Cambridge: Cambridge University Press.

Treffers, A. (1987) *Three Dimensions: A Model of Goal and Theory Description in Mathematics Instruction – The Wiskobas Project.* Dordrecht: Reidel.

Treffers, A. (1993) Wiskobas and Freudenthal: Realistic Mathematics Education. *Educational Studies in Mathematics*, 25 (1/2), pp. 89–108.

Tufte, E. R. (1983) *The Visual Display of Quantitative Information.* Cheshire, CT: Graphics Press.

Tuomi-Grohn, T., Engestrom, Y. and Young, M. F. (2003) From transfer to boundary-crossing between school and work as a tool for developing vocational education: an introduction. In T. Tuomi-Grohn and Y. Engestrom (eds) *Between School and Work: New Perspectives on Transfer and Boundary-crossing.* Amsterdam/Oxford: Pergamon, pp. 1–15.

Tymms, P. (2004) Are standards rising in English primary schools? *British Educational Research Journal*, 30 (4), pp. 477–94.

Usiskin, Z. (1982) *Van Hiele Levels and Achievement in Secondary School Geometry.* Chicago: University of Chicago.

Van Hiele, P. N. (1986) *Structure and Insight. A Theory of Mathematics Education.* Orlando: Orlando Academic Press.

Vergnaud, G. (1983) Multiplicative structures. In R. Lesh and M. Landau (eds)

Acquisition of Mathematics Concepts and Processes. New York: Academic Press, pp. 128–75.

Vygotskii, L. S. (1987) Thinking and speech. In R. W. Rieber and A. S. Carton (eds) *The Collected Works of L. S. Vygotsky.* New York: Plenum.

Vygotsky, L. S. (1978) *Mind in Society: The Development of Higher Psychological Processes.* Cambridge, MA: Harvard University Press.

Vygotsky, L. S. (1981) The genesis of higher mental functions. In J. V. Wertsch (ed.) *The Concept of Activity in Soviet Psychology.* Armonk, NY: Sharpe, pp. 134–43.

Wartofsky, M. W. (1979) *Models: Representation and the Scientific Understanding.* Dordrecht: Reidel.

Wells, C. G. (1999) *Dialogic Inquiry: Towards A Socio-Cultural Practice and Theory of Education.* Cambridge: Cambridge University Press.

Wenger, E. (1998) *Communities of Practice: Learning, Meaning, and Identity.* Cambridge: Cambridge University Press.

Wertsch, J. V. (1991) *Voices of the Mind: A Sociocultural Approach to Mediated Action.* London: Harvester, and Cambridge, MA: Harvard University Press.

Williams, J. (2005) Gestures, signs and mathematisation. In H. L. Chick and J. L. Vincent (eds) *Proceedings of the 29th Conference of the International Group for the Psychology of Mathematics Education,* Vol. 1. Melbourne: University of Melbourne.

Williams, J. and Ryan, J. (2000) National testing and the improvement of classroom teaching: can they coexist? *British Educational Research Journal,* 26 (1), pp. 49–73.

Williams, J. S. and Ryan, J. (2002a) Argumentation and teacher's role: the general and the particular. In J. Winter and S. Pope (eds) *Proceedings of the British Society for Research into Learning Mathematics,* Vol. 22. University of Durham (March) and University of Bristol (May), pp. 53–8.

Williams, J. S. and Ryan, J. (2002b) Making connections at Key Stages 2 and 3. *Mathematics Teaching,* 178 (March), pp. 8–11.

Williams, J. S. and Wake, G. D. (2007a) Black boxes in workplace mathematics. *Educational Studies in Mathematics,* 64 (3), 317–43.

Williams, J. S. and Wake, G. D. (2007b) Metaphors and models in translation between college and workplace mathematics. *Educational Studies in Mathematics,* 64 (3), 345–71.

Williams, J. S., Linchevski, L. and Kutscher, B. (under review) Situated intuition and activity theory fills the gap in concept development: the cases of integers and two-digit subtraction. In A. Watson and P. Winborne (eds) *New Directions for Situated Cognition in Learning Mathematics.* Kluwer-Springer.

Williams, J., Corbin, B. and McNamara, O. (under review) Finding inquiry in discourses of audit and reform in primary schools. *International Journal of Educational Research.*

Williams, J., Ryan, J., Hadjidemetriou, C., Misailidou, C. and Afantiti-Lamprianou, T. (2004) Credible tools for formative assessment: measurement and qualitative research needed for practice. *Annual Conference of the American Research Association*.

Williams, J., Wo, L. and Lewis, S. (2005) *Mathematics assessment for learning and teaching: an overview of the age standardisation model ages 5- to 14-years*. Paper presented to the Conference of the British Society for Research into Learning Mathematics, St Martin's College, Lancaster, UK, November 2005.

Wood, D. J. (1998) *How Children Think and Learn: The Social Contexts of Cognitive Development*. Oxford: Blackwell.

Yackel, E. and Cobb, P. (1996) Sociomathematical norms, argumentation, and autonomy in mathematics. *Journal for Research in Mathematics Education, 27*, pp. 458–77.

Yeo, D. (2003) *Dyslexia, Dyspraxia and Mathematics*. London: Whurr.

Index

Related books from Open University Press

Purchase from www.openup.co.uk or order through your local bookseller

---

LANGUAGE FOR LEARNING MATHEMATICS
ASSESSMENT FOR LEARNING IN PRACTICE

Clare Lee

Assessment for learning is a powerful way to raise standards and improve learning. However, as this book shows, effective assessment for learning in the mathematics classroom depends on pupils being able and willing to use mathematical language to express their ideas. When discussion, negotiation and explanation are encouraged, teachers use assessment for learning creatively, the work quickly becomes more challenging and the pupils come to see themselves as successful learners.

Many pupils find it difficult to express ideas in mathematics because of problems with the language that is used to convey mathematical concepts. This book shows teachers how to help pupils express what they really know and understand, so that assessment for learning can be used. The book:

- Discusses what mathematical language is, and what it is not
- Suggests practical approaches to introducing more discourse into the classroom
- Explores the ideas of assessment for learning – rich questioning and dialogue, effective feedback, and peer and self assessment – and suggests how these can be used effectively in mathematics classrooms to improve learning

Language for Learning Mathematics is key reading for teachers and trainee teachers in mathematics, as well as assessment advisors at LAs.

Contents
Acknowledgements – How this book tells its story – Increase discourse: Increase learning – Mathematical Language: What it is and what it isn't – Starting to talk in the mathematical classroom – Assessment for learning – Going further with purposeful communication in mathematics – The source of the ideas: Delving into theory – Looking at practice more deeply – References – Index.

136pp
978–0–335–21988–9 (Paperback)   978–0–335–21989–6 (Hardback)

TEACHING FOR LEARNING MATHEMATICS

Rosamund Sutherland

- Why do students find learning mathematics difficult? Can anything be done about this?
- What can we learn from mathematics lessons in which students are motivated to struggle with difficult mathematical ideas?
- How can teachers make sense of the research which is available, and use it to improve practice in real classrooms?

This book explores the factors that influence young people's learning of mathematics. It uses a holistic, socio-culturally informed approach to show how all young people can be encouraged to engage with and learn mathematics.

Rich examples from classroom practice are used to connect theory and practice. The role of mathematical tools, including information and communications technologies, is discussed. A key focus of the book is the link between teaching and learning, including different ways in which teachers can design and orchestrate mathematical learning environments.

This important, accessible and relevant book is essential reading for student teachers of mathematics as well as all qualified mathematics teachers in secondary schools.

Contents
Acknowledgements – Teaching, learning and mathematics – Cultures of mathematics education – Ways of knowing mathematics – Ways into the world of mathematics – Teaching and learning as reciprocal activity – Digital tools for learning mathematics – Designing for learning – Learning geometry – Theory as a way of seeing – Integrating research, policy and practice – References – Index.

168pp
978–0–335–21390–0 (Paperback)   978–0–335–21391–7 (Hardback)

RAISING ACHIEVEMENT IN SECONDARY MATHS
A MULTIDISCIPLINARY APPROACH TO CHRONIC CHILDHOOD ILLNESS

Anne Watson

This book brings together research and professional knowledge to enhance the teaching of lower attaining students in secondary mathematics. Attainment in mathematics is an important social issue, since underachievement can make a difference to future life choices, particularly amongst certain groups of students.

Raising Achievement in Secondary Mathematics shows how well-meant teaching strategies and approaches can in practice exacerbate underachievement in maths by making inappropriate demands on learners. As well as criticizing some of the teaching and grouping practices that are considered normal in many schools, the book also offers an alternative view of attainment and capability, based on real classroom incidents in which 'low attaining students' show themselves to be able to think about mathematics in quite sophisticated ways.

The author argues that teaching could be based on learners' proficiency, rather than on correcting deficits in knowledge and behaviour. She describes how a group of teachers who believed that their students could do better with higher expectations developed a range of principles and strategies to support their work – the students showed significant progress and the teachers felt they were doing a better job.

With numerous case studies, ideas and teaching strategies, this book is for anyone who is teaching, or learning to teach, mathematics.

Contents
Acknowledgments – Learning about school mathematics – Abilities and understanding – Teachers' judgments – The impact of differences in practice and belief – The fallacy of 'getting to know' learners – Thinking mathematically in low-attaining groups – Approaches to reconstruction: test cramming versus developing proficiency – Identifying deep progress – Construction, reconstruction and renewal – References – Author index – Contents index.

208pp
978-0-335-21860-8 (Paperback)   978-0-335-21861-5 (Hardback)